THE PULSE APPROACH

THE PULSE APPROACH

Physical Improvisation for
Theatre-makers and Directors

TANYA GERSTLE

methuen | drama
LONDON • NEW YORK • OXFORD • NEW DELHI • SYDNEY

METHUEN DRAMA
Bloomsbury Publishing Plc, 50 Bedford Square, London, WC1B 3DP, UK
Bloomsbury Publishing Inc, 1359 Broadway, New York, NY 10018, USA
Bloomsbury Publishing Ireland, 29 Earlsfort Terrace, Dublin 2, D02 AY28, Ireland

BLOOMSBURY, METHUEN DRAMA and the Methuen Drama logo
are trademarks of Bloomsbury Publishing Plc

First published in Great Britain 2026

Copyright © Tanya Gerstle, 2026

Tanya Gerstle has asserted her right under the Copyright, Designs and
Patents Act, 1988, to be identified as Author of this work.

For legal purposes the Acknowledgements on p. xvi constitute an
extension of this copyright page.

Cover image: *Invisible Stains*, 2009 Photo © Jeff Busby

All rights reserved. No part of this publication may be: i) reproduced or transmitted in any form, electronic or mechanical, including photocopying, recording or by means of any information storage or retrieval system without prior permission in writing from the publishers; or ii) used or reproduced in any way for the training, development or operation of artificial intelligence (AI) technologies, including generative AI technologies. The rights holders expressly reserve this publication from the text and data mining exception as per Article 4(3) of the Digital Single Market Directive (EU) 2019/790.

Bloomsbury Publishing Plc does not have any control over, or responsibility for, any third-party websites referred to or in this book. All internet addresses given in this book were correct at the time of going to press. The author and publisher regret any inconvenience caused if addresses have changed or sites have ceased to exist, but can accept no responsibility for any such changes.

A catalogue record for this book is available from the British Library.

A catalog record for this book is available from the Library of Congress.

ISBN: HB: 978-1-3505-2455-2
PB: 978-1-3505-2454-5
ePDF: 978-1-3505-2456-9
eBook: 978-1-3505-2457-6

Typeset by Integra Software Services Pvt. Ltd.
Printed and bound in Great Britain

Online resources for this title are available at: https://www.bloomsburyonlineresources.com/the-pulse-approach.

For product safety related questions contact productsafety@bloomsbury.com.

To find out more about our authors and books visit www.bloomsbury.com
and sign up for our newsletters.

In memory of Mary, her courage
and the trail she blazed

For Jarrah
who keeps her flame alive

CONTENTS

List of illustrations ix
Preface xi
Foreword xiv
Acknowledgements xvi
About the author and the interviewer xvii
List of interviewees xviii

Introduction 1

PART ONE TRAINING WORKBOOK 5

1 The Pulse Canvas 7
   How to use this workbook 7
   Before you begin 9

2 The Pulse phases 15
   Phase One: Developing kinaesthetic awareness 15
   Phase Two: Making connections 17
   Phase Three: Working attitudes 18
   Phase Four: Learning a shared language 24
   Phase Five: Expanding the action vocabulary 29
   Phase Six: The Pulse Sketch 33
   Phase Seven: Adding sound to the physical world 40
   Phase Eight: Speaking on the Canvas 44

3 Ensemble practice tasks 51

4 Skill focus tasks 63

5 Integrating design elements and audience 95

6 Alternative applications 105
Independent practice 105
Frameworks for Pulsing 108
Making new work: Strategies 109
Towards an original performance text 114

PART TWO DIRECTING WORKBOOK 123

7 Inner life revealed through action 125
How to use this workbook 125
Rehearsal practice 127
Rehearsal process 131
Rehearsal concepts 144

8 Case Studies 157
Using Pulse as a rehearsal device 157
    Time management and magical solutions 159
Immersion 160
    The Mill on the Floss – Recurring motifs and metaphoric resonance 160
    Pericles Punished – Non-scripted physical storytelling 163
Mapping 167
    Five Kinds of Silence – Depicting confronting content 167
    Stage Beauty – Corsets, wigs and social norms 171
Rendering 174
    Manbeth: Macbeth Amplified – Fluidity of space, place and character 175
Future considerations 181

Afterword 183
Notes 185
References 187
Index 189

ILLUSTRATIONS

1. Joshua Ryan, Emily Thomas, Kevin Fa'asitua Hofbauer and Kade Greenland, *Invisible Stains,* October 2009 5
2. Emily Thomas and Grant Cartwright, *Polygraph,* July 2018 13
3. Matt Furlani, Nikki Shiels and Kyle Baxter, *Invisible Stains,* October 2009 111
4. Mike Steel, Joshua Ryan, Kevin Fa'asitua Hofbauer and Emily Thomas, *Invisible Stains,* October 2009 112
5. Hannah Liddeaux and company, *Invisible Stains,* October 2009 112
6. Emily Thomas, Alice Sainsbury, Lia Davies and Maj Thomsen, *Invisible Stains,* October 2009 113
7. Meredith Penman, Grant Cartwright, Terry Yeboah, Carl Nilsson-Polias and Tim Potter, *Yes*, October 2007 123
8. Meredith Penman and Anne Louise Sarks, *Yes,* October 2007 156
9. Ella Watson-Russell, *New Anatomies*, June 2005 160
10. Grant Cartwright and Zahra Newman, *The Mill on the Floss*, August 2016 162
11. Oliver Coleman, Rachel Perks, Nicholas Kato and Tristan Barr, *Pericles Punished,* June 2013 164
12. Rachel Perks, *Pericles Punished*, June 2013 166
13. Ella Watson-Russell and Grant Cartwright, *Five Kinds of Silence*, October 2005 169
14. Grant Cartwright and Alice Parkinson, *Five Kinds of Silence*, October 2005 170
15. Rosie Lockhart, Tom Heath, Matt Whitty, Christian Grant, James Townsend and Sam Young, *Stage Beauty*, October 2012 173
16. Mike Steel, Lachlan Woods and Alexander England, *Manbeth: Macbeth Amplified*, August 2008 174

17 Gabriel Partington and Thomas Conroy, *Manbeth: Macbeth Amplified*, August 2008 180

18 Lachlan Woods and Alexander England, *Manbeth: Macbeth Amplified*, August 2008 181

PREFACE

Turning points of an evolving practice

How can I facilitate a group working with Pulse? How will I know if I'm doing it right? What comes next? Where is the book? These are some of the questions I was asked by performers over the thirty-year evolution of Pulse. During those years I was too busy developing the practice to write it down. Then former students began creating companies and integrating Pulse into their own professional practice. I knew of some who were teaching Pulse, although they had only completed a week-long intensive, and I was fielding phone calls from others asking what to do next. It was clear to me that an instruction manual was needed. This book was borne of my desire to contribute to Pulse as a 'living practice'.

Pulse is a performance strategy based on improvisational structures that can be used to train performers, develop original performance material and rehearse a dramatic script. The understanding of rhythm, kinaesthetically, and that of space, compositionally, are essential skills for actors and directors, but they are most often acquired through training in music and dance. Pulse offers a way for actors in a performance ensemble to develop these skills. During a text-based rehearsal process it is common for actors to struggle with the transition from the freedom of improvised speaking to the relative constriction of speaking interpretive text. As the improvisation during a Pulse rehearsal is wedded to the scripted text, this transition evaporates.

It was in the autumn of 1989 in New York that the idea of Pulse was born. I was working on a collaborative project with Lawrence 'Butch' Morris, a composer and jazz cornetist. During our creative development, Butch, who was also artist-in-residence at the Whitney Museum of Modern Art, invited me to observe his week-long residency with an ensemble of new music improvisors. He was evolving a vocabulary of signs and signals called Conduction, an innovative ensemble compositional method that he was sharing daily with the musicians. He would stand on the podium, and with a series of hand/body gestures and mid-air notations, 'compose in action' from the offers that the improvisors gave him. The performed result was called a Comprovisation (Composed Improvisation). As I witnessed, listened and watched, I questioned, imagined and invented. How could I conduct a group of improvising theatrical performers? How could I get each actor's attention? What are the performance principles and then, the accompanying signals that need to be communicated to actors from a conductor/director? I wondered if an ensemble of actors could improvise a nonlinear narrative but give it profound structural coherence. Could a theatrical improvisation be held together primarily by aesthetic form?

Could actors be the creators and the creation at the same time by internalizing a director's instructions? And would that be a satisfying experience for an audience to watch? Pulse evolved in my attempt to answer these questions.

Over the next ten years through collaborations with students and fellow actors, I found a way to remove the conductor's presence yet still have dramaturgical influence over the structure and aesthetic of the piece. I developed a system of concepts and principles that enabled a group of actors to internalize structure – be their own conductor/director. I searched for principles from abstract art forms such as music, dance and painting, and I discovered that actors, when given tools, could easily work with poetic association and create coalescing performative fragments instead of improvising narrative-driven realistic scenes. In 1999, when I began teaching at the Victorian College of the Arts (VCA), Melbourne, Pulse synthesized into an improvisation training for the first-year actors. They were already versed in Lindy Davies's Impulse work, so Pulse could build upon this understanding. But it was my introduction to Davies's 'kinaesthetic approach' to the speaking of text – the process employed to train an actor at VCA at that time – that significantly informed my directorial practice. It was this rehearsal training that gave me the key to bring Pulse towards a process for scripted plays – the horizontal layering of rehearsal, actors working in 'extended time', the trance nature of vertical immersion and working in the physical abstract with language were revelatory to me. Certain aspects of the way an actor in Davies's process works to internalize and externalize the text came together with my compositional Principles, and my focus on rhythm and the heightened body to create a physical approach when staging a play text. I had found a way to energize the stage when actors were speaking and, as I had the opportunity to direct two and sometimes three plays a year with actors who had trained with me in Pulse, the rehearsal room became my laboratory.

I was searching for an alternative to the dominant staging style of dramatic realism (where realistic behavioural gesture constitutes the physical 'world' of the play), and I realized that I had developed a training approach, Pulse, to create the 'physical acting' that I wanted to see as a director. At the same time, Anne Bogart, an American theatre director was addressing similar concerns. Friends were returning to Australia from New York and speaking of the parallels between Pulse and Viewpoints. Both had evolved in different parts of the world, with different initiating influences – Pulse from new music and Viewpoints from post-modern dance – and yet the similarity in training concepts, the language used to describe process and ethos, and the impetus to disrupt the entrenchment of psychological realism is striking.

In 2008 I founded OpticNerve Performance Group, a performance/research company based in Melbourne, to continue working with a community of actors and designers who had trained with me and were then working in the profession. We trained, produced work and offered Pulse workshops and masterclasses as well as insights to the Pulse rehearsal process where audience members were invited to explore the script from page to stage by viewing rehearsals, talking vision with the director and process with the actors.

When I first met Mary Luckhurst through her research into global actor training methodologies, our collaboration began and ideas for the writing of this book took shape. In 2013 she conducted interviews with actors and directors who had trained with me in

PREFACE

Pulse and with colleagues who offered reflections on viewing Pulse-created productions. The polyphonies of personal impressions revealed to me the essentials of Pulse and helped me understand it from diverse perspectives. Their voices framed the experienced outcomes of the work, so I have placed extracts from these interviews throughout the workbooks. Sometimes they explain, elucidate or reinforce a concept, they might describe struggles or the richness of an actor's inner life, but they are always insightful.

This book is written from a practitioner's point of view – what to do and how to do it. It offers a physically embodied alternative to Stanislavski-dominated approaches to text for actors and directors. Experimental ensembles have always used improvisation for collective creation but now the Pulse approach maps a focused, pragmatic and rigorous journey towards the integration of improvisation into the very fabric of a text-based theatre rehearsal.

> In Europe there are companies which place emphasis on movement, but they haven't necessarily solved the challenges of working text in with movement.
> The Pulse approach explores that relationship constantly and, I believe, pushes it to exciting frontiers.
>
> Richard Murphet

FOREWORD

I met the formidable Tanya Gerstle when I was leading the UK Higher Education Academy's largest ever research project on actor training, investigating methods offered in both conservatoires and universities. To be accurate, I should say, I unashamedly buttonholed Tanya and asked her straight out whether she would come to England and disseminate her training methods as there was an urgent need for them. This exchange occurred at a conference at Melbourne University in 2010. Having heard her deconstruct the challenges facing actors; articulate the skillsets actors need and the importance of a shared analytical vocabulary; discuss her techniques and emphasize the intellectual and physical rigour required for applied improvisation; I knew I had found the person and an approach to acting that I had been seeking my whole career. Tanya found my request strange but, fortunately for me, was intrigued. In Australia she had answers to many of the conundrums directors and actor trainers have been battling for decades. But European and Northern American practitioners knew nothing about Tanya's approach. It was a life-changing meeting for both of us. Tanya came to England, became a pivotal part of my research project, and taught Pulse principles in the UK and Europe. Three years later I moved to Australia and to a post at the University of Melbourne to further my research, to watch Tanya at work, and to interview some of the many actors trained by her. I began to appreciate the extent to which Australian approaches to actor training have been widely neglected in Europe and the United States. In turn, Tanya began the project of articulating her practice in written form for this book. Anyone who has ever tried to translate physical techniques into words will know how painstaking a task this is. To articulate a life's work and a philosophy of acting into a succinct, accessible account is monumentally difficult and has been brilliantly achieved.

    The Pulse approach offers a new way forward for actors and directors of theatre and screen who want integrated training based on improvisatory techniques that can be applied to both theatre and screen performance. Tanya's method offers strong structural and choreographic foundations, and a precise critical vocabulary for explaining those foundations and the evolution of an actor's development. In many forums improvisation has traditionally been presented as a tool that is detached from play texts and film scripts. Tanya's unique improvisation method can be used to make purely physical pieces or those that involve text or sound; but importantly, this method can also be applied to the production of pre-existing classical and contemporary texts. This multiplicity of applied uses is highly unusual – indeed virtually unknown in Europe. Tanya provides an exciting proposition by which improvisation becomes an applied technique for performing play/film scripts. She also offers a highly evolved critical vocabulary rooted in the body.

It is a pleasure and a privilege to be asked to introduce Tanya and her techniques to new international audiences. I have no doubt that this book will go on to transform even more lives and shape even more careers in the performance industries.

Dr Mary Luckhurst
Honorary Professor of Theatre and Screen Performance,
Bristol University

ACKNOWLEDGEMENTS

Pulse as a practice has been forged by many collaborations over many years. Every training session and every rehearsal and production moved the notion of Pulse forward, each teaching me something new. For this I am grateful to all the students I have taught and to the actors I have directed. I particularly want to thank the following people for their contributions to the practice of Pulse and to the writing of this book.

From the beginning of this creative journey, Lawrence 'Butch' Morris, who was the inspiration for the idea of Pulse and Lindy Davies, whose influence was instrumental in its realization. Richard Murphet and Geraldine Cook-Dafner, both colleagues, who became my artistic collaborators and offered both unconditional and practical support as the practice of Pulse evolved. Adrian Holmes who gave generously of his time, skill and friendship to make a film of my rehearsal process, and Mary Luckhurst whose encouragement, insight and collaboration set me on the path to writing this book.

Carol Woodrow for my first taste of improvising with heightened text, Astrid Grant, Chrissie Koltai and Deborah Lennie-Bisson for their long-time artistic collaboration, and Darren Natale and Loraine Little for their unwavering belief in me and their indispensable practical support. OpticNerve ensemble artists: Gary Abrahams, Luisa Hastings Edge, Zahra Newman, Meredith Penman, Ben Pfeiffer and Lachlan Woods, who gave generously of their talent and skills to develop and expand Pulse over the years; in particular, Grant Cartwright, a Pulse champion, and Stephen Phillips and Hannah Liddeaux, for their passion for Pulse and for training another generation of practitioners. To the OpticNerve associate artists for their valuable contributions to the realization of performance works as well as all the practitioners who gave generously of their time to be interviewed for this book.

I would like to acknowledge the University of Melbourne and the Faculty of Fine Arts and Music for giving me the opportunity to develop and articulate my ideas towards further practice. My gratitude goes to Yoni Prior and Zachary Dunbar for their guidance during the development and writing of this book and to Anny Mokotow and Diane Brown for their advice and editing expertise.

Finally, with deep respect and love, Jarrah Gerstle-Smith for her support and travelling this long road with me.

The author and publisher gratefully acknowledge the permission granted to reproduce the copyright material in this book.

Online resources to accompany this book are available at: https://www.bloomsbury onlineresources.com/the-pulse-approach.

ABOUT THE AUTHOR

Dr Tanya Gerstle is an actor trainer, theatre-maker, director and performance consultant. She was Senior Lecturer in Theatre and Head of Acting at the Victorian College of the Arts, the University of Melbourne, and is currently Honorary Senior Fellow. She has been teaching artist-in-residence at the Universities of Penn State, USA; York, UK; and Caen, France; and an international consultant on a UK research project investigating global actor training practices. She is founder and artistic director of OpticNerve Performance Group, a training and performance ensemble with a focus on the physical staging of narrative text.

About the interviewer

Dr Mary Luckhurst is Honorary Professor of Theatre and Screen Performance at Bristol University, UK. She is a theatre historian, pioneer in dramaturgy and an expert analyst of acting and directing. She is the author of fourteen books and many articles on theatre and performance. She is co-founder of the Department of Theatre, Film and Interactive Media at York University, UK and has been Research Professor at the Universities of Sydney, Melbourne, CUNY, Oxford and most recently, in 2023, at Trinity College, Cambridge.

INTERVIEWEES

All interviews were conducted by Mary Luckhurst, and took place in Melbourne and Sydney, Australia, from April to July 2013.

Gary Abrahams is a playwright, director, performer and theatre-maker. He is currently Executive Director of Kadimah Yiddish Theatre. Collaborations as an actor and director include *Angels in America: Part One, Yes, Pale Blue Dot*.

Grant Cartwright is an actor, voice-over artist, narrator and arts leader. He currently works as a producing artistic director based in New York. Collaborations include *Five Kinds of Silence, Yes, The Mill on the Floss* and *Polygraph*.

Luisa Hastings-Edge is an actor, voice-over artist, physical theatre-maker and producer working across stage, screen and in innovative new works. Collaborations include *Top Girls, Stockholm* at Red Stitch Actors Theatre and *Pale Blue Dot* and *The Mill on the Floss* with OpticNerve.

Richard Lawton is a theatre director and voice trainer currently working as a master voice and presentation consultant. Richard has observed the development of Pulse over the past thirty years.

Hannah Liddeaux is a contemporary performance maker, physical performer, actor and director. Hannah is a Pulse trainer and workshop leader for OpticNerve. Collaborations include *Invisible Stains*, *Pale Blue Dot* and *The Mill on the Floss* which she produced.

Dr Richard Murphet has been engaged in writing, directing and creating contemporary forms of theatre for five decades and is currently an Honorary Senior Fellow at the University of Melbourne. Richard has followed the development of the Pulse approach over the past twenty-five years.

Darren Natale is a creative professional and entrepreneur and currently works as a senior executive and strategy consultant. He trained in Pulse, was an actor/maker in *Zivot* and produced OpticNerve's *Yes* and *Five Kinds of Silence*.

Zahra Newman is an actor working across stage and screen with Australia's major theatre companies, and international film and television networks. Collaborations include training and performing in *The Taming of the Shrew* and *The Mill on the Floss*. She actively incorporates tools and skills from the Pulse methodology into her other work.

INTERVIEWEES

Meredith Penman is an actor and playwright working across stage and screen. She currently works as an English and Drama teacher and freelance writer. Collaborations include training and OpticNerve's *Yes,* which remains one of her most powerful creative experiences.

Stephen Phillips is a theatre-maker, actor, voice-over artist and teacher. He is currently Artistic Director of 5 Angry Men Theatre Company and is a Pulse trainer and workshop leader for OpticNerve. Collaborations include teaching Pulse and convening weekly Pulse Jams at VCA, and actor/maker in *Zivot* and *Pale Blue Dot*.

Sam Strong is a director, dramaturg and arts leader. He is currently Executive Director of Creative Industries at Creative Victoria. Sam encountered Pulse as assistant director and performer in Caryl Churchill's *Vinegar Tom*.

Kaz Therese is an interdisciplinary artist and cultural leader in authentically diverse arts practice. They are currently a lead programmer at the Museum of Contemporary Arts, Australia. Kaz first encountered Pulse at the beginning of their performing arts education in 1997. Pulse became a foundational tool for devising and creating their work.

Lachlan Woods is an actor, theatre-maker, photographer and arts leader. He has worked across stage and screen on contemporary, classical and new writing. Collaborations include as an actor/maker, *Invisible Stains*, *Pale Blue Dot, Polygraph* and actor/producer, *Manbeth: Macbeth Amplified*. His training in Pulse remains a cornerstone of his approach to performance.

INTRODUCTION

What is pulse?

A group of performers undertake Pulse training by improvising together with a shared language of working concepts. The concepts are combined with a performance and compositional vocabulary that I call Principles. As the Principles are introduced to the ensemble, one by one, they are worked with and embodied by the performers, enabling them to recognize and play with structures. Performative material may include language, action, image, sound or song; elements that can be combined to create a performance improvisation or Pulse Sketch. The content of a Pulse Sketch is associative and poetic, rather than linear or narrative driven. Once performers have trained and gained skill, Pulse structures can enable an ensemble to develop original performance material. When performers take ideas, themes and research into the Pulse improvisation, images, recurring motifs, scenarios, vignettes, monologues and dialogues emerge that can be recalled and repeated to make new work. When it comes to working on a dramatic script; the approach to ensemble practice and the embodiment of working concepts, Principles and ethos of Pulse training inform the rehearsal process. Pulse, in the rehearsal context, involves one layer of ensemble improvisation in response to the reading of the dramatic text (in which non-verbal scenarios and relationship images occur), and another layer in which individual actors improvise as they verbalize their character's thoughts (revealing a character's inner life through action), producing a heightened physicality which is then used for the staging of the work.

This book was conceived as two complementary practical workbooks, one for training an ensemble using Pulse and the other for directing and staging text-based plays using the Pulse rehearsal process. Ostensibly, they are two separate activities connected through the evolution of process. These workbooks can be read and used independently, but the content of each workbook enhances understanding of the other. If you only want to rehearse a play using the Directing Workbook you will need to read the Training Workbook to understand the premise of the work, and probably facilitate some phases of training with your actors to introduce them to the application of Pulse improvisation. If you are simply training a group of actors using the Training Workbook, it is helpful to understand practical outcomes and possibilities for the work, which case studies in the Directing Workbook will give you.

The Training Workbook speaks to emerging practitioners, from those who may never have taught before or teachers who have not encountered Pulse before, to actors who want to train in a group or to actors who want to become facilitators of Pulse training. The Directing Workbook will be of interest to actors who wish to direct and want to be physically engaged on the rehearsal floor, but also for any practitioner searching for a physical approach to the staging of text. These workbooks address practitioners wanting to work within the context of ensemble practice, such as conservatoire trainers and directors, drama and acting teachers at high schools and/or in the university sector, groups of actors training outside institutions and independent theatre practitioners directing with ensembles. The Pulse approach presents a model for ensemble practice where large cast size and diversity are a given and where learning the skill of collaborative practice is essential. I will not go into detail here about what you will find in each chapter as the nature of each workbook needs its own description. Chapters 1 and 7 begin with instructions on how to use respective workbooks (Training and Directing), where I have clearly set out how the content is organized and offer advice on how to proceed. Here I will give a brief overview of what you will find in each workbook and what you will not find.

The Training Workbook begins with advice on preparing the group and the training space. Chapter 2 guides you through the eight phases of Pulse training, focusing upon the application of Performance and Compositional Principles from group improvisation through to execution of Performance improvisations. The aesthetic of this practice is implicitly encoded in the style and structure of the work, as are the ethics of practice that underpin the application of each phase. Chapter 3 contains a series of ensemble practice tasks that prepare a group of individual performers to begin the Pulse phases. Chapter 4 supplies skill-focus tasks, offering a condensed and more defined context in which to practise specific skills. Chapter 5 outlines how to integrate design elements into the final phases. This integration will be useful if an ensemble is training to execute performance improvisations for an audience. Chapter 6 gives information on how to practise Pulse independently without a trainer; it also offers strategies for the development of new work and culminates with a case study of the creation of an original performance text – *Invisible Stains*. The Training Workbook takes a particular approach to improvisation rather than instruction on a specific system or acting technique. It will enable an ensemble to structure an improvisation for the purpose of presentation. And it is through the learning of this process that each ensemble actor becomes trained in spatial and dramaturgical composition, sensory engagement, working with ambiguity and non-literal association, rhythmic awareness, and the capacity to perform and create simultaneously. The resultant performance style is physical, the body and action are central and the skills have been embodied kinaesthetically.

The Directing Workbook describes in detail how to apply Pulse improvisation to the rehearsal of a scripted text. Chapter 7 outlines the four layers of the rehearsal process: Intuitive Investigation, Immersion, Mapping and Rendering. It builds on the shared language of process and skills developed by an ensemble and a trainer/director through Pulse training. Accompanying the rehearsal process, I discuss culture, attitude and structure, as well as rehearsal concepts and how they interface with the process. Chapter 8 shows how I have applied the process outlined in Chapter 7. Using case studies of productions – classical and contemporary texts – I describe how each of the rehearsal layers was used by offering detailed examples of rehearsal outcomes. A short documentary was made during rehearsals of one of the case studies, *The Mill on the Floss* produced in 2016. It offers examples of actors working through Immersion, Mapping and Rendering towards the final production and will help you visualize the physical nature of the work. It can be found on the Bloomsbury companion website (https://www.bloomsburyonlineresources.com/the-pulse-approach).

The Directing Workbook is not about conventional play directing and does not intend to be inclusive of all rehearsal demands. It does not involve the type of rehearsal where actors focus primarily upon script analysis and character development and where the director 'blocks' the play. It gives pragmatic instruction to a director wanting to use improvisation to realize a dynamic, energetically staged outcome with an ensemble of actors. In this process, character evolves through physical actions that emerge during improvisational layers. The staged outcome will involve heightened physicality if the director's curatorial choices are aligned with the Pulse aesthetic. If, however, the physical 'world' of the play is based on 'realist' principles, this approach will still assist the actor to develop the physical embodiment of character.

The evolution of Pulse is rooted in the Australian performance training ecology but there are many methods and artists that employ physical improvisation on scripted text; for example, Stanislavski's Active Analysis, Michael Chekhov's psychological gestures and practitioners such as Anne Bogart, Mike Alfreds and Mike Leigh come to mind. You can also work with emotions using the body through Alba Technique and the Perdekamp Method. The Pulse approach is simply an account of how I have systemized my use of such performance tools. As the reader may be an emerging practitioner and not yet experienced at guiding a performance group; I have erred on the side of caution and perhaps at times been overzealous when repeating advice about working safely and with consent. This is the difference between doing it and writing about it. The best I can do is give the reader my perspective and alert them to possible challenges.

A group of improvisors must be responsive to what happens, moment to moment. The 'call and response' from trainer to ensemble, director to actor, cannot be planned or anticipated, and the development of skill in an ensemble happens for individual players at different times. There is an organic evolution of group consciousness that moves the work forward, but the work can also crash without warning. With Pulse improvisation, the application of Principles, concepts and structures is not linear, and yet I must describe these complex phenomena in a linear fashion when I translate them into writing here. The pragmatic delivery of information on the page cannot encompass the intuitive subjectivity of a trainer or director who 'reads the room' and must make choices about what the group needs next. Notions of chance, timing, subjective perception and random associative collisions affect what happens on the Pulse floor and serve to dislodge attempts to create a prescriptive methodology. In its written and performative form, Pulse must be considered as an approach that is fluid and will evolve to serve the needs of every practitioner who uses it.

I searched for many years for a way to articulate the progression of this organic process. At the very least, I hope this book provides a conceptual and practical framework to refer to while you are exploring and playing with Pulse, and that it encourages you to create your own collaborative performance culture.

PART ONE
TRAINING WORKBOOK

Figure 1 Joshua Ryan, Emily Thomas, Kevin Fa'asitua Hofbauer and Kade Greenland, *Invisible Stains,* October 2009.
Credit: Photo © Jeff Busby.

1
THE PULSE CANVAS

How to use this workbook

The Training Workbook is a practical, step-by-step guide through the phases of training on the Canvas (the playing space), referred to as Pulse Canvas work. In this chapter I explain how Pulse is different from free improvisation; I provide advice on how to introduce this approach to your ensemble as well as how to prepare the space before you begin to work. In Chapter 2, 'The Pulse Phases', I introduce each of the eight phases of Canvas work consecutively. I describe how to set up each phase, give definitions of each Principle to be introduced and suggest what to say when side coaching the actors as they are working. I identify the most common challenges and how to debrief each Pulse to take the actors to the next stage.

The nature of Pulse training is organic and evolves as the group absorbs the Principles. As the conceptual and ethical framework of Pulse is fundamental to the work, I have described these aspects throughout the delivery of phases rather than explaining them at the outset. Key working concepts and advice to the performers and trainer are also dispersed throughout the progression of the phases and not found in a separate category. It is important that some concepts and attitudinal strategies are not introduced too early and that others are only introduced when the trainer perceives the need for them. Each phase builds upon the one before. An overview may appear in this way. In Phase One a group begins moving choreographically in silence which develops through Phases Two and Three. By Phase Four Performance Principles are introduced, in Phase Five, physical action and gestures, and in Phase Six, Compositional Principles are layered. From Phase Seven onward, vocal sound and speaking are integrated. I have described the Canvas tasks in the general order in which they usually happen, but the best way for a trainer to use this workbook would be to read it in its entirety, gain an understanding of why I have put the phases in this order and then work instinctively as the phases evolve.

In Chapter 3, 'Ensemble Practice Tasks', you will find a series of exercises that will instil the notion of ensemble practice in a group. If you are unfamiliar with Pulse work, or working with a group of individuals who have not worked together before it is a good idea to start with these tasks. Do a couple of sessions with selected tasks before you begin the Canvas work. I have suggested certain emphasis with side coaching and debriefing, to introduce Pulse concepts, and alerted you to a performer's tendencies that can be learning opportunities. Chapter 4, 'Skill Focus Tasks', also has a set of exercises, but of a different nature and design. They all involve practising integration of words, physical gesture, emotion and speaking. These group exercises offer an opportunity to focus on a particular element that is about to be introduced in one of the phases on the Canvas. There are clear instructions in Chapter 2, during Pulse phases, about where and how to do this. As the Pulse Canvas work progresses you will need to continually dip into them. I have included extensions (supplementary exercises) for most of the tasks, so each time you return to them there can be a development. If you are not in a position to commence the Pulse Canvas work but you want to train an actor's physical imagination and verbal improvisatory skills, all the exercises in Chapters 3 and 4 will serve that function. Chapter 5, 'Integrating Design Elements and Audience', will take you through the practical aspects of introducing objects, costume, music, light and audience if Performance Pulse is the outcome you desire. Chapter 6, 'Alternative Applications', offers frameworks for independent practice, strategies for making new work and a case study – *Invisible Stains,* describing the process of making an original performance text including the challenges faced.

I have written through the lens of my own teaching and side coaching in a class. This means I am talking to the trainer or the person guiding the group. Occasionally, mostly with the tasks in Chapters 3 and 4, I find myself directly addressing the actors, as if I am teaching. I drift and become the trainer's voice in a class: 'Focus on your breath and watch it returning to its normal rhythm.' Occasionally, I will address both trainer and actor simultaneously: 'Notice how using these shapes on the edges of the Canvas can lead to "story" moments.' Hopefully, writing in this mode reflects the very nature of Pulse where performers move fluidly with ease from micro to macro and from subjective to objective, constantly dancing with this duality.

The language of training

In Pulse, a tension may appear when describing the notions of 'intellect', 'rational', 'instinct', 'intuition', 'emotion' and 'imagination' separately, as this is not what is literally happening; the divisions are metaphorical. During training, however, referencing them separately is a way of prioritizing an aspect and bringing greater focus to it. When the actor has gained skill, the *feeling* of coalescence is a sign for them that embodiment is occurring. There are no literal boundaries to begin with, but as embodiment takes place the metaphorical boundaries dissolve. Neurologist Antonio Damasio (2000, 26) refers to the 'feeling of knowing', which may be another way of recognizing synthesized skill. Such kinaesthetic perception is a useful training benchmark for the actor.

Communication through side coaching while actors are working needs to be simple and precise. The physiological processes involving the brain, mind and consciousness that take place during a psycho-physical training[1] such as Pulse are complex. Your choice of words needs to be practical, as the actor must be able to immediately process the idea. For this reason, my use of language is mostly metaphoric and creates an image to pursue rather than a concept to enact: words that focus the actor on *feeling* rather than literal understanding or analysis of process. Using a phrase such as 'by-pass the rational mind' means to let go of trying to make logical connections between what is happening. It encourages an actor to make poetic associations. 'Activate your composer' refers to the part of the performer's consciousness able to focus upon composition while the actor's body is in action. I refer to the actor 'playing their instrument' (their integrated selves) and ask them to access their 'physical imagination' (prioritizing imaginative physical responses).

You will find that I have, at times, given examples for tasks that refer to gender identities (a man chases a woman) or that are heteronormative (she/he kisses them). This is purely to emphasize to practitioners the generic (not personal) nature of the imagery emerging. You may wish to replace the pronouns. In practice, Pulse begins with an empty Canvas, and will reflect diversity and social/gender fluidity of the world we live in. The Canvas work reflects, includes and uses, as material, whatever identities (gender, sexuality, ethnicity) exist within the ensemble that are brought to the floor.

Many of the exercises I have described in Chapters 3 and 4 were originated by others. The way I use them is specific, and this is important to note. They have been passed down as a legacy in the great tradition of artists absorbing ideas and making them their own. I don't remember how they came to me. Perhaps a workshop with Richard Schechner, Pina Bausch, Playback or KISS Theatre Research Group, but I know that I experienced these exercises decades ago when I was an actor, and that I adapted them, shifted their focus and then repurposed them to supplement Pulse Canvas training. You might even recognize or practice some yourselves. For this I am eternally grateful to my theatrical ancestors. I hope that contemporary emerging practitioners will similarly take Pulse in their own direction.

Before you begin

Doing Pulse is participating in the training.
A *Pulse Canvas* is the playing space.
A *Pulse Sketch* is a structured improvisation which takes place on the *Pulse Canvas*.

This workbook takes you through the full sweep of Pulse Canvas work: from beginning with four actions in the space with a group who may never have worked together before, to finally executing a multilayered performance improvisation in the form of a Pulse Sketch. Below, I have outlined an integrated framework that will train an ensemble to embed performance and compositional Principles and key working concepts incrementally. The following phases can, however, be explored separately and independently, and although the training uses the idea of an audience (observers) and is conceptually performance oriented, you can also use these tools simply for rehearsal and the creation of material.

Improvisation and Pulse

Often improvisation used in theatrical rehearsal is free and open-ended with no parameters. In his book *Free Play: The Power of Improvisation in Life and the Arts*, Stephen Nachmanovich describes it like this:

> Play is different from 'game.' Play is the free spirit of exploration, doing and being for its own pure joy. Game is an activity defined by a set of rules, like baseball, sonnet, symphony, diplomacy. Play is an attitude, a spirit, a way of doing things, whereas game is a defined activity with rules and a playing field and participants.
>
> (Nachmanovich 1990, 43)

In our context, I think of free improvisation as 'play' and Pulse as 'game'. Free improvisation is like a bunch of friends going to the park to chuck the ball around. Pulse is like playing a championship match with objectives, rules and strategies. 'The most common form of improvisation is ordinary speech. As we talk and listen, we are drawing on a set of building blocks (vocabulary) and rules for combining them (grammar) … the sentences we make with them may never have been said before and may never be said again' (Nachmanovich 1990, 17).

When we converse, we communicate successfully with each other because we recognize and apply the same rules. Different languages have their own rules. Within the world of improvisation practice, Pulse has its own vocabulary (actions) and grammar (Principles), and just as language has a style – poetic, prose, heightened or ordinary speech – Key Working Concepts influence the style of improvisation. Principles, like the grammar of language, are applied by a group of improvisors to the actions that are taking place in the space. The culture of Pulse is built through the performer's kinaesthetic understanding of the 'grammar', which makes future collaborations with any performer who knows this 'language' possible. The Principles can be understood dramaturgically under the following categories:

SPACE Geometry of Space, Architecture of the Space, Depth of Field
RHYTHM Sustaining Action, Development to Climax, Dynamic Tension, Shattering the Space, Plateau
STRUCTURE Commencement, Jo, Ha, Kyu, Denouement, Form and Chaos, Finding the Ending
CONTENT Contrast, Repetition, Unit of Action, Recurring Motif, Juxtaposition

They will be introduced to the group of improvisors once the group has established the action 'building blocks' (Scales), in Phases One and Two.

The floor of the studio on which you are about to work is called a Canvas. In the literal sense, it is an empty space where actors improvise, but the language I use for describing Pulse work is intentional. I want the actor to look at this space as if they are visual artists contemplating their canvas. As the painter applies different coloured paint or collage materials to the canvas they will apply performative elements in a spatial composition comprised of movement, vocal sound and language. It may help them to imagine seeing the Canvas from the perspective of a drone hovering above the space. In this way they can practise becoming aware of the picture they are in. The four fundamental actions practised on the Pulse Canvas are called Scales. Just as the actors visualize the space through the lens of a painter, I'd like them to hear and sense the rhythm of the actions like a musician. The musical scale is a set of tones from which you can build melodies, harmonies, disharmonies and musical phrases. Similarly, the four actions are the building blocks of a Pulse Sketch. It is a Sketch because it is fluid, spontaneously executed and it takes place upon the Canvas.

In re-iterating notions, that will be familiar from abstract art forms, I am hoping that they will seep into the actor's creative sensibilities. This will encourage them to be associative rather than linear in their thinking, and attend to shape and form rather than content and narrative with language dominating. When I teach Pulse to dancers and musicians they understand it instinctively. For actors to take on Pulse they need to initially put down their theatrical tools – dialogue, character, behavioural gesture and psychological congruence – in favour of attention to shape, position, rhythm and sensation.

The Space

You will need a studio space where the group can run full pelt and fall to the floor safely. Safety is the most important guiding parameter; but working with physical freedom is key; so, until the participant's physical awareness develops sufficiently, the space must be large enough for each member of the group to safely take risks. In my experience Australian training spaces are much larger than those in Europe and North America, so use your discretion. All this is relative depending upon the size of the group. If it is a group of twenty, I would recommend working in halves. If your group is larger, split the group into four. Often a dance studio can work well. If there is a wall of mirrors, make sure there is a curtain to cover them. It is important that the actors are not watching themselves work. The space needs to be empty, preferably with three clear walls. The actors who are observing will sit watching from the invisible fourth wall side of the space. A sprung wooden floor is optimum. Concrete is too harsh on the joints and carpet too rough on the skin.

The Light

Whenever possible I work with theatre lights. Working in a bright and sunny studio will be fine for initial phases of training, but as performance improvisations (Pulse Sketches) begin to consolidate, try to create performance conditions. I have been known to black out the windows and use a few lights fixed on floor stands or trees if I can get them. Of course, you can progress without these conditions, but I discovered early on that actors were braver and less tentative when Pulsing under stage lighting. It creates a 'theatrical womb' that makes them feel safe, unself-conscious and less exposed. It also helps them to pretend they are performing to an audience. The other benefit is that stage lights create an aesthetic bubble; everything looks beautiful and actors will play with the shadows, creating a generative source for content as well as a spatial dynamic.

The Body

It is preferable to Pulse in loose, relaxed clothing of a block colour. All black is useful to begin with, as it neutralizes individuality and focuses the group's attention on form.

Later, wearing different block colours can become a generative source for a Pulse theme. Don't wear clothes with writing or symbols on them. This would introduce content into the improvisation. Similarly, florals and patterns are too visually busy. Performers will be absorbing an understanding of structure by witnessing others work and visual clarity makes this easier. The space you have set up is like a blank canvas. Whatever goes onto it will create meaning. It is best to work with bare feet, but if that is not possible, soft shoes are essential.

Respect

I suggest that there is no social conversation after entering the space. The working space is a sacred place dedicated to the support of an ensemble consciousness: a heightened awareness of the state of the 'other'. Learning to be comfortable with silence in a group is a valuable skill for an actor and needs to be practised. Sharing with words takes place in the form of group verbal reflection at the end of a task. If a session begins in silence, it creates a ritual commencement, which sets the tone for working, as it encourages respect for the space and for the preparative creative state each performer must find before commencing the work. Choose a task such as Walk/Stop (Task Two) in Chapter 3 to frame the early working sessions. This clearly announces that Pulse is a group physical experience rather than one where static thinking and talking are the primary modes of learning.

Safety and shared responsibility

It is a good idea to 'commence the way you intend to proceed'. Begin the conversation about personal and group safety before it becomes a necessity. When the imagination takes hold of an inexperienced actor, they can lose all sense of limitations. This is the glorious thing about improvisation. 'Letting go' is crucial to the performer's kinaesthetic learning, but it can also present some risky behaviour. The performer's will and imagination can push them beyond their physical limits. As a facilitator you will learn to anticipate this from certain individuals. You should also bring this to the attention of the ensemble to make them aware of this tendency. Once, I was facilitating a blindfold exercise and an actor ran into a concrete wall. After that, the safety conversation became a priority. I learnt that lesson so you don't have to.

When engaging in improvisation the 'what' and 'how' are not prescribed. If an actor is triggered by emotional content or a physical action, let them know they should leave the floor. If they are physically entangled, they should call your name, and you can go onto the floor and remove them. Counselling can take place when the session has finished. There is a difference between feeling 'uncomfortable' and feeling 'unsafe'. Feeling unsafe is a matter for the individual. Usually, it will be about something tapping into an actor's physical or emotional lived experience. Only they can recognize this. In early Pulse sessions most actors will be uncomfortable because they will be working outside their 'comfort zone'. Many will feel scared when they are in the unknown. The more Pulse they do the more comfortable they will become. It is about stretching this zone. I think of it a bit like 'good' pain and 'bad' pain. Only they will know if it is about safety or discomfort.

Figure 2 Emily Thomas and Grant Cartwright, *Polygraph*, July 2018.
Credit: Image by Pier Carthew.

For actors to risk being open and vulnerable they need to trust you and trust the group. Creating an environment of permission – allowing critique but not judgement – will create psychological safety in the room. If the ensemble feels 'held' by you, they will do their best work.

Physical intimacy and consent

The notion of consent must be raised before any exercises or Pulse Canvas work begins. This is now a common prerequisite for any group physical work in performance environments, and as improvisation makes it impossible to obtain consent within the context of the work, establishing a general protocol about touching is advised. My suggestion is to have a frank and open dialogue with the group, eliciting a sense of stress levels for various individuals. Let them know that this work is about physical action in groups and relationships so it will inevitably involve touching, perhaps caressing, grabbing, lifting and dragging each other's bodies. When executing these actions, they must be respectful, or trust will be lost. As stated above, stress clearly that it is their responsibility to leave the floor if they feel unsafe. Create a signal, a hand gesture towards you, which will let you know they are coming off the floor for that reason and you can follow up later. I would suggest that, as they begin to experience the nature of the work, if they are feeling vulnerable at the start or during a session, that they become observers rather than go onto the Canvas. In some cases, you may have to modify the work considerably which is a choice that you can make.

2
THE PULSE PHASES

Phase One: Developing kinaesthetic awareness

This first phase introduces Pulse Scales – running, walking, standing and falling – which enables the development of kinaesthetic awareness: the ability to activate change in response to external stimuli. The aim of this task is for the actors to experience physical intuition by 'listening with their body', receiving information through their senses and responding with action – to practise letting go of decision-making with the rational mind (intellect). Encourage the actors to work with their *first impulse* (instinctive drive/urge) and to commit to that action.

Working in the micro

In preparation for the full Canvas work, ask all the participants to practise the action of falling to the floor safely by keeping their body loose, as if 'melting'. You should allow five minutes per group to ensure that everyone understands how to fall without hurting themselves. Split the group in half with one half working on the Canvas (Group A) and the other half (Group B) observing from the invisible fourth wall.

Side coach with the following instructions:
Group A, find a place in the space to begin. Stand still, close your eyes and focus on your breathing, waiting for an impulse to move. When you experience an impulse, you can do one of four actions: run, walk, stand or fall. Once you have moved into action and when something in the space affects you, allow yourself to be changed, which will lead to another action. There is no mental rationale for moving, stopping or falling.

Group B, *actively* watch Group A. Practise imagining yourself in the space. As you watch, have a sense of what might change *you*.

While the actors are working, point out what might stimulate *change* – the moving or falling of someone close to them, light shifting in the space, feeling a breeze from someone running, the sound of feet or the silence after bodies have fallen. Encourage the actors to take every opportunity to be changed. Invite them to focus solely on their own experience and what they are doing: working in the micro. They are only using the activity of the group and what is happening in the room as a stimulus. These actions are like primary colours, or notes in a chord; they should be clear and precise, not embellished with a supplementary narrative, for example walking backwards or falling in slow motion. Encourage them to focus on 'when' not 'how'.

Group A works in this way until the experience has been established. Group B swaps with Group A and the exercise begins again. After both groups have Pulsed, ask the whole group to reflect on their experience.

Group reflection and debrief

The observations of both watchers and participants are a core part of training and they are not incidental. Reflections embed the Pulse vocabulary and train the analytical eye. During reflection, participants try to translate their kinaesthetic and intuitive experiences into words using a cognitive process. This dance between kinaesthetic and cognitive underpins Pulse as a physical training with an analytical vocabulary. Responses to what they have seen or experienced should be immediate and brief, so as not to stay 'in their heads' for too long. At this point emphasis should be on the *doing* rather than the talking. The following is a guide to some useful questions to begin with:

- Did you look for opportunities to be changed and then take them? If not, why not?
- While watching, did you notice opportunities for change being missed?
- Were you stuck 'in your head?'
- Did you find yourself trying to recognize or define an impulse?
- Did you tend to favour one action over others? Why do you think that was?
- How much did internal sources (adrenaline rush, feeling lazy after lunch) play a part in how you moved?
- What happened to your awareness of the action in the space when you fell to the floor and remained there for some time?

I have found that participants can sabotage themselves by setting the bar for sensing an impulse too high. They get stuck trying to define what an impulse is and then decide that unless it is of significance they will not be affected. Point out that you can choose to be affected by a breath across your skin, or you can wait until a brick falls on your head. It is up to you. You must *want* to be affected. That is what I mean by the actor searching for something to change them. They are *active* rather than *passive* in the space. Working in the micro is a framework to enliven and heighten the senses. It is the fundamental task for practising *being changed*. It is a good way to begin group work on the Canvas, but even an individual working solo will find it a useful tool for bringing themselves physically and mentally into the present moment. As we move forward with the Canvas work, the Pulse Scales – running, walking, standing and falling – are the materials (building blocks) upon which we apply the Principles. They also act as the safety net, the default position, the home page. They are where everything begins.

Phase Two: Making connections

In this next phase the ensemble extends their sphere of awareness from their own interactions with the environment to the dynamics of the group: working in the macro.

Working in the macro

Split the group into A and B in the same way as above.

Side coach with the following instructions:
Group A, find a place in the space to begin. Stand still, close your eyes, focus on your breathing and wait for the impulse to move. Use the four fundamental actions, Pulse Scales, and work in the micro. (Let this go for about five minutes.) Continue doing the Scales but take your attention away from your personal sphere and become aware of what others are doing in the space. Without making eye contact, make connections with the other group members through proximity, rhythms and action. Create patterns. You are still working from impulse, but instead of the impulse being an immediate reaction let it become a response conditioned by the imperative to join with others. Group B, while watching Group A, become aware of the patterns that begin to form.

While the actors are working, point out what patterns you see emerging, for example when someone runs others start running; a fall creates a domino effect of falling; someone standing against a wall evokes an impulse in others to join them making a line. Remind them that attention to the making of patterns overrides any other impulses. They are searching to do as others do, joining in or initiating. They are making connections, not trying to be different.

Once Group A has grasped working in the macro, briefly ask for reflections from Group B. What patterns did they observe? Did they see missed opportunities? Swap the groups over and repeat the task. The groups may go back and forth, Pulsing for five to ten minutes at a time for the whole session.

Emerging roles

As the groups swap back and forth and become familiar with making patterns you will notice that formal elements are emerging. When everyone is still and one actor is activated, they are 'doing a solo'. When two performers create a connection through action or in space, they are 'doing a duet'. When a small group works in unison against the action of a solo or a duet, they are working as a chorus. Side coaching is a good opportunity to draw the ensemble's attention to this. For example, 'everyone has fallen but one person is left standing, they are doing a solo', 'I'm seeing a duet of two people standing while all the chorus run the diagonal of the space'. At the beginning of each Canvas session work in the micro, and after a while ask them to open their attention to the group and to start making connections. It is important to give the ensemble practise at consciously shifting attention between micro and macro. You might use instrumental music as a soundscape for this task. If you want some guidance doing this, see Chapter 5.

Key working concepts for the performer

Commitment to action and *What does it need*? These are two of the three key working concepts that are part of the Pulse shorthand, and they are constantly referred to when side coaching. The other is to *'smell' the dramatic potential* (which is introduced when content becomes a priority). Also introduced later, *breaking the fourth wall* and *working in parallel* are two other key concepts which help define the Pulse performance style, but they are not used for side coaching. From here on, whenever mentioned, the concepts, and later the Principles, will be in italics to visually imprint the shared language.

Commitment to action
Introduce the performers to the idea that committing totally to an action, which is a response to having been affected, is what creates authenticity and watchability. Once they are in the action, encourage them to bring their physical, imaginative, mental and psychic energy to its execution and to let go of any doubt; be completely in the action of that moment and not in what came before or where it might lead. The authenticity of an act is to do with commitment not 'feeling'. Focus and energy equal commitment. Bringing attention and performance energy to a moment makes it believable. Establishing this notion with the Scales is important to do before Verbal and Emotional Gestures are introduced to the Canvas. The only way to make an emotional gesture believable on the Canvas is through *commitment to action*. For a full explanation, go to Chapter 4.

What does it need?
The addition of each new Principle will cause the dropping of some others. Learning to juggle takes time. But as the actors are practising, the Pulse still needs to be kept 'alive'. I continually ask the question while side coaching, *what does it need*? This invites the performer/composer to bring their focus into the macro. Often performers say they don't know what to do or where to go, or I see them offer not *what it needs* but what they 'feel' like doing. It means they are self-focused and working in the micro. This question acts as a compositional tool. It helps the performer to focus on the work and not on themselves. As Michael Chekhov observed, 'true freedom in improvising must always be based upon necessity; otherwise, it will soon degenerate into either arbitrariness or indecision' (Chekhov 2001, 38). Eventually, *what does it need?* becomes the performer/composer's mantra. The answer will be their next action.

Phase Three: Working attitudes

Before moving on to Phase Four, where the action and content will take on complexity, it is time to introduce the following notions or working attitudes. They will need to be in place to continue working effectively on the Canvas, so stay with alternating the groups and working with Phase Two until you have covered them. You might bring them up in debrief when you notice the issues arising or introduce some as you side coach. They will become part of the collective understanding and culture of the work.

Advice for the performer

Personal and creative impulses

Point out the difference between *personal* impulse and *creative* impulse. A *personal* impulse is a discriminating response from the 'human'. For example, I'm tired, I don't feel like moving, I don't like working with that person, I'm bored with this task, I'm ideologically opposed to that. The passive being: waiting to be moved. The *creative* impulse comes from the 'actor' and overrides anything personal; it springs organically from an association (thought, sensory, kinaesthetic or intuitive) in the space and so is connected to the bigger picture, the macro. The *creative* impulse emerges out of an actor's *active* search to contribute. For example, they are running – I'll run too, or they ran past me – I felt the breeze – so I'll fall.

Connection not feeling

Being connected to your creative self, to the energy in the space and to the other actors, is about breath and attitude. This is different from *feeling* connected. Participants will often say that they are not *feeling* connected; they are passively waiting for an emotional signal to move them. Encourage them to change from a state of passive reception to being actively curious and outwardly focused. It will help later if the actors can already detach from the idea of only being affected if they *feel* something. Invite them to be affected by proximity, rhythm and synergy of action.

Chords versus individual notes

Embellishing the four actions at this stage activates personal desire: doing a funny walk or a mannered run. Try to focus the actor's attention on the group sensibility of making patterns. It is not the action or the actor themselves that should draw attention. It is not the single note we are concerned with but the combination of notes that make the beauty of the chord.

Courage and surrender

Actors may unconsciously avoid lying on the floor after falling or standing at the fourth wall with all the action happening behind them, because these actions obscure the major sense for information gathering – sight. It takes courage to surrender to the unknown. Getting them excited about being there is what we want to happen. Encourage them to trust their other senses and gradually they will be able to 'intuit' what is happening: anticipating group action without cognitive understanding.

Fear

All improvisation involves working in the unknown; this is likely to activate the performer's amygdala, the part of the brain that is responsive to threats in their environment. This will result in a fight/flight or freeze bodily response: the heart beats faster, the breath shortens and the palms get sweaty. Some people enjoy the arousal of these sensations when they are not literally under threat – that's why horror films and roller coasters are popular. While performers may experience the physical sensations of fear, there is another part of the brain that knows they are in a safe place. If the studio was on fire they would respond in a different way. Point out to those who seem debilitated by such sensations that it might be useful to interpret the body's response as excitement rather than fear and that they can choose to enjoy the arousal.

Everything is disposable

When performers are holding on tight and trying hard to make it happen, they are hostage to the rational mind and to the ego trying to be in control of everything. Sometimes it helps to talk straight to their ego. Instead of reinforcing what they are not doing, 'release the tension', 'go with the flow', I have found it helps to suggest that 'everything is disposable'. I have been told years later by former students that this simple phrase unlocked them. Using this as a mantra gave them permission to let go of the responsibility for the outcome and allowed them to become curious about what might be.

Dual consciousness

From the moment we introduced working in the macro on the Canvas we activated the actor's compositional awareness. We made them aware of an overriding group objective and gave them a desire to create form by focusing on the making of patterns. They are performing at the same time as composing; they are the creators and the creation. This is what I mean by working with dual consciousness: the ability to split awareness but work in an integrated way. In Phase One, the actor experienced working in the micro and in Phase Two, the macro. But from now on, the actor will need to juggle both states concurrently to be able to do a Pulse Sketch. The art of acting demands that an actor plays their part authentically; they must suspend their disbelief of the artificial performance context they are in. They must be inside an imaginary 'world' and yet be aware of the practical realities of lights, the audience or the camera. On the Canvas the performer and their 'composer' (the part of the performer's consciousness focusing upon composition) are symbiotically connected. I will be referring to the 'composer' in this way from now on. The performer must be seen to be *committing to action* while the part of them that is the 'composer' simultaneously focuses on compositional imperatives. If two levels of awareness are continually practised the dual state becomes reflexive and stamina is developed.

The performer/composer

Having worked through Phase Two (working in the macro) the 'composer' in each performer has been activated. This happened because they had to make 'choices' to make connections. From now on the actors will be exploring what it means to *postpone* an impulse. They will still work from impulse (an action emerging from a 'need to do') but not their *first* impulse. A first impulse is really an instinctive reaction. Working with the Principles in the following phases forces the actor to respond rather than spontaneously react. To respond means that the *cognitive* (imaginative) and *instinctive* aspects of consciousness are in the process of synthesizing, which is how the 'compositional consciousness' of a performer becomes developed.

The following are some examples of what might be happening as the synthesizing process takes place. A performer might recognize their first impulse, but because their 'composer' is working with Principles and looking for what the space needs, they will postpone it. They will wait until the time is right, or for an opportunity to arise or they will drop the impulse because the 'story' has moved on. Many impulses or ideas will pass through the 'composer' of an actor, but they must continue performing in the action of Pulse until their offer is needed. At another time the actor may be compelled to act immediately upon a spontaneous connection with another because their informed intuition tells them that the action is needed now. Alternatively, their awareness may be drawn to the balance of the space, which informs them that the composition needs them to hold their stillness 'in the picture' regardless of their 'personal' urge to move.

As you introduce the Principles in the following phases you will witness the actors struggling. Making this shift will be a confusing time for them. The kinaesthetic fusion process is uncomfortable, so explaining what is happening can be useful. It doesn't mean, however, that they will be able to do it at once. It will take much practice. Be careful not to talk too much about it. Actors inevitably try to intellectually understand instead of working through it on the Canvas. This synthesizing process will continue at a different pace for each individual actor right through the Canvas work.

> Side coaching is an important aspect of Pulse but, as a performer, I often have no recollection ... I know that I responded but I cannot recall the instructions because I was immersed totally in the work... Effectively the paradox is that you can exercise rationality while 'feeling' in an unconscious state – it happens the more you do Pulse. And what you learn as you become more advanced is to make the choice that is the most interesting for the art you are making together.
>
> Hannah Liddeaux

Embedding the principles

Embodiment through repetition creates physical/neural pathways and body memory, enabling us to drive a car, play an instrument or type without conscious application. Each of the Pulse Principles can be understood theoretically, but to Pulse, the Principles need to become embedded to the point where the actor is 'thinking with their body': the gap between cognitive thought and physical impulse closes until physical intelligence takes over. I often talk about doing 'flight hours'. For a pilot to get their flying license they must fly a set number of hours. If actors want to 'fly' when they do Pulse, they need to put in time on the Canvas – just as an athlete, dancer or musician does with their daily practice.

Advice for the trainer

The following are some training imperatives to keep in mind as you move further into the Canvas work.

Why are watching and side coaching important?

By working and then observing the same work being done by others the actors are consolidating their understanding of each Principle through 'active' observation. The observers connect with the Principle by witnessing the result of side coaching and when they are on the Canvas they connect the Principle to a kinaesthetic experience. In this way the ensemble learns the shared language of Pulse. Watching and doing are different and yet complementary experiences. By engaging in both perspectives, performers arouse a dual consciousness and begin to activate their 'composer'. This mode of discovery also moves the work along more quickly. Each time a group comes to the Canvas having watched the previous group; they take a leap forward, already knowing what they are working towards.

Focus on structure and form

In these early stages of developing a structural instinct, giving attention to meaning and content will get in the way of freely responding to the evolving form. Actors have an entrenched desire to constantly search for psychologically congruent meaning. They are accustomed to prioritizing content and will try to emphasize that aspect in the early phases on the Canvas. Gently discourage this desire. Pulse, as an ensemble compositional language, can only hold content successfully if the structural Principles are embedded and strong. When the physical vocabulary starts to expand, meaning and 'story' will organically emerge on the Canvas. It will be time then to pay attention to emerging content and bring it into conscious focus. In my experience, unless there is total attention first to the development of form and structure by discouraging attention to content, the ensemble's structural language will not develop.

Imprinting the learning: debrief and journal

Talking in a focused way straight after a task or a Canvas session brings together embodied experience and reflective practice. Having listened to the side coaching, the observers associate what they have *seen* with what they have *heard*. They are practising dual perception, learning to be 'in the body' of the performer (noticing opportunities and possibilities), and at the same time understanding what an audience is perceiving. In a debrief they articulate their discoveries then get on the Canvas to synthesize the experience. Doing, watching, listening, speaking then writing completes the cycle. Keeping a journal throughout the training journey will assist this process. Encourage them to talk to *themselves* by writing about their discoveries, challenges and questions, inviting them to self-evaluate as they look back over their development from the beginning of the work.

THE PULSE PHASES

Sharing experiences can invite comparisons, so guide the debrief away from criticism, always framing it as critique and calling on respect as the guiding principle. Someone once said, 'the learning occurs in the doing – the teaching occurs in the debrief'. The debrief is a time for you to contextualize the work/task/key working concept: the why. It is important that the conceptual framework is understood. If it remains elusive and unstated the performer is dependent solely upon the quality of the experience. If this is the case, they will not be able to perceive the 'bigger picture' nor translate the work into other contexts or environments. However, herein lies a paradox. It is important to keep talking sessions to a minimum and to be clear, precise and succinct when speaking. If in doubt don't *speak* – *do*. In this early phase the way you communicate and the language you use are highly influential and these set the tone of the debrief and the culture of the training room. By role-modelling non-judgement in your debriefing style the actors will follow your lead. Language can be ambiguous, so try to dispel assumptions and projected expectations. Reinforce the idea that they are in a state of constant discovery and that 'everything is information'.

Pulsing with the performers

Make sure that you introduce a concept or Principle because you have witnessed something on the floor that brings it to your attention. The introduction of each new Principle and concept should be initiated by what you see someone in the group already doing, not because you are following a lesson plan. You are Pulsing with the participants, so your next action is also determined by information you receive.

When the pulse falls apart

If the Pulse de-constructs and the group seems to have lost focus, connection and flow, it is a good idea to wind back, do the Pulse Scales and begin adding the layers bit by bit again. It also gives the ensemble a way of measuring their progress. It can be inspiring for them to go back to the basics, experience the embodiment and remember how difficult it was when they started.

Duration

The groups may change over in these phases many times until they are comfortably working from impulse without activating the rational mind. You will discern the pace you need to work at from both debriefs and what you witness on the Canvas. Each group is different. Some participants will move faster than others, which can help the ensemble progress. This is not a linear process, but you will notice when the dynamic of the group has shifted. Generally, if more than 50 per cent of the group has embodied the instruction you'll need to move on.

The training paradox

The performers are being asked to work from impulse and not the rational mind: the intellect's ability to reason and understand. Yet, to absorb the Pulse Principles while working from impulse they must access their intellect. We are asking them to be in the moment and anticipate the next move of the group or their duet partner. Having to hold two opposing notions at the same time is related to the state of dual consciousness. Whether they are juggling opposing ideas, states of consciousness or Pulse Principles, it is through doing 'flight hours' that they will accomplish integration. There is another paradox that will emerge at this stage of the training. If they try too hard to *do,* they will not succeed. If you see them working with effort and holding tension, they are unconsciously trying to control outcomes in a situation where that is impossible. When the ego loses control of a situation it feels like it is dying and the body panics. The key to balance is letting go of what you can't control. Encourage them to pay attention to the present moment. Ask them to change their attitude from 'I'm going to make this happen' to one of curiosity and intrinsic satisfaction in the task.

Pulsing without a trainer

Once an ensemble is Pulsing with the Scales, one of the witnesses can facilitate the introduction of a Principle or a leader can call out different Principles while they are working from inside the Pulse. Alternatively, a group may elect to focus on one Principle before they go onto the Canvas. When all the Principles have been introduced the ensemble will be able to Pulse autonomously.

> One's pulse is the basis of rhythm, and the rhythm is the receptive mechanism for the audience – it's also the hardest thing to teach. The understanding of rhythm is the strongest quality that a Pulse actor builds up. I'm talking about all the levels of rhythm: where to move, when to move and how, how long to stay silent, at what point you speak. Movement can be the flash of an eye or a sprint across the space.
>
> Richard Murphet

Phase Four: Learning a shared language

The introduction of each Principle is an evolving process dictated by *what* is needed *when* to build a piece of collaborative art. You will be introducing the Principles in two sections: performance and compositional. Performance Principles focus primarily on what the *performer* is doing and compositional Principles on what the *group* is doing, and the overall shape and dramatic structure of the Pulse.

Each session begins as usual, with a group on the Canvas working in the micro then moving to the macro. It may take a whole session or several with the two groups swapping back and forth for the ensemble to get a sense of each Principle. The introduction of the next one will depend on the pace of working and the openness of each group. There will be leaps forward towards a new Principle even before it is mentioned and there will be messy, chaotic moments when the Pulse falls apart. This often happens when a new Principle is introduced; everyone wants to play with the 'new toy' and all the others get neglected. When this happens go back to the Scales. It will take some practice before a group can add another Principle without losing awareness of the others. Don't worry – as sessions progress information accumulates, and the pace of uptake and integration increases.

> For me Pulse is instrumental work. Performing is fundamentally about being in a space and not knowing what is going to happen next. It is the stuff of theatre – there is no better training for that than Pulse.
>
> Stephen Phillips

Introducing the performance principles

Get Group A working the Scales on the Canvas, making patterns and finding solos, duets and chorus forms. As they are moving on the Canvas, use side coaching to introduce the first Principle. When you see that the group has kinaesthetically experienced integration, swap groups with reflection in between. Use your judgement about when to introduce the next Principle. You might see it emerge on the Canvas through the actor's actions; that's when I usually add the next one, but I will generally use the order below. Under each Principle there is a definition, a side coaching suggestion and supplementary observations that might be better left until debrief, or they may just be for your information. You decide how to use it.

Geometry of space

Attention to movement in the space in its geometric form: straight lines (up and down, side to side, diagonals) and circular motion.

Side coach Let go of focusing on patterns for a moment and become aware of the geometric shapes possible on the Canvas. Straight lines (vertical, horizontal, diagonal) and circles. Focus your attention on moving along these lines. Movement on the Canvas is now no longer directionless or random. Search for movement in a shape joining with others.

Debrief If someone falls on the diagonal line, another goes to the line and falls, then another and another. If someone initiates running on the vertical line: from upstage to downstage and back, everyone may join in. You will notice from these examples that the group is beginning to combine an awareness of both patterns and geometry.

Sustaining action

Individuals override the tendency to stop an action, such as running, based on an entrenched individual or group rhythmic pattern that develops. The continuing or pursuing of action is based on what the Pulse needs.

Side coach   Notice the rhythm of movement in the space. Notice your tendency and the other performer's tendency to run or walk for a short while and then stop for no reason. The rhythm of the herd is contagious. Draw your attention to sustaining an action once you are in it until something happens in the space that makes you stop.

Debrief   If you are running, continue running until you can't anymore; through exhaustion, obstruction or a stronger offer demanding your participation. At this stage make falling the end point of running. Falling acts like a full stop. Sustain lying on the floor or standing still until what the Pulse *needs* is for you to move. The *sustaining of action* is the Principle that overrides your internal impulse to stop when you haven't been affected by external influences.

Development to climax

An action grows without losing its essence. It increases in tempo, size or volume and intensity (the action itself does not change its form – running does not turn into skipping) until it reaches its peak. At the climax of the action, individual or group, there is a fall. A kinaesthetic experience of jo, ha, kyu (see below).

Side coach   When you find yourself *sustaining the action* of walking or running with others in the space, turn your attention to increasing the pace and intensity of the action. Whether walking towards running or running and getting faster, let the group energy drive the action until it reaches its peak where it can go no further, then fall to the floor.

Debrief   Once the action is at its peak, it must release. The performer falls to give the action a sense of completion. It is like a full-stop at the end of the sentence and the finish of the *jo, ha, kyu* (next Principle). The end of a climax must always be a fall because this is the only action that will create an abrupt release of energy and a still point. It is also the action that will create the most striking kinaesthetic effect on the actor's body as it imprints the rhythm of *jo, ha, kyu* or signals the end of the cycle. At this stage, gradually reducing pace and slowing to a walk, will only dissipate group momentum (this can happen later in the Canvas work once the group has more skill). To always commit to the fall as a mark of completion is also important for other reasons. During this early phase it helps reassure fellow performers that they can anticipate what will happen, builds trust in the developing language and initiates the group into the 'reading' of the score.

Discuss with the group if they reached a climax or if they let go too early. Did they fall at intensity level seven instead of ten? Did they stay at seven for too long, stuck in a *plateau*? (see Principle below). Draw their attention to sensing the rhythms in the space and the notion of duration.

Jo, ha, kyu

In this structure, you start slowly, then gradually and smoothly accelerate towards a very fast peak. After the peak, there is usually a pause and then a recommencement of the acceleration cycle ... Almost any rhythmic physical activity will tend to follow this pattern if left to itself.

(Oida and Marshall 1997, 31)

> **Side coach** Tune in to the rhythm of the Pulse. The *sustaining of action* builds the tension to the release, and then the beginning of the whole cycle again. Tune into this rhythm and notice its inevitability.
>
> **Debrief** Remind the group of their recent experience of *development to climax* – running, developing pace and intensity, reaching a peak, and then releasing, falling into stillness. Playing with *dynamic tension* (see Principle below) follows the same pathway but with its opposite outcome – being in the centre of rising tension through stillness and when it reaches a peak, releasing it by bursting into action. At this stage of training *development to climax* and *dynamic tension* introduce a rudimentary kinaesthetic sense of *jo, ha, kyu*.

Much has been written about the use of *jo, ha, kyu* in music, dance and theatre. In occidental performance forms, we can refer to it loosely as beginning, middle and end; but the concept of *jo, ha, kyu* is much more subtle and nuanced. It is also in everything, from a single gesture or breath to a monologue, a fragment or an entire Pulse Sketch: jo – *commencement*, ha – *development to climax*, kyu – *climax*. After the peak there is a pause (in Pulse this is represented by 'falling') and the cycle begins again.

Plateau

This is the tendency to remain constant in pace and volume resulting in a monotonous rhythm. The plateau will generally occur during repetition, where there is a tendency to 'tread water' stopping forward momentum.

> **Side coach** Notice during your *development to climax* how you are running but not accelerating towards a peak. Focus on the action always moving forward. Don't get stuck in a groove.
>
> **Debrief** There will always be a tendency for individuals to attach themselves to the group and wait for someone else to make a move: to 'hitch-hike'. When many of the performers are doing this there is no drive to push forward. This will cause a plateau. Ask everyone to take personal responsibility to reach the climax in the most efficient way possible. The sooner the group pushes towards the peak, the sooner they can

stop running. Practise this notion now within this simple framework; when this issue arises later it will be more complicated. You can then refer to this task.

Contrast

A performer makes an offer in opposition to what is taking place. Contrast can be applied to: the body (movement / stillness), the voice (vocal sound / language), tempo (fast / slow), volume (loud / soft / silence) and ensemble action (solo / duet / chorus).

> **Side coach** Notice the notion of *contrast* that surrounds you as you work. You are already doing it. This kinaesthetic understanding is already in your body. When everyone falls there is always someone left standing. When most of the group is running there is always a solo or duo standing still: movement and stillness. When a small group or chorus is clumped together in the space, notice the solo individual/s standing on the other side balancing the space – chorus and solo. Notice contrasts in levels: lying down and standing; in shapes: vertical and horizontal; and in tempo: fast, slow, still. Now that your attention has been drawn to contrast, activate your 'composer' to work with this Principle in the space.
>
> **Debrief** This Principle may seem obvious now but embedding an awareness of *contrast* in action will help them make the leap to the more complex notion of *juxtaposition* that will be introduced when we are dealing with content.

As this Principle becomes absorbed, like the others, it should take its place in the 'palette' and only be activated when the Pulse *needs* it. There may be a tendency, however, for some or all performers to be continually *contrasting* with the main group because they want to stand out. If this is the case, draw their attention to it and suggest they drop their focus on *contrasting* and instead, work for cohesion.

Dynamic tension

The building of intensity, experienced as tension, in stillness before its release. Introduce this Principle when you see the entire group is still (standing or lying).

> **Side coach** Tune into the sense of group cohesion. Enjoy the stillness and the silence. Experience it as punctuation. Now feel the tension building towards action. Be inside the tension like an animal poised to leap. Experience the group synchronicity of needing to break this tension. Be ready to act immediately.
>
> **Debrief** When all the players on the Canvas find themselves in this still moment, it is a moment of cohesion. It is powerful. Everyone knows something will happen, but no one knows what, when or how. It is to be listened to and taken advantage of, not to be ridden over by someone 'deciding' to move. There must always be vibrational energy and physical anticipation in the body, so it is not time to rest. It is important, however, to avoid the 'deadness' of *plateau*. If performers are not tuned into the rise of group tension, they will 'miss the wave' and the moment to move. If this happens,

the whole group will feel it through the dispersal of tension and lack of vitality in the movement that eventually happens. If they are tuned in and 'catch the wave' at the peak of tension they will usually make the strongest group offer, which is to run. When you see this, point out that they are kinaesthetically sensing *what it needs* or *'smelling' the dramatic potential* (key working concept). If they keep 'missing the wave' you can help them by side coaching. When *you* 'feel' the tension rise and your rhythmic sense says 'go', call it.

Repetition and the unit of action

A fundamental tool used as a Performance and Compositional Principle. A sequence of gestures, which when combined, is repeatable (physical and/or verbal). The order of the actions within the unit may change but the content remains the same. The unit may be a solo, duet or create a pattern for others to join.

Side coach Experiment with the idea of *repetition*; falling/standing/falling/standing, or running/falling/standing, running/falling/standing. This introduces the *unit of action*. It will consist of a minimum of two but usually three or more actions put together. Still focus on what the Pulse *needs,* but when you 'find' yourself in a solo or duet play with *repetitions* of a *unit of action*. Repeat them three times before moving onto another moment.

Debrief Encourage others to join in on someone's *repetition*. This may become a duet or a whole group action. The repeatable *unit of action* is called a motif. When it occurs at intervals throughout the Pulse it is called a *recurring motif* (Compositional Principle). When repeating *units of action* there might be a tendency to *plateau*. Bring in the notion of 'same but different' (apply the same *unit of action* to different contexts – somewhere else in the space, with a different person, at a different pace).

Phase Five: Expanding the action vocabulary

Having integrated the above eight Principles you will need to pause for a while. It is about now that you will notice, if you haven't already, the performers trying to break out of the limitations of Scales. It is time to bring other actions to the Canvas. The following individual actions should be introduced into the Pulse Scales separately, just as you did with the above Principles. Don't introduce the next one until the group has found multiple ways to work with the new action. This gives the ensemble a new element to integrate, broadening their 'physical palette' while they are still doing the Scales and juggling the Principles.

With the introduction of each new action/gesture, you will notice the seeds of possible narrative lines emerging. Don't draw too much attention to that yet. While they are integrating an expanded physicality they need to concentrate on form. If you introduce the notion of 'story' too soon, the rigour of formal experimentation with gestures will cease, and shape and spatial composition will get sloppy. Content will be the next layer of focus and this is introduced only when all physical gestures are on the Canvas. 'Story' will inevitably keep emerging, so remark on it, but don't put too much emphasis on it yet (see Evolving 'story' and attitude below).

In moving forward there will be more action, gesture and visual complexity on the Canvas, so you will need to make the working groups smaller. Of course, this depends on the size of your main group, but seven is a workable number. Seven is an odd number which allows for a solo to happen. If the group is small, start with five or three people on the Canvas, making sure there are at least a few participants left to witness and give feedback.

Physical gestures

- Head-turn to the audience from the standing still position (in the direction of the fourth wall).
- The action of a hug.
- Dragging a body that has fallen.
- Carrying a body in the space.

Head-turning

When the actors are tuned into the Pulse, they will notice their rhythmic compulsion to add a head-turn from standing at the conclusion of a *jo, ha, kyu*. The head-turn, just like falling, acts as a punctuation point. Draw their attention to the notion that rhythm now feels like a compositional tool. Secondly, this action has the consequence of *breaking the fourth wall*, which introduces performers to the Pulse aesthetic of relating directly to the audience and draws the audience's attention to an image or action that has just happened on the Canvas. It will often draw laughter.

Hugging

One of the reasons to work with strict action limitations is to exercise the physical imagination 'muscle'. It may take a long time for the actors to stop simply hugging someone with the other person hugging them back. Remind them that the task is to create the 'same but different'. Invite them to hug themselves, hug an imaginary body, hug a horizontal body or hug a body part. Hugging is an action just like falling, running or walking. There is no psychological intention behind the execution of this action, and there is no expectation of a conditioned response. Once they click into this, you will see someone falling out of hugging arms or someone running away from the hugger. Remind them that all gestures and action on the Canvas must be executed with physical commitment. You might also mention that no one should insist on imposing an offer on another person. The general rule is that you do not control another's offer, you only respond to whatever happens. In this way you are never trapped inside a scenario you don't want to be in.

Dragging and carrying

With both actions the same parameters apply. If the physical action on the floor becomes messy and incoherent the Pulse cannot be diagnosed or 'read'. If this happens, go back to the Scales and build-in the gestures again. This restriction of action and gesture is to solidify the actor's physical – and through watching – visual understanding of the power of clean, efficient gesture on the Canvas. Later, when the physical vocabulary has expanded again and all actions are permitted, individuals will draw on this kinaesthetic understanding when making physical offers.

Emerging training challenges

Micro and macro

At the beginning of the Canvas journey the performers practised working in the micro with total focus on the self, and then shifted states to make connections with others by working in the macro. During the last four phases they have been focusing entirely on the macro; accessing their 'composer', embedding the Principles, attending to what the Pulse needs, and developing their awareness of the space and the ensemble. As we move forward on the Canvas, the performers will need to flip into the micro to commit fully to a performative offer; a physical, vocal (sound) or verbal (words) motif. The challenge now will be for the performers to stay working in the macro and only enter the micro when they need to, not the other way round. This is a tricky transition in the process. When vocal and verbal gestures are introduced, the Pulse is likely to de-construct as the actors will shift their focus away from the macro. Remind them that the constant shift from one to the other is what makes the Pulse possible.

> The performer is simultaneously the doer and the maker, and you operate on both micro and macro levels continually. The performer is both in the space and creating the space of performance. These dualities are a fundamental principle of acting. Pulse teaches you the mechanics of how to achieve them.
>
> Darren Natale

Recognising the score

Once they become familiar with initial Principles the actors will sense developing themes and might resist continuing to prioritize the practice of structure. Actors are not accustomed to gaining precision through repetitive physical training. They can find it frustrating to work without literal meaning. Humans innately search for meaning and the actor's insistence upon intention and motivation can inhibit them from surrendering to the acquisition of form. The difference between free improvisation and Pulse is the structural score. The hidden cues instigate an invisible, internalized dramaturgy that allows performers to follow directives given by, and to, each other. These cues enable an ensemble to freely improvise, knowing that every performative moment will be successful. But it does, however, rely on everyone playing the game according to the rules. For example, if the chorus you are in begins to run, you must run; if a performer in the line drops, and then another, then another, creating a pattern; you have no choice but to fall. If you have a solo you must *develop to climax,* so the chorus knows when to step in. It is the shared language that allows the ensemble to be on the same page. If you can't rely on a collaborator to pick up the signal and do what is agreed upon, then you can't trust them. The whole point of training structurally in the context of improvisation is to increase trust and minimize variables as much as possible. It will be in the debrief of each Pulse that you, as trainer, can point out key moments that were missed and opportunities not taken, like those I have mentioned in the example above. Make sure you also affirm for observers and players when they are picking up cues and converting them into action.

Pulse working style and aesthetic

You will notice, as the work progresses, that the working style which is dictated by the Principles and Working Concepts creates a particular aesthetic. Many other improvisation practices strive to be neutral concerning performance design, encouraging the individual performer to develop a personal aesthetic. That is not the case with Pulse because it has a distinctive signature. I invented this structure for the purpose of performing in front of an audience based upon what I wanted to see: a performance improvisation as a 'moving poem'. Adherence to the style is how a group learns to 'read' the score. It is worth mentioning to performers, at this stage, that this working style facilitates agency. If they find themselves engaged in a scenario they don't want to be in, they can abdicate without the audience noticing, because leaving an image unfinished is part of the aesthetic. They can fall, run or walk away. It is built into the form.

Evolving 'story' and attitude

Introduce the idea of playing with attitude around gesture or action. Until now the ensemble members have been on the Canvas with neutral expressions. Encourage them to randomly attach attitudes to their actions. The observers might begin to see hugging that is hungry with desire, that is tender or angry, or hugging that is disinterested. They may see head-turns that contain a smirk or a glare. Actors may run fearfully away from a hug or seem to die when they fall out of a hug. When someone drags a body in the space it will seem as if the body is dead, and when someone carries another, it could look like they are in love, or it could be that the other is hurt. As I mentioned before, it is important to prioritize form over content in the early phases, but now that meaning is creeping into the consciousness of the actors it is time to turn our attention to the 'stories' that will emerge. The performative gestures and attitudes will now create relationships between people, and you will see themes evolving. Draw their attention to this development and invite the observers to describe what they saw and how it made them feel in the debrief of each Canvas session. They will see moments and describe 'story' fragments that performers didn't know they created. Until now, the emphasis of the Canvas work has been on embedding a shared structure and form and developing performance fitness. With the emergence of 'story' it is time to turn our attention to the Pulse Sketch.

Phase Six: The Pulse Sketch

In this phase we begin to make theatrical art. With the introduction of the next set of Principles the ensemble practises creating complete pieces of spontaneous performance. Each Pulse is called a Sketch. Think of them as short performance poems, Haiku, rather than Coleridge's *The Rime of the Ancient Mariner* (twenty-six pages). These compositional Principles allow the performers to focus on the overall structure of the Pulse Sketch. We want the ensemble to have some extended practise with the shape of a Sketch before we get really involved in making content.

> Pulse requires the performer to act, direct and write a story all at the same time. You can't skate on the surface with Pulse; it requires a deep engagement with the emotional and physical life of the unfolding actions.
>
> Lachlan Woods

Introducing the compositional principles

If you haven't mixed up the groups already, do so before you move into this phase. Give the performers an opportunity to work with all members of the ensemble. I usually say, 'seven on the floor' and they randomly jump onto the Canvas to work. The duration for each Sketch is flexible depending on what is emerging; however, approximately five to ten minutes would be a good start. Explain as little as possible before introducing each Principle, so as not to interfere with the group's attempt to discover how it works from within. They must make this journey themselves to enable a kinaesthetic imprint. As you have discovered, this is an organic, nonlinear process, so if you observe the group on the edge of a certain Principle, then that is the one to do next. Be curious and responsive. Try not to impose too much from the outside. The learning takes place by them trying to solve the riddle of how it works. Do the teaching in the debrief. As you have already introduced the Performance Principles, you know how your group responds. Introduce the Principles below in the same way. The debrief information will help you learn to 'read' the Pulse Sketch and will give you suggestions for feedback to the group.

Commencement

The starting point of the Pulse Sketch where performers enter the playing space, place themselves in a composition on the Canvas and from stillness begin the Pulse. It is the jo of the jo, ha, kyu.

> **Side coach** Enter the space and find a still composition on the Canvas from which to launch your Sketch. Be aware of each other taking a position and be willing to adjust your own choice according to *what it needs*. Do this without talking.
>
> **Debrief** The group is mutually searching for a strong place to start. It will have been found once everyone is static in the space. Remind them about what they had discovered from working with *Geometry of Space*: the shapes and the strength that lies in group cohesion. Now would be the time to explore with them 'power places' on the Canvas – difference between standing still in the centre and doing the same on the edge. They need to know that when they make an offer they want the group to take up, it is also important from *where* they make it. A cluster in the centre or a line-up against the back wall: both examples of strong *commencement*. It is a good idea to begin unified in some way. Let them explore a little at the beginning of each Sketch.

Architecture of the space

Use the characteristics of the playing space (the walls and floor) as generative elements for the Pulse. Shape, dimension, protrusions and gaps offer imaginative possibilities for action.

> **Side coach** Draw your attention to the architectural characteristics of the space and explore their possibilities. Are there any protrusions, gaps or ledges in this space? For example, windows or doors that can be opened and closed? Give attention to the architecture while you are making patterns with others.
>
> **Debrief** Notice how using the architecture can lead to 'story' moments. It can act as a generative element for creating group action leading to a theme.

Depth of field

The three parallel bands of an end-on playing space, usually used simultaneously: foreground, middle ground and background. The ensemble is responsible for taking care of the 'balance of the space'.

> **Side coach** Draw your attention to the three parallel playing spaces on the Canvas. There is the foreground (closest to the audience), the middle-ground (the central band) and the background (the space in front of the back wall). As you are Pulsing try

to place your actions in a zone that balances the space. If there is a chorus running horizontally from wall to wall in the middle-ground, stand still against the back wall or fall and stay down in the foreground. If a group is working the horizontal line against the back wall, make your way to the middle-ground.

Debrief By getting used to playing in the three zones, the ensemble embeds an awareness of playing *to* the audience. Their actions are oriented towards the fourth wall, they know they are working with simultaneous imagery and that their actions need to support and complement those of the others on the Canvas. Their 'composer' starts to identify which actions have priority on the Canvas. They will notice that the size, intensity and placing of actions are generally what determine the primary focus of the Sketch. This is where the concept of '*what does it need?*' guides their 'composer' when balancing the space.

Recurring motifs

A motif (unit of action or image) which belongs to an individual performer or to the group that is 'stored' and returns at least three times during the Sketch. If the group picks up a motif it will most likely become the thematic source for that Pulse.

Side coach Search for a motif to become the theme of your Sketch. It will emerge in the form of a repeated *unit of action*. If you become aware of one, join it and make it a group action. Let it build to a climax and then move on. Bring it back so that it recurs at intervals during the Pulse, either as a solo, a duet or a chorus action.

Debrief Establishing a *recurring motif* involves members of the group first recognizing and second, memorizing the sequence. When someone makes an offer of a motif, they must do it at least three times. It takes three or four *repetitions* before others in the space register that the motif has potential, and can join in. The most common tendency is for actors to not back themselves. They make the offer once or twice and if others have not joined them, they lose faith, get nervous and drop it. Often it is a great offer, but no one saw it because it happened on the margins of the Canvas or was not executed with commitment. Encourage them to jump on the first strong motif that is offered in the space, not to judge or resist it or to look for a better one. Remind them that at this stage they are practising the act of group composition, of 'reading' the Canvas and creating a score. They need to embed the *recurring motif* as a structural tool before they start to discriminate content or theme.

Denouement

The ensemble consciousness towards the sense of duration has developed and the group becomes aware that the Pulse must finish. Whilst maintaining the stage action the group finds a way to bring back the recurring motifs before closure.

Side coach The group has *developed to climax*. You have experienced the *jo, ha, kyu*. Feel the rhythm of it as a turning point in the group 'story'. You can all now sense that you need to conclude the Sketch – to *find your ending* (see Principle below). Before it comes to an end, bring back any *recurring motifs* solo, duet or group that have emerged during this Sketch.

Debrief The *denouement* is the part of a narrative towards the end. It usually occurs after a climax when the strands of a plot are drawn together. In a linear narrative form, it is where matters of plot are explained or resolved. In Pulse, it is the poetic and rhythmic resolution we are searching for. When group motifs are brought back as a structural device towards an ending it gives us closure. The group's sense of duration is developing through this process and the idea of a beginning, middle and end becomes a kinaesthetic experience. The group is beginning to embody dramatic structure. Once they have a structural understanding of the shape of the *jo, ha, kyu,* they can play with it as a modular construction; you might suggest that they do a *development to climax* or *jo, ha, kyu* three times before they begin the *denouement.* There are several ways for the group to practise moving into *denouement.* By using modular construction (they will be practising the groups autonomous sense of duration), or when the trainer says *find your ending* or by using time as a structure. Ring a bell at four minutes, giving them a minute to wrap up.

Find the ending

A group searches for a thematic and rhythmic conclusion whilst keeping the Pulse 'alive'. Once all performers have come to stillness, the group knows they have finished the Sketch.

Side coach When everyone has come to stillness and those who are standing are looking towards the audience, you have found your ending.

Debrief The ending is as much about the compositional shape of the bodies on the Canvas as it is about the rhythm of the conclusion that gives us all a sense of closure. Can you feel the rhythm of this image? Everyone is running, they all fall, three performers are left standing with their backs to the fourth wall, one falls, then another falls, and the third turns their head to the audience. All remain still.

Shatter the space

A performer may initiate a physical or verbal rupture in the space, creating a dislocation or change in direction. When this happens, everyone drops their current action and goes into the 'unknown'.

Side coach Notice the lack of focus on the Canvas. The rhythm and dynamic of action on the Canvas is flat, directionless and has *plateaued.* Nothing is connecting. Something must be done. Everyone run.

Debrief Hopefully someone tunes into the macro, senses *what it needs* and takes responsibility to lead. The group picks up the signal and everyone runs, sustains and *develops to climax*. They *shatter the space*. It is like throwing all the cards in the air to see where they land. It works as a re-set. From here they can begin with Scales, find a connection and search for the beginning of the next sequence.

Form and chaos

A formalistic juxtaposition. When a pattern of movement is established creating symmetry and choreographic form the group may shatter the space to create chaos in contrast to the previous sequence. When there is chaos on the Canvas, performers then take steps to bring the Pulse back to form.

Side coach Can you sense the chaos on the Canvas? You have slipped out of form. The Pulse seems lost. See if giving your attention to the search for patterns and questioning *what it needs* will lead you back to form.

Debrief It is not wrong when the Pulse becomes chaotic, as it inevitably will; it is only a problem if it gets stuck in that state and becomes unwatchable. Encourage the ensemble to recognize the unstructured, unfocused Canvas action as soon as possible so they can give attention to returning to form. If employed consciously, the seesaw from form to chaos and back again can inject a vital dynamic and energy into the Sketch.

Emerging themes

Due to the *recurring motifs*, performers have identified themes within the Sketch. An example motif could be, a performer runs to a fallen body, drags it across the space, then falls. This sequence (*unit of action*), if repeated three times, will encourage others to join in. The theme of the Sketch might then become death and dying. By extension, when the Sketch is comprised of several modules (*jo, ha, kyu*) there may be a few *recurring motifs* moving in and out of the Sketch. There might be one major group motif and several minor solo or duet motifs recurring throughout. In association with the example above, a pair of performers may create a duet: one hugs another, that person falls out of their arms, the hugger runs away. They have added the theme of love and loss to death and dying. The performers represent 'every person'. The generic, the universal. A woman/man is running, a man/woman runs behind (chasing them). A cluster of men/women fall, the women/men drag their bodies. A group of people turn their heads to look at us (the audience). The heightened vocabulary of actions and gestures that the performers have at their disposal when used in multiple combinations suggest big themes – love, loss, death, betrayal, war, revenge and longing – all sit well with the poetic nature of the fragmented imagery.

Another generative source for theme development will be the characteristics of the working group. As the seven random performers jump onto the Canvas, point out the 'story' potential that may be contained within the group. Like the stimuli offered within the *architecture of the space* think of this as the 'architecture of the group'. For example, there are six men and one woman on the Canvas, there are seven women with long hair or four short and two very tall people. In this way we are encouraging them to practise transforming the given visual stimuli into a performative idea. They are 'bricoleurs, artists of limits' (Nachmanovitch 1990, 86), making art with seven people in a blank space. They must be able to see every possibility before them to make something out of nothing.

Expanding the physical vocabulary

After a while you will notice the performers incrementally adding other physical actions to the Canvas: crawling, rolling, waving, touching, holding hands. From now on the physical vocabulary can expand to serve the evolving themes.

> **Side coach**   You have noticed other actions and gestures creeping onto the Canvas. Determined by *what it needs*, allow this to happen but keep all movement heightened, clean and specific.

It is around this time that I introduce them to the idea of bringing codified movement sequences to the Canvas. There will be performers who have a movement practice or who studied dance like ballet, flamenco, tap, break dancing or belly dancing – still alive in their bodies. These forms have a codified technique with a particular style and series of movements that are repeatable. Similarly, sequences from other physical practices such as any of the martial arts – skating, skiing, boxing, soccer and netball – might appear. A sequence from such a technique is already a *unit of action* and, when repeated, might become a solo *recurring motif*. If you are lucky, there may be someone on the Canvas who also knows that technique and can do a duet. If it is not too complex others can join in – like performers who all know the same song. Get them to explore its potential a little now, but it will probably emerge more significantly later when they are speaking and working with *juxtaposition*. As the training continues, from the *commencement* of each Pulse Sketch the group's objective now is to identify a theme introduced by a physical motif or characteristics of the working group.

Associative imagery and meaning

The performer does not intentionally invent meaning by using any specific action. They create action based on Principles and possibilities. Actors will be used to the notion of having an intention and then performing an action to communicate its meaning. With Pulse, it's the reverse. An action happens that may imply meaning and intention; however, it is the audience who attributes meaning to what they see. That is why it is important to have half the group act as witnesses. Pulse is an exercise in creating physical or vocal action that does not emerge from psychological intention, narrative consequence or emotional logic, but from poetic association. Because it works on association, the resultant imagery is consequently fragmentary – like dream imagery in which you find yourself in a room but you don't know how you got there, and then suddenly, you find yourself by a river. You don't think your way from state to state. As mentioned, this has created a particular working style. The embedded practice of doing Scales means that at the climax of an emotional or storytelling moment the actor knows that they can fall, walk away or run, leave the 'story' unfinished and join a totally different image, playing a different role. A Pulse Sketch is made up of many associated 'unfinished' images delicately balanced upon a framework. Meaning is not given to the viewer in a linear fashion. They must collect their own impressions from a series of fractals. There will be some recurring images and ideas which give the Sketch a through line, but ultimately, it is a collective poetic meditation on a theme.

> In Pulse the structures can be jagged, sudden, precipitous, slow, calm, frantic. You don't have to 'round off' a scene and you're not forced into the mode of dominant narratives or dramaturgies. You can have abruptness, and an ending can smash or collapse … Geometrically, I see a play as a line. Pulse is a glowing planet which fizzes with energy and light.
>
> Kaz Therese

Key working concepts for the performer

By now the performers have become used to side coaching instructions of, *commitment to action* and *what does it need?* As content is becoming a focus on the Canvas, we can introduce the last shorthand concept *'smell' the dramatic potential* and the two working concepts, *Breaking the Fourth Wall* and *Working in Parallel*.

'Smell' the dramatic potential

When I observe an offer on the Canvas that has depth, significance and resonance with 'story' potential, I will call out *'smell' the dramatic potential* and encourage the group to pick up that theme. The shorthand has value for several reasons. The observers will become accustomed to what has dramatic potential and understand why; they will see what I see and translate that to the Canvas when they are working. By looking through this lens, the performers will make and adopt offers that are heightened and have universal themes. Later, when they work with emotion and speaking such choices afford a 'palette' of bold colours.

Breaking the fourth wall and working in parallel

These two working concepts are stylistic markers that contribute significantly to the creation of the Pulse performance aesthetic. I introduce them as soon as I notice the actors working towards each other, cutting out or closing off the observers. Both concepts involve the performers focusing their action towards the audience.

Breaking the fourth wall (which began with the head-turn) is about the actor building interaction with the audience through their focus, intention and actions. Verbal gesturing is directed to the audience, not to another performer, by singing, speaking monologues or even one-sided dialogues. The audience is their playing partner, even if verbally they are referring to someone in the space. In this way, the performers are working *with* each other not *to* each other. This is called *working in parallel.* For example, a duet could consist of a performer delivering a monologue to the audience, 'I loved you once ... ', while another performer is wrapped around their ankles crying or hugging the speaker, falling, running away and then repeating the motif. Both performers' actions can be executed independently. They are in their own 'realities', but they recognize each 'reality' as part of a duet. They are being affected by each other through poetic association and proximity rather than conventional relating.

If the ensemble has been training consistently you will probably find they are developing Canvas fatigue by now. So before applying the vocal (sound) and verbal (words) gestures to the Canvas, shake things up and introduce the act of speaking in a series of tasks where they don't have to keep the Pulse 'alive' at the same time. Once the group has become familiar with the new element you can bring it back to the Canvas.

Go to Chapter 4: Words and the Physical Gesture. There are four tasks to choose from, ascending in degree of difficulty, so it is up to you and your assessment of the group's progress as to how long you decide to remain off the Canvas.

Phase Seven: Adding sound to the physical world

Hopefully, having practised the Principles in a different context the ensemble returns to the Canvas refreshed. Although they have been speaking phrases in the Skill Focus Tasks, on the Canvas you should begin with vocal sound and build from there.

Vocal gestures

As themes are growing from the physical actions and motifs, invite the performers to vocalize their effort and reveal the inner life of the gesture. Encourage them to allow the sound of breath and vocal sounds to accompany their actions; panting while running, a scream when falling or in conflict, or breath and sounds of protest while being dragged. Now sound has entered the space and breathing becomes the soundtrack. Get them used to integrating physical action and vocal (sound) expression before introducing the following verbal gestures (words).

Verbal gestures

Think of verbal gestures in the same way as we initially thought of Scales. They are tools with which to practise the Principles. Encourage the performers to think of them as sound texture so as not to be weighed down with literal meaning. We are avoiding the pressure of having to improvise speech at this stage. Introduce each gesture in separate Sketches.

THE PULSE PHASES

Once gestures have been explored, they belong to the performer's vocabulary and can be used by the 'composer' on the Canvas when needed.

- Whispering
- LOTE – Languages Other Than English
- Singing

Whispering

Whisper anything (gibberish is best), making sure the observers cannot hear it. It is an action that can be executed as a solo, a duet or in a chorus – to another performer, to themselves, to the audience, while lying, standing, running or hugging.

LOTE

This is only for those of the group that are fluent in another language. They can speak nonsense or any kind of stream of consciousness. If they are not fluent speakers, they will probably struggle to improvise and become self-conscious, activating the rational mind. In most cases observers will not understand the language. It is about sound texture rather than meaning for them. It does, however, stimulate mood and atmosphere and will enhance the Sketch thematically. For example, if a performer walks through a cluster of fallen bodies speaking Indonesian, Russian, Hebrew or Arabic and we recognize the sound texture, there is 'story'.

Singing

Lyrics of a song can reinforce any theme that has emerged through a physical motif. For example, if the theme of the Sketch seems to be love and betrayal, when the opportunity for a solo arises, a performer might sing, 'when a man loves a woman', or 'please don't take him just because you can', and then run or fall or walk away. The phrase then becomes an established motif that can recur throughout the Sketch. That performer or others can now play with that lyrical phrase, treating it as they would a physical motif. They will need to sing a larger section of the song at another point and then bring the phrase back in the denouement to assist *finding the ending*. If another performer knows the song, they will be searching for an opportunity to do a duet. It is not about singing the song; however, it is about using fragments of that song as a compositional tool, a *recurring motif,* for the structure and theme of the Sketch. The song must not dominate, only complement the Sketch.

Singing from outside the Sketch

Before the Sketch begins, ask the observers if there is anyone who wants to sing. The singer pays attention to themes evolving in the Sketch and when appropriate (best in a moment of stillness), sings their offer. The singer explores how to Pulse with the players from outside the Canvas. This gives them an opportunity to work from a different point of view, seeing and sensing when their offer will enhance the mood and rhythms of the

Sketch. They must not dictate the direction of the Sketch, but support and assist when their offer is needed. Using singing as a gesture works best when singers are skilled and confident.

Music as playing partner

Now is a good time to introduce the use of music. Singing may have become part of the performer's vocabulary but what if there are no good singers in the group? Working with sourced sound lyrics in repeated phrases works the same way. Chapter 5 outlines how to Pulse with music.

Renewed focus on the solo, duet and chorus

During these Sketches, pay some attention to the roles that have emerged: solo, duet and chorus. Point them out and suggest possibilities. We remarked on these early on; when the performers were the only ones moving or standing, they were doing a solo, if two performers were running together while everyone else was still, they were doing a duet. Later, physical motifs gave them the opportunity to further explore all three roles. Now, with an increased physical vocabulary and vocal and verbal options, the solo can become a monologue comprised of sound or song, and soon, emotion or words; it can be a physical motif that is joined in duet with another performer speaking words; or the chorus may be in a line of performers all whispering simultaneously while a gestural solo or duet is taking place in front of them. There is no limit to the combinations possible. They will need constant reminding that it is the structure and form of the Sketch that holds it together, dictated by the Principles and performers delivering *what it needs*.

Emotional gestures and the Principle of juxtaposition

Emotional gesture

The Principles are applied to the sounds of crying and laughing exploring their compositional possibilities musically, as opposed to their connection to psychologically induced emotion. Commitment to action serves to create believability for the viewer.

Take time out from the Canvas at this point and go to Chapter 4: Committing to Emotional Gesture. There you will find the conceptual foundations for expressing emotion in Pulse, as well as a suite of tasks to choose from. For more advanced tasks, choose from the section in Chapter 4: 'Words, Silence and Emotional Gesture'. Having taken the group through some exercises using emotional signifiers (the sounds and physical actions of crying and laughing), when they return to the Canvas, they should be less self-conscious about authenticity and will be able to use crying and laughing as physical/vocal expressions. They will see the gestures as 'moving energy' on sound and realize that it is their *commitment to action* that makes them believable. Get them back on the Canvas doing Sketches with all the variations of crying and laughing.

> Emotion is a physical aspect of what you are doing. It is part of an action or series of actions, and it is not privileged above your other physical responses … you cannot indulge your emotions or allow them to cloud your responses … Pulse gave me the capacity to find form for emotion.
>
> Kaz Therese

Art can encompass both contradiction and paradox. Paradox is about 'holding' two diverse qualities, aspects or notions simultaneously. In formal terms on the Pulse Canvas, it is expressed through the Principle of *juxtaposition*.

Juxtaposition

An offer is made in relation to content rather than form creating opposition, for example, tragic/humorous or literal/abstract. Elements may be layered against each other so that the resulting meaning arises from the clash of disparate elements.

Side coach Notice the potential of working in *contrast* but with content. All the performative vocabulary is permitted on the Canvas now but give some attention to the use of emotional gestures to explore *juxtaposition*. Explore the emotional sounds for their rhythms and textures.

Debrief Use side coaching to draw the performer's attention to the possibilities of crying and laughing in solos, duets and in chorus. For example, in the centre of the Canvas a performer has fallen to the floor, another performer stands above them crying while a duet laughs as they walk a horizontal line in the background. Remind them that believability, while using emotional gestures on the Canvas comes from *commitment to action*.

I am introducing *juxtaposition* at this stage because the emotional gestures supply oppositional content to work with. *Contrast* is concerned with opposition in physical and spatial form, whereas *juxtaposition* is making an offer in relation to content. It is a major compositional tool now that 'story' building is becoming the focus of each Sketch. It is important to practise this Principle with crying and laughing first, as it limits the options; when we bring speaking onto the Canvas, the complexity will increase. For example, juxtaposing the tragic with the humorous – crying over a body while another tells a joke, or someone singing a love song while several others fearfully run and try to hide; juxtaposing the literal with the abstract – one speaks a monologue from the centre of the Canvas to the audience about childhood abuse, four others box the air in a line across the back, another giggles whilst jumping hopscotch around the speaker, and in the corner a woman clutches her pregnant stomach softly singing 'Danny Boy'.

> There is consonance and there is dissonance ... the notes that jar, are just as important in jazz as the notes that are in harmony. In Pulse those tonal shifts might be thematic, visual, or vocal.
>
> Stephen Phillips

You might find it useful at this stage to introduce chairs to the Canvas. Chairs can be moved around the Canvas during the Pulse to offer different playing levels: standing on them and crawling under them. Experiment with their integration and explore different possibilities, for example a line of chairs against the back wall or in the middle ground, or on the side to begin with (see Chapter 5: Working with Objects). It will take a few sessions to integrate the chairs. If you find they are not helping, leave them till later.

Phase Eight: Speaking on the Canvas

Now go to Chapter 4: Improvised Speaking and Yielding and work your way through a selection of tasks. When the group is ready, head back to the Canvas and integrate speaking into a Pulse Sketch.

When to speak?

When a performer 'finds' themselves doing a solo – they are in a strong place in the space and the focus is on them – instead of a physical or an emotional gesture motif, they can now speak. Alternatively, a performer may have to take the solo and introduce speaking because that is what the Pulse *needs*.

What to speak?

The generative source for speaking will be the theme that has been established in the Sketch. To begin with, speaking should not happen until there is an association to what's physically happening on the Canvas. It is essential to maintain this rule until the ensemble has developed the ability to pull a theme out of a physical image/source and translate that idea into literal speech. It is a collaborative searching endeavour. You may notice a tendency for an individual performer to decide what they will speak about, jump on the Canvas, and begin a monologue that will furnish the Sketch with several themes. Of course, this is the easiest option. When language arrives, it tends to dominate. In fact, when Pulse is used to develop material for performance making,

THE PULSE PHASES

bringing pre-conceived material and ideas to the Canvas is essential. During this early training phase, however, it is valuable to practise using generative sources other than speech for inspiration.

How to speak?

Be open to discovering how words can work in the Pulse landscape. This is a new frontier. The performers have a new tool to play with so undoubtedly the Sketch structure will be compromised until speaking has been integrated. Be patient but also prepared to be surprised and delighted. Speaking can take many forms on the Canvas; however, these are three possibilities.

- Verbal solo
- Compulsive monologue
- Fragment.

Verbal solo

If a performer must take the solo and speak because that is what the Sketch *needs,* but they have no impulse to speak, what do they do? They are encouraged to open their mouths, see what comes out and turn it into a performative moment. The 'composer' gets ideas from what their 'performer' does and vice versa. For example, the performer sighs (marking time) splutters, and is then breathless. By association, they speak, 'I ... I can't breathe, suffocation (they are looking for "story") ... in the dream I am drowning ... ' etc. They continue to build a story punctuated by their inability to breathe.

Compulsive monologue

Associating off an established theme in the Sketch, the performer faces the fourth wall externalizing thoughts in a 'stream of consciousness' or they address the audience directly. This can turn into a duet or a chorus moment as others line up beside the speaker and simultaneously monologue to the audience, all within their own reality. They may repeat the words of the original speaker or associate off those words to find a different story or choose to *juxtapose* that content.

Fragment

Any performer in the space can extract a section of text (at least three or four lines) that has emerged from a solo and repeat it, thus turning it into a group *recurring motif.* You will find that in the early stages, performers may find a phrase or a sentence and keep repeating that. This does not work rhythmically, compositionally or thematically on the Canvas. A phrase often echoed around the space becomes meaningless through its repetition, performers are not technically invested, and it does not add information that others can explore at a deeper level. If they are going to speak, encourage the performers to invest imaginatively in that moment and to *sustain* speaking until something happens in the space to make them stop.

Why speak?

A European colleague of mine used to refer to himself as an 'artist in the first person', meaning an actor who has something to say rather than an actor who interprets other people's words. I've never forgotten that description. The responsibility of every artist, regardless of the art form, is to have something to say. Encourage actors to pick something about their existence that they don't understand, do some research and bring it to the Canvas. Ask them what they feel passionate about and give them permission to bring it to the Canvas. They will need to have all those sources inside them, so they have something to feed off when the opportunity arrives to speak. When the ensemble can fluidly incorporate speaking within the structure of the Sketch, invite them to bring political, social, psychological, literary or historical matters to the Sketch to create more complexity and depth with content. This will involve a certain amount of pre-meditation. Encourage performers who are thinking deeply about something not to talk about it, but to explore it performatively. Practising improvised monologues off the Canvas is a good idea. It is not a simple task to finally bring speaking onto the Canvas as part of the performative vocabulary. Those performers who already enjoy improvised speaking will surge ahead, but for those who are struggling, encourage them to use performative and compositional Principles with speaking because it will help them enormously. To do this, go to Chapter 4: Translating the Principles to Speaking on the Canvas.

Where are we now?

The shared understanding amongst the ensemble and the momentum of the work has naturally taken the performers to the next level. An extensive palette of actions and gestures (physical, emotional and verbal) is now at the disposal of the performers. The vocabulary is expanding as the ensemble moves from Sketch to Sketch, and reliance on the use of the Scales is dissipating. Understanding structure and form is now embedded so the 'composer' can pay attention to the development of content. It is inevitable that the ensemble will unconsciously drop earlier Principles, but their ability to 'read' the score keeps the structure solid. Owing to the necessary repetition involved in all psycho-physical practices, Pulse may at times seem like a 'blunt instrument'. Now that a level of reflexive proficiency has been gained, the performers should turn their attention to working with nuance and detail. Now, when you debrief the Sketches refer to the balance of light and shade and discuss precision and accuracy. Now that the *jo, ha, kyu* has been kinaesthetically imprinted the performers can experiment with subverting the *development to climax* and see if the group can incorporate that. They know the rules, so they can play with breaking them. As a Pulse trainer Stephen Phillips says, 'when Pulse really works there is a continual breaking of the vocabulary and a continual rescuing' (2013). Encourage them to expand their performative offers, incorporating personas that may emerge and dialogues that may come out of duets. The following may help to maintain the health of the Pulse and serve as a prompt for you to keep advancing the ensemble's fluency.

Compositional consciousness

The part of the Pulse performer that is the 'composer' strives for balance on the Canvas: balance of the space, of performative elements and of each performer's participation. If a cluster is happening stage right, your offer needs to be on the left. If most action is at the back, your next offer needs to be in the foreground – *depth of field* and *contrast*. If there are only physical gestures on the Canvas, it needs words. The notion of 'layering' means bringing the different 'performance languages' (song, speaking, action, gesture) onto the Canvas and activating them simultaneously but in cohesion; using different activities but all working towards the same theme: *What does it need?* The answer will be balance of space and action. Similarly, exclusively enjoying the position of soloist or only melting into chorus connections will not serve the ensemble or the Sketch or the training of the individual performer. The idea is to gain fluency in both roles so that when the Pulse calls on you, you can and will respond to that call.

Collaboration not consensus

Collaboration, to me, means efficiently and effectively building something together. This does not mean there is no dissent. It means using a framework that successfully includes diversity. In my early years as a performance maker, I became frustrated with the common practice of 'talking' the ideas rather than 'doing' the ideas. If someone disagreed with an idea, based on personal politics, bias or aesthetics, it was discarded and never tested out performatively. I like to take an idea, explore it performatively and try turning it into something else. The alchemy is where my interest lies. Subsequently, some of the most striking images in my work would have sounded implausible and been rejected if I had spoken about them instead of executed them. The Sketch is a performance, which means you can't stop what you are doing and argue or dismiss the idea (unless you did that performatively on purpose), you must engage in the artifice of being watched and continue to work. It doesn't mean you have to agree or like what is offered, but you must 'taste' it before you abandon it. Because the style of Pulse is fragmentary, and the means of content development is through association, every performer has the agency to transform any idea.

A legacy of performance pulse

Improvising as if you are performing (being watched) will be a different experience for those who have mainly improvised in a rehearsal where the focus is on research and discovery. If the culture of your ensemble practice is one of safety, permission, non-judgement and 'no such thing as a bad idea', the performance imperative produces some quite surprising benefits. When there is pressure to deliver, performers develop the skill of 'doing the work while they are doing the work', rather than being in constant preparation for the work. I don't mean not preparing, that is essential. I am referring to the actors that procrastinate and don't *commit to action*. In such cases you never know if the idea can work. With some kinds of pressure, the work advances more quickly. Conventional wisdom might state that placing the performer under (performance) pressure is a sure way to shut down their creativity. Through experience I have found the opposite. Although some performers are held back by fear, others thrive on what I call 'released pressure'. Usually, when performing in front of an audience an actor brings total commitment because they have rehearsed it and feel prepared. During Pulse, performers must bring just as much energy and commitment to an improvised moment despite knowing it is not for public consumption.

Courage to juxtapose

When you witness an inspired Pulse Sketch there is nothing quite like it. Some images are seared into my retina. I have a memory of such a Sketch that took place in 2007. I was training a group of students, and we were investigating the notion of the 'artist in the first person' creating content that was meaningful to them. As a random group of seven jumped onto the Canvas to begin, I challenged them to take the opportunity to make their politics performative. The group comprised of a First Nations female performer and six white men. What happened next can only be described as extraordinary. Fragments and monologues told a story of dispossession and stolen generations, and images of violence and mistreatment became *recurring motifs*, but the *juxtaposition* of tenderness and regret emerged during the *denouement* to *find an ending* that spoke of hope and reconciliation. The standing ovation from all of us lasted a long time.

    I tell this story for two reasons: it speaks of trust and courage. The Sketch could not have happened if the First Nations performer had not trusted the Principles and the motivations of her fellow performers. She allowed her persona to be victimized knowing that at some point she and they would turn the victimization around. She served the Pulse. It would not have happened if a male performer had shied away from representing white colonialism. He took the solo and become the unpalatable protagonist. He avoided the vanity and ego that often inhibit courageous work, committing totally to the ugly persona he had to become to tell the story. He served the Pulse. Without such a *juxtaposition* it would have been a Sketch without political resonance.

> Pulse gave us an identity as an ensemble and gave us a sense of our own resourcefulness, of our own body as our greatest resource. We came to understand how to shape a moment, to understand the power of silence and stillness as opposed to frenetic energy, and Pulse put us in touch with our inner poetry.
>
> Meredith Penman

Where to go from here?

If training is your focus, continually returning to the Canvas will make the work stronger and maintain the ensemble's performance fitness. You can also take the ensemble through the extensions of the Skill Focus Tasks in Chapter 4. If you are interested in Performance Pulse you will want to integrate objects, costume, music, light and audience; go to Chapter 5. For ideas on setting up different Pulse frameworks, how to continue Pulsing independently, and how to bring research and themes onto the Canvas to make new work, go to Chapter 6. If you want to take Pulse into your rehearsal culture to direct scripted text, go to Chapter 7.

3
ENSEMBLE PRACTICE TASKS

This section is comprised of exercises that will prepare a group of individual performers who have not worked together before to begin the Pulse Canvas work. They assist the transition to ensemble consciousness where individuals in the group let go of self-consciousness and focus their attention on serving the group creation. These preparatory tasks serve several functions: they give performers permission to touch and hold each other, they introduce fundamental notions of ensemble practice and they give the trainer an opportunity to begin mentioning some Pulse terminology and Principles. The following tasks can be used in any order, except to say that vigorous tasks can also double as a physical warm-up and should be used to commence a group session. They will get the blood pumping, the breath active and bring the participant's mind into the present. As the trainer you will be responding to the energy and focus of the group. Work instinctively to feel what they need. Trust your choices. Try to segue from each task seamlessly, allowing for reflection briefly. Keep participants standing active in the space for as much of the session as possible rather than debriefing by sitting and talking.

It is important with all these tasks that the group receives enough instruction to execute the aim of the task but only enough to frame it. We want the participants to be working in the unknown without second-guessing how to do it. Encouraging them to work towards the objective of the task without alerting them to anything else will give them the freedom to problem solve creatively. Right and wrong don't exist with this kind of experiential learning. There is only discovery and everything is information. At the conclusion of most of these tasks there is a section called Extensions. I thought it might be useful for you to see how you can elaborate upon a task or distil the essence of a particular skill you want the group to practise. I generally move into an Extension if I perceive that the group has a command of that task and needs to be challenged further. Sometimes if I use that task repeatedly as a warm-up or to drill the group in that skillset, the task becomes familiar, and the actors disengage. Most often an Extension builds upon the degree of difficulty involved, so offering one will re-engage the actors.

Task 1: Fields of awareness

This meditation develops stamina of focused awareness, called 'attention', and introduces the concept of the detached 'observer'. Ask participants to find a place in the space and sit cross-legged with their spine aligned and eyes closed. Introduce each field of awareness one at a time at five-minute intervals.

- The body
- The surrounding sounds
- Thoughts.

Ask them to focus only on that field for the required time and then ask them to shift their attention when you introduce the next. After the third field, suggest they experiment by shifting their attention from one field to another. Moving attention from one field of awareness to another quickly will give them the sense that they are holding all three fields of awareness simultaneously, inducing the notion of being an 'observer' of their own awareness.

Challenges

When focusing your attention on the fields of the body and/or surrounding sounds, thoughts may continually distract you. They are usually superficial thoughts. The mind does not like to be empty. It is habituated to being constantly alive with thoughts. When they do invade, try not to engage with or resist them. Just notice them and allow them to pass through, returning your attention to the field you are focused on. Imagine you are sitting at the window in a café observing people passing by. You don't feel the need to go out and engage with each of them, do you? You just watch them as they pass by. Think of your thoughts in the same way. Watch them and let them pass. If you do this meditation daily, unwanted thoughts will diminish. You will build your stamina of attention.

Extension

This task takes the developing skill of focused awareness and combines it with physical imagination and endowment. Each performer finds a place in the space and stands still with their spine aligned and their eyes closed. You will talk them through a creative visualization. Leave time between each image, and each question, for them to visualize and then sensorially endow each part of their body.

- Take your attention to your right arm. Imagine that it is a feather. How big is it? What colour is it? Is it still or moving?
- Now take your attention to your left leg. Imagine that it is the trunk of a sapling. What type of tree? See the bark.
- Imagine that your right leg is a pipe. What is it made of? What colour is it? Is it hollow or full of something? Is it hot or cold?
- Imagine that your left arm is a ribbon. What colour is it? What size is it? Is it still or floating on the breeze?
- Now take your attention to your pelvis. Imagine that it is a bowl full of liquid. Is the liquid transparent or opaque? What colour is the bowl and the liquid? Is it hot or cold, still or moving?

ENSEMBLE PRACTICE TASKS

- Move your attention up your body to your chest. Imagine that your chest is a bird cage. See the cage. Is it empty or is there something in it? Is the door open or closed? Is the cage old or new? What is it made of?
- Imagine that your head is a helium balloon. Feel it float. How big is the balloon? What colour is it?
- Now gently release your attention from the balloon and let it travel through the cage down to the sapling, then from the sapling to the feather and from the feather across to the ribbon, then through the bowl to the pipe. Let your awareness fluidly move from one focus to another until it feels as though you are holding all of them simultaneously. Be the observer of these physical sensations.

Task 2: Walk/Stop

This exercise begins the ensemble's journey towards 'listening' through the senses, being affected and acting on an impulse. The Pulse trainer instructs the group from within while participating in the task.

The group walks in the space with each performer moving towards an empty area. When they reach it, they move towards another empty area. This will circumvent a group's tendency to walk 'herd like' in a circle. Everyone continues to do this as they negotiate the bodies in space without collision. Their gaze should not be on the floor but straight ahead, with a soft focus, gazing towards their personal horizon.

Gazing ahead, not watching the trainer, the individuals try to stop moving when the trainer stops. They remain still and start to move again when the trainer moves. Ultimately everyone in the group is attempting to stop and start at the same time. It may take many attempts to come together. The trainer keeps stopping and starting until it appears as if members of the group have mysteriously come to stillness together.

This task is about sensing the subtle shifts of energy within the dynamic of the group and responding through action. The performers will need to access information from senses other than sight to achieve the group outcome. Notice their tendency to mentally fixate on the task and try to strategize an outcome with their rational mind. You may need to remind them that they can only achieve unity if they are working in the present moment and not anticipating. *Debrief:* Ask the group to reflect on their journey from their individual struggle to the sensation of group unity.

- What did you experience?
- What did you learn about yourself?
- Why would an actor practice this task?

Here, I would introduce the notion of 'closing the gap' between perceiving external stimulus and responding with action: from sensing the energy change in the room to standing still. With practice the performers will get quicker and quicker at doing that.

When they all respond to the impulse instantly it will appear that the group has stopped in unison. This simple exercise is the most basic way of experiencing an important aspect of Pulse: while working from their own reality the actor is hungrily searching for any opportunity to be *affected* which will allow them to *change their state*.

Extensions

It is important with all extensions that stopping and starting in unison remain the aim of the task. If the group loses this connection, go back to the fundamental task, and build towards the extension again. When the ensemble achieves the fundamental task, offer them an extension to raise the degree of difficulty, and add variety and challenge to the repeated practice of the same principle. Introduce the extensions in order, so the group can build their skill base. Be aware, jumping straight to number four would ambush them, defeat the layering process and could be dangerous.

- The trainer passes the initiating role onto another, by imperceptibly brushing the body of another member of the group while passing. The new initiator takes on the stopping and starting and then passes on the initiation to another in the same way; the group has no idea where the stop and start will come from.
- Let the group be self-determining, working on stopping and starting with no initiator.
- Increase the pace to very fast walking without sacrificing connection in unison. This will sharpen response time and develop the ability to work from impulse with speed.
- Work blindfolded. Only try this if you can make the space safe. Walk in slow motion which means that no one will be hurt if collisions occur.

Task 3: Counting

Form a circle with shoulders touching but allow enough room not to feel squashed. Look slowly around the circle allowing your gaze to rest momentarily with eye contact, and then move on. Observe what your breath is doing, don't control or change it, just notice it. Notice the rhythm of your heartbeat and any sensations you feel in your body. Notice thoughts that pass through your mind, release them, and come back to the present moment. Release any tension in the jaw and around your eyes. Try to be open and transparent. Allow yourself to be seen. This continues for about five minutes or until the group releases tension and seems comfortable with the silence.

Introduce the following task

Your objective is to reach the number twenty. Counting starts from one and the numbers must be consecutive. Anyone can say a number, but if two or more people say a number

ENSEMBLE PRACTICE TASKS

at the same time the group goes back to the beginning and starts again from one. This exercise should be repeated until the group discovers together how to accomplish the task.

The following points may be useful to discuss in reflection after the task: being in the moment and not projecting towards an outcome; becoming aware of the tendency to invent strategies to 'win'; leaving space and allowing everyone to participate; becoming aware of the subtle energy shifts and breathing in the group; and being comfortable with waiting and being in silence.

Extensions

- Don't stop at twenty. Keep going as far as you can. Each time you do the task try to reach a higher number.
- Pick up the pace but don't lose the connection to the moment or group awareness.
- Replace numbers with words and create longer and longer group stories, for instance: a participant says 'when', another says 'I', another says 'learned', another says 'to', another says 'love' and so on.

Task 4: Blindfolds

Any kind of blindfold task is useful preparation for Pulse. By removing visual and verbal facility the need to use smell, hearing and touch becomes essential in the gathering of environmental information. As we continue to practise tasks blindfolded, our senses become heightened, and we begin to trust and then learn to act upon our intuition (sixth sense). These tasks also introduce us to the notion of immersing and yet functioning in an altered reality.

Split into pairs and find a place in the space to begin. It is essential that there is no verbal communication during this task. One person puts on the blindfold and the other is the guide. As the guide, hold hands lightly with your partner and walk slowly in the space. Introduce a particular hand squeeze, which will become the signal to stop moving *immediately*. Walk gently in the space, testing the signal to make sure your partner understands the instruction. Once this is established, lead your partner around the space and use the signal to avoid collisions with other couples, walls or objects. As trust increases pick up the pace and encourage gentle running, safely, in the space. Take your partner on an adventure into the unknown. Vary pace and direction. Come to a standstill and swap roles.

Blindfold tasks cultivate trust between partners and a sense of responsibility towards the group at large. They enable the actor to take 'safe' risks and push past perceived fear thresholds, or at least question them. In the debrief mention that the notion of a shared, non-verbal language is fundamental to the Pulse work they will be experiencing.

Extension

- Change partners and decide who will be blindfolded and who will be the guide. Without holding hands, if you are the guide move your partner around the space by calling their name. When you call it, your partner walks towards you. Experiment with a particular way of using their name, and without talking, communicate this as the signal for stopping. By varying the pace, tone, pitch and volume of the way you call their name you can work in subtle ways. The person wearing the blindfold has freedom to experiment with personal risk taking, whilst feeling 'held' and protected by you.

Task 5: Hug sculptures

This exercise asks the performer to express ideas with their body rather than words, evoking the performer's physical imagination. It introduces important notions for the Pulse Canvas such as trusting the unfolding of an idea through action and responding to ideas using physical intelligence rather than the rational mind. This task encourages performers to act first with their body and leave words and the search for meaning till later. It also lays the ground for physically intimate work. In a monitored and contained scenario, performers will become accustomed to touching, being touched and trusting each other's touch.

Split into pairs and with your partner find a place in the space with enough room around you to work. The space should be 'dotted' with pairs. Decide who is A and who is B. The trainer should choose one of the participants and demonstrate the initial set-up of the task taking the role of performer B.

Hug each other in a relaxed way feeling both bodies melt to create one form. Performer A becomes still, fixing the shape and releasing their hug a couple of centimetres away from their partner's body. Performer B very carefully and delicately, without disturbing their partner's shape, disentangles and stands clear. All A performers in the room look like still sculptures floating in space. All B performers then wander through the space, choose another body to work with and begin to wrap their body into a shape around that physical form. When performer B feels they have a finished shape, they become still, which is the signal for the person who was the sculpture to gently find their way out of the form, leaving performer B as a free-standing sculpture in space. That person then moves around the space to find another empty sculpture to repeat the task. The exercise continues to flow as all performers repeat the action, again and again, changing roles from sculptor to sculpture, from creator to creation. It is essential that there is no verbal communication during this task.

Side coach the following adjustments as the work evolves

1. Work with the sensitivity and grace of a hug, but make sure the joint sculpture the two of you create does not resemble a conventional hug.

ENSEMBLE PRACTICE TASKS

2. The source for your imaginative response is the shape of the sculpture in front of you. You are wanting to imaginatively respond with your body. If the shape you find yourself making feels familiar or pedestrian, keep gently moving until you find a shape that feels unfamiliar. Do this each time you meet a new standing sculpture. Challenge your physical imagination and create shapes that may involve delicate balance or physical exertion. You may find yourself lying on the floor and working on different levels. Work outside your comfort zone.

3. The only necessary parameter for connecting your two shapes is that one part of each body must be touching.

4. Don't stand in front of the sculpture thinking. You are practising 'problem-solving in action' so begin by entering the space of the sculpture and let each placement of a body part lead to the placement of another, not knowing what the outcome will be. It is important to allow the work to evolve from within, without jumping ahead to the final shape. Build it incrementally. Let each step in the process lead you to the next. Enjoy the idea that you don't know how it will end and make space for yourself to be surprised by the outcome.

5. When you are satisfied with your final shape, finish working. If you are not satisfied, keep adjusting your body by bringing awareness to each body part (e.g. feet, hands, fingers, gaze). Work towards the detail within the whole shape.

Something to add

- Introduce music as another source of inspiration. A sculptured body shape in space together with music will now inform the imaginative response. Start with genres that do not rhythmically disturb the gentle flow of work in the space (e.g. subliminal sounds and atmospheric music).

- Building on the above, you could experiment with familiar ballads where lyrics are known.

Working with two generative sources (image and sound) simultaneously introduces performers to responding to the blend of different sources. This aspect is built upon extensively in the later layers of Pulse training.

Extensions

Extensions for this task involve language and can be found in Chapter 4: Words and the Physical Gesture.

Task 6: Physical transitions

This exercise cultivates imaginative autonomy where performers learn to recognize offers from their own actions: imaginative responses inspired by what their own body is doing.

It demands that the performer, whilst in the 'doing' is open to receiving the first idea they can transform into action.

With the group standing in a circle, one person approaches the middle and begins to move in any way they choose. While they are moving, their 'observer' is inside the action watching what they are doing. This is the idea of the detached 'observer' that we met during Task 1. Their 'observer' is waiting to receive an offer from the action they are doing that could turn the abstract movement into something literal (e.g. arms moving up and down in front of the body in unison may remind them of shaking out a sheet). So that everyone can clearly identify the action, they might need to fold the sheet up and then shake it out again. Once the literal action is established, they pass the literal action, perhaps the sheet, onto someone in the circle. That performer enters the circle, slowly dissolves the sheet into abstract movement and then works to find their own literal action. This continues until all members of the group have done the task.

Challenges

- To genuinely enter the circle in the spirit of investigation without conjuring up an idea before you enter.
- To move for as long as you genuinely need to, resisting the pressure to rush and finish or of being watched – to let the literal action evolve *organically*.
- To recognize the first offer that your movements make and to accept it without judgement.
- To develop and clarify the literal action by giving it detail and precision.

When watching from the circle, participants will see many offers in the movements of others that are not being acted upon. It is easier to see a missed offer when you are a witness. Getting better at recognizing and accepting offers is a skill that Pulse develops. The beauty of this exercise is that it can also be done alone, anytime, anywhere.

When you are witnessing this exercise from the circle, recognize the power of the 'moments of transition' where the action is 'becoming', but no one knows yet what it will be. Notice how engaging that moment is, how riveting. Both the performer and the witness come together in the unknown, suspended in that moment, until an idea takes shape and the tension is released. This exercise picks up the already introduced idea of working with duality: the performer and the 'observer'. Once we get onto the Pulse Canvas, we will meet duality again in the form of the performer and the 'composer'.

Task 7: Hug tag

Game structures are often used to train actors because they encourage a sense of play and the suspension of disbelief: both essential states for the actor to work within. Games allow actors to play with a light heart while practising serious technical skill. There is an

ENSEMBLE PRACTICE TASKS

objective to achieve, and they must creatively solve problems to achieve it. Games give actors inherent permission to behave in a 'child-like' manner. I use this task whenever I begin with a group, especially if the individuals don't know each other. It gets them physically active and very quickly brings them into the present. While their bodies are activated, I can verbally introduce (side coach) the fundamental concepts of ensemble practice, at the same time as they are experiencing them.

Introduce the common idea of Chasing Tag to the group. Whoever is 'in' chases the group and tries to catch someone. When they catch them that person is 'in'. The difference with Hug Tag is that you can avoid being caught if you are hugging someone. The game begins with the trainer being 'in' and they chase the performers. In fact, as the trainer, I never actually catch anyone because I talk as I move the group around the space. I want them to engage with theoretical concepts and kinaesthetic experience concurrently. Soon they realize that they are not actually playing a child's game but developing ensemble consciousness.

As you are 'in', moving in the space, you will notice certain group tendencies, some of which are included below. When you see a tendency, stop for a moment, ask them what they think is happening and point out what you have observed. Be brief and succinct. Begin moving again. As you are not trying to catch anyone you do not need to run. Work at a measured pace. By taking speed out of the equation you will reduce their tendency to panic. The interventions below are training points which you can mention as the group is working. You may also stop briefly whenever you want to introduce an intervention because you notice a tendency, or you need to catch your breath, or you want to move onto the next adjustment. Do whatever you feel comfortable doing, but be aware not to fall into talking without moving for too long. Instructing while you and the group are working introduces the process of side coaching. This is an essential skill for working on the Pulse Canvas where the performer needs to transform a side coaching instruction into action, whilst being in the 'reality' of the Pulse.

Keep the Hug Tag going until the group is moving seamlessly and all the interventions have been incorporated. If you decide to begin each session with Hug Tag you will find the extensions useful.

Tendency one

You will notice everyone is out to save themselves. Unlike the game of 'tag' this task is not about personal survival.

Interventions

Ensemble consciousness
Suggest the group works as a community against the outside threat – which is you. They need to be alert in every moment to the needs of all members of the ensemble. Ask them to be aware of someone running towards them, needing their help, and to look for opportunities to save others. They are trying to work as one body. If one person is in

danger, then everyone is. It is the group's responsibility to keep everyone safe. This notion builds group rapport and trust.

'Response' instead of 'reaction'
The performer's instinctive reaction will be to save themselves. Instinct drives 'reaction' which does not incorporate awareness or consideration. Once the notion of group consciousness has been introduced, ask them to ameliorate their reaction to incorporate this new awareness. The blending of instinct and awareness creates 'response'. By explaining the notion of 'responding' rather than 'reacting' we are introducing the conceptual process towards being a performer/composer. Ultimately, it is their 'composer' that will be responding to stimuli on the Pulse Canvas.

Personal detachment and physical touch
As participants are working with pace, physical efficiency and group objective there is generally little self-consciousness around holding and touching a group member's body. If they are nervous about this action, get them to focus on achieving the objective of the game as they will need to hug people to keep playing. In this task they are learning to work intimately with the body of another, in a detached way, where the individual's personality is not at issue, much like a masseuse or beauty technician. This task is very useful when working with a group of strangers.

Tendency two

An adrenalin rush may cause laughing and talking when the game begins. Bring their attention towards blending instinct with awareness. The game should be played in silence.

Intervention

Suspension of disbelief
Members of the group may squeal and panic when the threat comes near them, as if the person chasing them has a knife in their hand. They have unconsciously agreed to the contract of the game and suspended their disbelief of the actual reality. Point out that it is essential that actors have the capacity to do this, so that's great, but in this case the vocal and physical dispersal of energy is not matched to the stakes of the threat. The only thing that will really happen is that they will be 'tagged'. Encourage them through this awareness to replace the sensibilities of the child with those of a training actor. Suggest that they contain this energy and use it appropriately and efficiently when a burst of energy is needed.

Tendency three

Holding onto someone to stay safe instead of being active in free space.

ENSEMBLE PRACTICE TASKS

Intervention

Become comfortable in the unknown

Being in the unknown and responding to needs of the self and the group, from moment to moment, is the experience we are trying to create for the performers. Holding on to someone is safe and therefore comfortable. Sudden quick changes, spontaneously adapting to them and not knowing what will come next can be a frightening zone for some to be in. By encouraging them to continually take risks in this controlled environment, they will expand their comfort zone. Hopefully, what was frightening will become exciting. Playing on the Pulse Canvas is a distilled and intense version of being in the unknown. It is good practice for life.

Adjustment to the task

- If you stay hugging someone longer than three seconds you can be 'tagged'.

Tendency four

Participants not actively exploring the space and moving the game forward because they are staying near one another to be safe.

Intervention

Commitment to action

It is lazy to hug someone when there is threat, pull apart when it is gone, and then when the threat returns hug them again, all the time, hanging out on the fringes of the game. This means they are not playing the game; they are standing on the sidelines. When you see participants doing this, call them out. This task can be a mirror for life; they are not *committing to action* because of fear. They are self-absorbed, concerned only with their own safety. They are taking no risk, exerting no energy and pretending to be playing when they are only witnessing. Ask them if this is a tendency for them in their acting work ... in all things? Suggest that Pulse is a safe place to practise *commitment to action* despite feeling afraid.

Adjustment to the task

- Once you leave someone you can't go straight back to that person; you must at least hug someone else before you can hug that person again.

Tendency five

They only have a sense of working 'outside themselves', for the safety of others or for the objective of the game and not paying detailed attention to when the threat is upon them. If you were tagging people, you could have caught them many times.

Interventions

Kamikaze action

As opposed to the tendency to stay 'safe', some performers are driven to achieve the objective of the game and will want to 'win' at all costs. They will come too close to the threat, take unnecessary risks and want to be the hero in the room. Of course, because you are not catching anyone, they have unconsciously settled into complacency and have lost focus of their dual responsibility; to the group *and* to themselves. Remind them it is about balance, as well as the contract of the game, even if no one is being caught.

Dual consciousness: The micro and the macro

Individuals in the group must balance their sense of responsibility to others with their own well-being. It is no good taking so much risk for another that you incur your own demise. Tending to one's own performance (the micro) but remaining connected and aware of the whole event (the macro) is fundamental to Pulse. Here could be a good moment to ask the group these questions.

- Who has noticed that I am not catching anyone?
- If you have, has it changed the way you have been playing?
- Are you less engaged or does it make no difference?

Here you can mention one's attitude to the work. Training is about building skill without having investment in an outcome. Acting is about investing in imaginary high stakes so you can create illusion.

Extensions

- Once the group is working in silence in a seamless focused way, change the parameters of the space: reduce the space they are permitted to use to half the size.
- Ask them to take their visual focus away from the threat (the trainer) and place their attention totally inside the group's movement, using peripheral sensing only when the threat is near.
- Step out of the game, give the tag to a participant, and let the group know that the original rules of chasing and catching now apply. Ask the group to work with just as much precision, calm, efficiency and pace as they have been, but with the added stakes.

4
SKILL FOCUS TASKS

What is a skill focus task? I think of it as an 'oblique illustration' – a change of course at an angle, an indirect example. These tasks offer a contracted and more defined context in which to practise the Principles and additional elements before they are added to the Canvas. By limiting the variables, the performers can concentrate on the aim of the task without juggling the greater demands of keeping the Pulse 'alive'. This separation allows the actor a deeper focus, as well as offering you a chance for more conceptual exchange during and around tasks.

Reminder

While working through these tasks, you will need to draw on Principles and working concepts from the Canvas. They are listed below and will be useful as shorthand for side coaching.

Performance principles

- *sustain action*
- *develop to climax*
- *plateau*
- *contrast*
- *dynamic tension*
- *jo, ha, kyu*
- *repetition.*

Compositional principles

- *commencement*
- *recurring motif*
- *denouement*
- *form and chaos*

- *find the ending*
- *juxtaposition.*

Working concepts

- *What does it need?*
- *commitment to action*
- *breaking the fourth wall*
- *working in parallel*
- *'smelling' the dramatic potential*
- *shifting from micro to macro*
- *recognizing the score*
- *accessing your composer.*

Words and the physical gesture

Although we access all our brain functions when moving and talking, until now the work on the Canvas has largely engaged the right-brain, responsible for intuition, imagination, spatial perception, spontaneity, risk taking, symbols and images, and 'big picture' perception. We activated the left-brain minimally to access our 'composer' when concerned with forming strategies and sequential perception. The general understanding is that the left hemisphere of the brain is thought to be responsible for language and literal meaning, so as we enter the territory of words, we will be engaging it further. Our aim is to start incrementally with sounds, words and then phrases, finally building to continuous improvised speaking so that we can gently achieve balance and integration of the two hemispheres, and balance and integration of the physical and verbal. In Western performance culture, language is usually prioritized as a purveyor of meaning and in theatrical convention our eyes are generally drawn to the speaker. The physical, visceral meta-language we have strived to create on the Canvas must not diminish when words enter the picture.

The tasks in this section involve working with physical gesture as well as language in a phrase structure. They present the performers with the challenge of switching between right- and left-brain functions with the aim of developing cognitive balance. They also present an opportunity to explore the use of a heightened physical style layered with everyday speech, introducing the performers to using *juxtaposition* with form.

An inherent challenge in this work is to honour the musicality and meaning of spoken phrases whilst repeating them. The performers will tend to verbally flatten the phrase (speak in a monotone) as few, at this stage in the work, will know how to embody it with meaning whilst using it for rhythmic experimentation. It happens generally when imaginative and sensory impulse is disengaged from speaking. Bring their attention to the

SKILL FOCUS TASKS

monotone phrasing in each of the tasks so it doesn't become a habit. Eventually they will develop the capacity to do both concurrently.

Task 1: Hug sculpture extensions

You will find the fundamental Hug Sculpture task in Chapter 3. Introduce the ensemble to this task or re-visit if they have done it before. In my experience it is a well-loved exercise and its familiarity will be satisfying for them. With the extensions below segue from one task to the next without stopping. When you observe that the group has incorporated the previous instruction and it is evident they have understood the new challenge, they are ready to move on.

Side coach

6 Moving to the next sculpture; let your imagination be inspired by the form you are finding and make an association between your body shape and the other person's. Imagine that the joint sculpture is a snapshot of a circumstance that these two people might be involved in (e.g. lovers lying on a bed, a father holding a daughter, a couple searching for something lost or two people in physical conflict). Keep your discovery to yourself. It will be relevant to the next layer. Try not to invent the idea first and then use your body to illustrate the scenario. That approach creates a behavioural response; the body shapes become pedestrian, limited and predictable usually based on visual familiarity. Work from the body first, just as you did when your shapes were in the abstract, and when the shape has settled, only then allow yourself to imagine what the situation might be. In this way the physical response will remain heightened and detailed. The situation will appear inventive and unpredictable.

7 Once you are working with physical shape and you have found a circumstance, 'story' has entered the work. What I mean by 'story' is the imaginary given circumstances or the backstory of a situation between two people. With 'story' comes attitude and emotion. Until now your facial expression has probably been neutral as there has been no internal source to change it. After you have shaped your next sculpture, your physical response can be completely embodied, as your face will respond to the emotion and the circumstances in your 'story'.

8 Moving to the next sculpture, after finding the shape and then finding the 'story', allow a sound to emerge from the emotional circumstances and then repeat it. Make sure the sound evolves from the human relationship you have created (e.g. a sigh, a squeal of delight or a moan of pain), and is not an abstract sound disconnected from the reality of the image. When your partner leaves you, remain silent. When you are aware of another participant observing you and getting ready to make a shape around you, make the sound again, repeating it when necessary. Just as music was a generative source in the earlier Hug Sculptures, that performer is being affected by both your shape and your sound. When they

have made their shape around you and found their sound, leave them, and move to another sculpture to create a new shape and a new sound.

The above is an individual response task using the sound sculpture of another as your inspiration. It is a duologue only in the sense that two separate responses blend visually and rhythmically into one image, but there is no vocal consensus when creating this joint image. You have no idea what your partner is responding to or what circumstance they hold in their mind.

9   The next element to introduce is language. Continue the frame of the task as above but when moving to the next sculpture, find the shape and 'story' and then let a word emerge. Again, try to make the word come from the circumstance, emotion and relationship. It should not *describe* the situation (e.g. love, pain, anger). It is something you might say to another *in* that situation (e.g. help, smile, no).

10 After the word move onto a phrase (e.g. 'come here' or 'hold me' or 'are you sure?').

11 After a phrase move onto a long sentence full of detail and information about how you feel or where you are or what is happening (e.g. 'I can't believe you dropped that vase mum gave us for our anniversary, she gave us that just before she died … ').

12 From a sentence emerging out of the Hug Sculpture move into a spoken scene where, as a couple, you are liberated from your frozen image and come to life improvising the circumstances of your relationship.

For this last extension to happen in a room with ten or fifteen pairs working, you will need to ask everyone to take a 'memory snapshot' (remember their shape and phrase in that moment) and come out of the task to watch a selected pair working their scene. You can call *find the ending* after a few minutes and select another pair to begin working. Repeat with other couples.

The above series of tasks outlines how to integrate a physical and then verbal response. By focusing on them separately, it allows time and space to explore the variety and expansiveness of possible physical responses. In general, when naturalistic scenes are improvised, performers rely on plot which is driven by verbal eloquence. Little or no attention is given to the potential expressiveness of the body's language which can then make the physicality of the scene pedestrian and unpoetic. An opportunity is lost to reveal meaning. As the degree of complexity gradually evolves from the introduction of a sound to a word to speaking and finally, to a moving improvised scene the fundamental concept of the body being the generative source should remain the priority. In this way, hopefully the physical response continues to be imaginative and heightened as the verbal response evolves, authentically connected to emotion and the invented circumstance.

Task 2: Fluid sculptures

I originally did a fundamental version of this exercise with live musicians at a Playback improvisation workshop in the early 1990s. I adapted it and have been using this exercise

SKILL FOCUS TASKS   **67**

to train the Principles ever since. This task challenges the performer's ability to respond and adjust to rhythm as a source, to access their emotional/imaginal range and to integrate physical gesture with vocal (sound) and verbal phrases.

Four performers sit on chairs next to each other, a hip-width apart, in a straight line facing the fourth wall, in the centre of the space. The rest of the group form an audience leaving space in front of the chairs for the performers to work. Ask all the observers to imagine a situation which they will offer to the players. It should be in the 'first person', succinct and only describe what *happened*, not how they *felt* about it (e.g. 'I was on a plane, and I overheard one of the hostesses say, 'don't tell them, you'll just create panic' or 'I woke up this morning and there was an unfamiliar, naked man lying next to me').

Choose an observer to tell their story. The performers seated on the chairs listen to the story and at its conclusion all stand. One after the other they move downstage and offer a vocal or verbal and physical gesture response to the story. Their offer is a sequence they can loop and repeat.

The observers

The stories need to be brief. Those receiving the generative source can then breathe it in and register a response in one breath cycle. Too much language and detail will sabotage the performer's spontaneous response. Make sure the story 'snapshot' involves high stakes, avoiding mundane offers (e.g. 'I woke up this morning and I couldn't find my socks'). This has less *dramatic potential* than, 'I woke up this morning and when I put on my socks the left one was full of blood'. High-stakes and unpredictable events will elicit heightened responses.

The players

You are the protagonist, the person telling the story. You are not the naked man. Offer a physical gesture and either a sound or a phrase. The aim for the performers is to find four contrasting emotional attitudes. The following are some possibilities to the 'naked man scenario' mentioned above:

- Covering yourself – 'can you remind me what happened last night?' (embarrassed)
- Holding their imaginary face, kissing them – 'mmm' (seductive)
- Punching them – 'who the hell are you and how did you get here?' (angry)
- Hands in pleading position – crying 'what have I done?' (upset)
- Both hands to mouth – giggling (amused)
- Putting on pajama bottoms – 'Oh … hi, are you here to fix the tap?'(inquisitive)
- Slowly crouching – 'I promise I won't tell anyone if you leave now' (fearful)
- Jumping on the bed – 'I had no idea I was gay!'(excited).

If embarrassment is everyone's first impulse, when the first player steps forward and executes embarrassment, the others must choose another impulse. Each player that steps forward must deliver an emotional response in *juxtaposition* to the others. If you are the third or last player to step forward, you will not be working with your first emotional impulse which means you will have to *commit to the action* for it to be believable.

Finding your way in

As a group of four, your aim is to create a unified sculptural shape by placing yourselves in physical connection with each other, yet all players are gesturing and speaking to the audience. Walking from the line to the sculpture, identify what is spatially missing in the picture. The guiding concept here is not what should I do, but *what does it need* me to do. Pay attention to the shape, angle and playing levels (standing, kneeling, crouching, lying) that the sculptural composition needs and place yourself there. Don't try to make logical sense between the position you adopt and your gesture/sound. Each player will be repeating their gesture/sound on a loop. This is the emerging group score. Listen to the group's sound/verbal pattern that is already established and place your phrase or sound into it. Those already in the sculpture will adjust and make space for the new offer. Each time a new phrase or sound is added the sound pattern will shift until all four offers have found their order in the score. Once all four performers have joined the sculpture, keep playing the physical and aural score on a loop together.

From the example above, the sound pattern may happen like this; Players 1/2/3 have entered and established a loop: *crying* – what have I done? / mmm / *giggling*, *crying* – what have I done? / mmm / *giggling*, etc. Player 4 might insert their line – who the hell are you and how did you get here? after mmm or after *giggling*, or break it up, e.g. *crying* – what have I done / mmm / who the hell are you / *giggling* / and how did you get here, *crying* – what have I done / mmm / who the hell are you / *giggling* / and how did you get here, etc.

Working in parallel

Regardless of where you place your body in the sculpture, you must deliver your physical gesture and phrase/sound, looking towards the fourth wall. You are in your own reality and addressing an imaginary someone in the audience. At the same time, you are being affected by your proximity to each other and your attention to the composition of associations: rhythmic, score and shape. This imbues the sculpture with a sense of tight ensemble playing. You are playing *with* not *to* each other.

Finding the ending

Once you are all comfortable repeating the score, you will be looking to *find the ending*. Anyone can initiate and all players should respond to reductions in pace, or volume and intensity which will serve to elongate the rhythm towards stillness and silence. In searching for a sense of completion pay attention to the verbal and physical rhythm and try to finish the composition in a poignant way. For example, 'I had no idea I was gay (pause) I promise I won't tell anyone if you leave now, *the sound of crying* (extended pause) what have I done?' This last statement hangs in the air, all four faces look out

SKILL FOCUS TASKS

towards the audience and the sculpture freezes. End. The sculpture melts and the players return to their chairs to respond to another story. Change over players and repeat the task with two stories for each group until everyone in the ensemble has had a turn. If the ensemble is a small group, you could try this task with three players or even two.

For the observer, the same visual 'frame' contains four contrasting emotional states, playing levels and approaches to the event. Each fragment has been placed together randomly and yet as the score repeats itself, each observer will decipher multiple meanings emerging from the associations bouncing off each other.

Extensions

These extensions take the improvised, repeated structure – the score – into formlessness and challenges the players to find the form again; in a sense working with *form and chaos*. They execute this whilst in action remaining in their own performative reality.

- Once a group of four has responded to the event, and a repeated gestural pattern and sound score has been established, before *finding the ending,* ask the group to *develop to climax*. Individual players increase the intensity and size of their offer and the group's energy begins to accelerate. As this happens the sound score and gestural pattern will break apart and lose its form as the offers overlap and become loud, large and heightened. As this occurs, the sculpture must stay loosely connected spatially. The *essence* of the offer and the phrase remains the same, but other gestures and sounds may be added to create the intensity necessary to reach a climax. For example, crying may become wailing and self-harming, punching could turn into a violent rage, giggling will become hysteria, and a seductive kiss may become vigorous sucking. Once they reach a chaotic peak, the players slowly reduce the intensity, volume and pace of their offers and imperceptibly find the pattern again. Once they have achieved form and have re-created the recognizable score, they begin *finding the ending*. Having physically pushed their emotional expression to its peak and returned, the observer can see there is a change in the actor. They have experienced a physical transformation. Due to this, the tonal quality of the sculpture is different to its origin. At the final moment of stillness, the interacting individual offers will now represent an alternative reading.

- *Moving in space*

  A player may enter the sculpture and make an offer that is mobile in space, yet repeatable. For example, yelping, running and punching the air in a straight line from the sculpture to the side wall and back, repeated on a loop. A sculpture with four players will only be viable with one or maybe two mobile parts, otherwise the structure will collapse. Again, if all three parts are rooted in space, *what it needs* is for the fourth part to move. Invite the players to experiment 'in the doing' with balancing the need to be rooted as well as having mobility.

- *Continuous speaking*

    One of the verbal offers may be a continuous monologue which softly slides over and under the other vocal offers. There is no repeated physical gesture; fluid gesticulating accompanies the monologue. This is a *sustained action*, so it does not fit into the sound score in a pattern. The performer making this offer plays the thoughts like a percussive instrument, leaving space and jamming with the vocal/verbal score. An example might be, 'can you remind me what happened last night … I … um … ah, yeah, not sure how we got back here … I mean … I mean … I do remember the club … and those last three martinis … Are you a friend of Sam's? Rachael's? Do you know my name? … Do you speak English? Last night … did we … (gesturing), etc. The speaker can put this on a loop, cut it up, repeat sections or continue the narrative. Again, responding to *what it needs*, if there are three vocal sound offers, the fourth needs to be a phrase or a monologue. If the first offer is a monologue, then the other three offers need to be vocal sound or a phrase. The offer of two monologues in the one sculpture requires a great deal of skill. Accept the challenge if you dare and experiment with what must happen to keep it articulate, audible and watchable.

Task 3: Liquid jams – Solo

Take the material generated from the fluid sculptures above. Each performer will have at least two vocal/verbal and gestural units. An example might be (1) lying on the floor, holding onto your stomach and laughing, or (2) standing and pointing towards audience saying, 'I've absolutely had enough'. Get into groups of four and teach each other your two units. Everyone will then have a vocabulary of eight units. It is important that within each group's vocabulary of units there are at least two gestures that are not standing (e.g. crouching, sitting or lying) to facilitate working on different physical planes.

Find a place in the space to work by yourself. Working spontaneously at moderate pace, weave the vocabulary of units together in a continuous stream. Try not to put them in an order that becomes a repeatable pattern. You are working from moment to moment not knowing which unit will appear next. Continuously being in action is key. When you draw a 'blank' repeat the unit that you are on until a different one comes to you.

The sequence may look something like this: 1-2-3-4-1-1-4-2-5-4-3-3-3-6-1-3-1-6-7-7-2, etc. Or in action, like this: on the floor laughing, standing/pointing – 'I've absolutely had enough', crouching crying, hand gesture – 'I love you', on the floor laughing, (stand) on the floor laughing, hand gesture – 'I love you', standing/pointing – 'I've absolutely had enough', jumping up and down – 'I had no idea I was gay', hand gesture – 'I love you', crouching crying, (stand) crouching crying, (stand) crouching crying, pulling up pants – 'are you here to fix the tap?', on the floor laughing, crouching crying, on the floor laughing, pulling up pants – 'are you here to fix the tap?', hand gesture – 'mmm', hand gesture – 'mmm', standing/pointing – 'I've absolutely had enough, jumping – "I had no idea I was gay", "mmm", "mmm", on the floor laughing, "mmm", crouching crying, "mmm", on the floor laughing, standing/pointing – "I've absolutely had enough", pointing – I've absolutely had enough', pointing – 'I've absolutely had enough', etc.

SKILL FOCUS TASKS

Extensions

- When individuals have found fluency with their vocabulary, encourage them to pay attention one by one to a series of Principles. Side coach them while they are in action suggesting they experiment with *contrast, development to climax, jo, ha, kyu* and *finding the ending.*

- Until now you have been working spontaneously in a random pattern. A rondo structure means keeping one unit or a duet of units as a theme throughout the piece interspersed with other units (e.g. 1-2-1-5-1-3 or 1-5-4-1-5-8-1-5-3). As a choreographic structure the rondo form is strict but notice how this structure relates to the *repetition* of *recurring motifs*. Try doing a solo using the rondo structure.

- Now loosen up the form, access your 'composer' and only introduce the *repetition* when you feel it *needs it* (or when you blank). The rondo structure sets up a predictable pattern. Try to experiment with setting it up and then subverting expectations by dropping out of the pattern.

- Individuals have been scattered throughout the space working solo. Now each performer does a solo whilst being watched by the group. The trainer calls on the performers randomly, one by one, as they 'pass the baton' from solo to solo. Each performer *commences, develops to climax* and *finds the ending*. They bring their awareness to the observers scattered in the space and become directionally fluid so they can work in the 'round'.

Task 4: Liquid jams – Duets and chorus

Two performers with a shared vocabulary stand next to each other, a hip-width apart, with their gaze towards the fourth wall and one of them begins. Seated in the audience position the rest of the ensemble actively watches. The performers are 'alive' to what they can hear and sense but cannot directly see their partner. They are 'listening with their body' and *working in parallel.*

1. Using their vocabulary of units, they associate off each other. When they were working solo, they associated off their own previous gesture/unit. In the duet, they are associating off their partner's. They will find themselves in moments of synchrony and contrast during perpetual action. At the beginning there is a tendency to do solos beside each other. Encourage the players to slow the pace, breathe into pauses and surrender to being affected by the unit they sense is happening beside them.

2. Another player with the same vocabulary joins the line. Possibilities expand as the three performers associate while in motion. They will find multiple combinations. For example, performer A in one unit, performers B and C repeating a different unit together, A joins B and C, all repeating the same unit, then C changes to another unit and A joins them while B remains repeating, or changes to an

alternative unit. They are not planning or predicting any synchronicity. They notice when it happens and try to build upon it.

3   The last player with the same vocabulary joins the line. There is a higher degree of difficulty with four as the players on either end of the line cannot really sense all players. If each member of the group is associating off the one next to them, the impulse is carried along the line. With four players many more combinations are possible: four solos, two duets, trio with a solo and the quartet (chorus) in unison.

Extensions

- Each group of four with the same vocabulary creates a Liquid Jam Sketch, *developing to climax* several times before *finding the ending*.
- Two performers with a shared vocabulary and two with a different shared vocabulary stand between each other. During this task, the vocabularies will bleed into each other as the necessity to find synchrony will propel performers to adopt their playing partner's units. They can all use any units of both vocabularies.
- As ensemble members have been witnessing all the vocabularies, a random group of four can work together, drawing on any units they know, or have absorbed during the working sessions.
- Performers take themselves into the space leaving the line in a forward or backward direction, carefully making sure to stay connected and affected. For example, if one performer slowly moves forward, one or more might come too, or others may move backwards in *contrast,* and later all could end up in unison against the back wall. If the form falls apart, go back to the line and try again.
- Players begin to make not only formalistic associations but thematic ones with vocal (sound)/verbal gestures. For example, the *repetition* in *development to climax* of 'I love you' *juxtaposed* with crying at the end of the *jo, ha, kyu,* then immediately followed by 'do that again and you're dead' implies 'story'.

During this advanced stage of the work, it would be wise to give some attention to the expression of the repeated phrases. If they are monotone and sound like 'dead' thoughts, encourage the performers to slow down, and invest emotionally and imaginatively in those few spoken thoughts each time they say them.

Fluid Sculptures introduce the notion of an individual performer bringing material to collaboration during its creation and adjusting it rhythmically to fit within the whole. The Liquid Jams offer a frame for the performers to play with each other like improvising jazz musicians by utilizing a given vocabulary to find moments of connection through synchrony as well as juxtaposition.

I will generally work on Fluid Sculptures followed by Liquid Jams in consecutive sessions. I ask the players to make a note of their individual gesture/phrase units in their journals so they can bring them to the next session. Of course, you can also create gesture/phrase units from alternative material and play with them using the same Liquid Jam structure.

SKILL FOCUS TASKS

Committing to emotional gesture

Emotions are unconscious responses to our environment.
Feelings are private, internal sensations we experience because of emotion.
Emotional signifiers are the publicly observable physical manifestations of those feelings.
The word emotion comes from a Latin root meaning to move through or out.
E-motion means 'energy in motion'.

(Damasio 2000, 42)

In Anglo cultures it is generally considered unacceptable to externalize one's negative emotions in public. If it is pain, it will have the effect of burdening others and if it is sadness or fear, it is a sign of weakness and vulnerability evoking shame for the person experiencing it. Those that bear pain and negative feelings in silence are perceived as exhibiting strength of will and are therefore respected. In my experience, people are usually uncomfortable when feelings are expressed in front of them. When we cried as children, we may have been held but we were also met with 'shh ... don't cry' – the subtext being, you will be loved if you don't cry, or it makes me sad when you cry so don't do it. Most boys had it particularly rough when they cried. They may have been told not to cry in a disapproving tone or were called names and insulted. Sometimes grown men don't recognize they are having emotions as the reflex to express feelings has been so repressed. If women in public positions don't repress their expression of anger, they are seen to be aggressive, or seen to be incompetent if they cry. In general, the expression of intense emotion is seen as being out of control which indicates low status. Of course, these are gender generalizations based upon my experience, and I am hoping that for current and future generations this is/will be different. However, I have found this to be the social behavioural landscape that has informed today's actors in training which means there is usually unconscious anxiety, discomfort, confusion and fear around expressing emotions when acting.

This being the case, I do find it surprising that actor training in English-speaking countries, such as Britain, America, Australia and South Africa, is still dominated by early Stanislavski and associated processes (Luckhurst 2012), that involve accessing authentic experience and expressing genuine emotion rather than outlining a technical way to produce its enactment. Aiming to access genuine (real) feelings from one's own (lived) experience whilst acting is problematic for several reasons.

- Expressing emotions in public is fraught with negative social conditioning so it can be psychologically complex and to some people, detrimental.
- We as humans have repressed the expression of emotions so much so that associated feelings can be very difficult to locate and to activate.
- Accessing feelings from authentic experience may compromise the actor's ability to be 'present' and usually disconnects them from their imaginary world.
- When humans experience negative feelings, we instinctively try to hide them, so we shut down our capacity for openness. We physically and emotionally contract. If the actor cannot employ technical means to keep the body open

and vulnerable for an audience to see the raw emotion, then what's the point? Consequently, the performer's energy is focused on them feeling (internal) rather than revealing the emotion (external expression).

I have found a misconception among actors in training that being 'emotionally connected' means to *express* feelings rather than being committed to the internalized 'feeling state' of the character in the imaginary world. This leads them to emoting or trying to 'show' feelings in a forced and uncontrolled manner. If they think that this is acting, then anxiety around not being believable can be profound. They will generally go straight to personal life trauma to connect them with genuine feelings. This can be therapeutic but exploiting one's own emotional past can be psychologically compromising for many actors.

> Many performers assume that if they really feel the emotion then it means that the audience feels it too and they believe that the feeling of emotion makes them 'a real actor' …You must let go of that, and it is hard. It's a leap of faith. You must ask yourself, why does the expression of emotion provide catharsis for you, and is it becoming more about you than the work?
>
> Stephen Phillips

The line between theatre and therapy can easily be blurred in other ways too. Sometimes actors entrench themselves in such a process, unknowingly to fulfil personal needs rather than to gain artistic technical skills. There are several reasons why they might become attached to such a process.

- They are reluctant to give up this way of working because of how it makes them *feel*. When genuine feeling is experienced the body releases endorphins, oxytocin, serotonin and dopamine – the 'feel good' chemicals. This gives the actor a natural high and creates a sensation of well-being.
- They experience psychological release. Being permitted to express emotion publicly has enormous therapeutic value – authorized catharsis.
- They experience pride. By fiercely expressing emotion the actor gains a sense of achievement in having the courage to show such vulnerability.

Attachment to such an approach may not only be about how it makes the actor *feel*, but it may also be that the actor is unconsciously influenced by what they have observed. All our lives we have been exposed to film and television, so for most people our notion of acting comes from exposure to screen acting. When the screen narrative throws up emotion, we observe actors crying with seemingly real tears, raging with anger or quaking with fear, usually in a close-up. The realistic medium of film implies that everything we see

SKILL FOCUS TASKS

is real, including the expression of emotion, and yet mostly it is good acting enhanced with tools of the trade: menthol air in a blower for making tears and stunt choreography. Many screen actors do use an approach to recall genuine emotion. If they do, they only need to produce it for several takes. They will never have to play that scene again. The theatre actor cannot do that. In some cases, they must reproduce those feelings and express them eight times a week over many months. They might also need to have that emotion in one scene and then the opposite in the next. They must play the character's emotional arc fluidly in a through-line over the course of a couple of hours which may cover years in story time. When expressing genuine feelings, the vocal cords are constricted (raising the pitch of the voice) and the breath is disturbed making embodied sound not feasible. In film the microphone is just out of shot, so the actor can whisper or sound can be re-recorded in post-production. In theatre the actor needs to project performance energy and be vocally free to be heard at the back of a space. It is difficult, stressful and complicated to maintain genuine feelings and express them in the context of live performance.

The following section introduces an alternative approach to that of using one's past emotional experience to evoke actions for performance. Think of the expression of emotion as an integrated vocal and physical exercise, not as something psychologically motivated. It is just the 'moving of energy on sound'. If the actor brings commitment to this physical and vocal action it will be believable. When an audience witnesses this, *they* experience emotional 'truth' and have an empathetic response. The circle is complete.

How do we know someone is feeling something? Their physical and vocal actions signify their internal state. We see and hear the person *doing* something. I call these actions emotional gestures; shaking and nervous tension may imply anxiety or fear, explosive physical gestures and erratic breathing patterns will signal anger, sadness, grief, frustration may involve crying/wailing/weeping and squealing and laughing might mean joy or excitement.

Give the ensemble the following provocation: can emotional gestures be created believably without them springing from personal emotional memory? Ask them to enter the following tasks with a sense of investigation and not to pre-empt or judge what they might discover. This work will be physically and emotionally intense, so you need to monitor the energy of the group and perhaps spread these tasks over several sessions. Returning to some tasks, from time to time, will help build strong emotional and physical stamina.

Task 1: Exploring emotional gesture

Darken the room and ask the performers to find a place in the space to work by themselves. If the room is too light, they should work with blindfolds, or with their eyes closed. Invite them to lie on their backs and hold their knees to their chest focusing on their breath, breathing through their nose, observing it, not changing it. Ask the performers to respond to the following instructions:

1. tighten your eyes and drop the edges of your mouth
2. let your body roll gently and slowly from side to side or stay in foetal position

3 open your mouth slightly and begin to breathe through it
4 instead of a long, fluid in breath, 'catch' your breath several times on the way in
5 add sound to the inhale and exhale, imitating the sound of crying
6 let your body lead in exploring the sound and breath patterns of crying.

Detach your mind and become the 'observer'. Listen to the rhythm and texture of the crying. You may want to put your fingers in your ears to make it easier to listen to your own sound. Do not try to produce tears. If they come, don't stop them, but a crying sound scape has nothing to do with tears. By this point the body will recognize the organic flow of this action so let your physical intelligence take the lead.

After several minutes, call 'stop'. Ask the performers to let go of the task, let out a long sigh, release any tension and lie flat on their backs in a silent, still position. Give them a minute to focus on regular breathing. Now ask the performers to respond to the following instructions:

1 place your hands on your diaphragm and raise your shoulders and head off the floor, then release. Repeat a few times.
2 crinkle the eyes and lift the edges of the mouth
3 breathing through your mouth, suck in the breath and 'catch' it several times on the exhale
4 touch on sound as you 'catch' the breath on the exhale
5 increase the pace until the 'caught' sounds form a string of notes and the body recognizes the sounds of laughing
6 let the body take over the act of laughing and let the 'composer' explore different possibilities of sound.

After several minutes, call 'stop'. Ask the performers to let go of the task, let out a long sigh, release any tension and lie on their backs in a silent, still position.

Using this approach but getting them to work faster and more intuitively, move through the extensions. Encourage the performers to not create outcomes or compare themselves to others but to be in the centre of the investigation. The journey will be different for everyone and the point of this work is to discover how *their* body and *their* mind respond.

Extensions

- As with the task above, move from crying to laughing in your own time. Release into a neutral position in between to practice letting go. Repeat several times.
- Switch back and forth from laughing to crying without returning to neutral. Investigate the gradual segue from one to the other, paying particular attention to the nature of the sound and fusion.

- The trainer might call out each of these suggestions for performers to create a vocabulary of sounds: giggle, titter, chuckle, snigger, cackle, guffaw, roar, whimper, snivel, wail, weep, lament, howl.

Task 2: Applying Principles to e-monologues

An e-monologue is a structured solo comprised of emotional signifiers instead of words and thoughts. Set up the same conditions in the space as with Task 1 above, and explain that they will be activating their 'composer' by applying the Principles to compose a crying or laughing monologue. The choice of laughing or crying is up to them. The aim is to perform the reality of one who is crying or laughing, but instead of imagining emotion and circumstances, to focus on the making of authentic sound and use some of the Principles to create structure.

Outline the use of the following Principles before beginning the task and let actors explore on their own or side coach them through the different stages:

- *commencement* – investigate the evolving sounds from a very soft, almost imperceptible beginning
- *repetition* and *recurring motif* – try different kinds of sounds and rhythms drawing on the vocabulary that you evolved in the last extension of Task 1
- *dynamic tension* – try to suppress the sound – hold the breath and build the tension till it needs to break
- *development to climax* – let the repeated sounds build to a peak, then release
- *denouement* – bring back a *recurring motif*
- *finding the ending* – let the sounds slow down and become intermittent towards silence.

Solo crying monologue

This task follows on from the one above. The stakes are raised as they are no longer working in their own bubble, and although they are still anonymous, they will be heard by the rest of the ensemble. From now on there is a focus on crying, as in my experience, actors are generally most frightened of being inauthentic whilst crying and they get little practice at doing it publicly.

Begin with the same conditions as the task above. The trainer will touch someone on the foot which is the signal to begin the crying monologue informed by the previous task. When they have *developed to climax* or reached a turning point, the trainer touches another performer who then begins their e-monologue. Hearing another voice in the space is the signal for the first performer to work on *finding their ending*. The rhythm of the whole is like a relay where the baton is passed just before completion. Continue until all performers have had a turn.

Debrief: Due to the intensity of the task, performers will need some breathing space to come out of that zone. Responding to questions sitting in a circle and facing each other is a good way to encourage this. The following questions will be useful:

- When focusing just on the sound of another performer, what did you discover?
- Could you read the score, identify the composition?
- Did crying sometimes sound like laughing?
- Did the sounds activate any 'feeling states' within you when you were listening?
- When composing your own e-monologue, what did you discover?
- Did images and intense sensations emerge while you were working technically?

What often happens when you begin to work with emotional gestures, specifically crying, is that genuine feeling can be evoked. Your physical intelligence recognizes familiar physical and vocal patterns, a message is sent to the brain and a state is activated which brings forth a feeling response. It is produced by physiological changes and not connected to thought. You may define the feeling as sadness (Damasio 2000) because you are using crying gestures, but really it is purely an intensity of sensation. Because it has no context and is not connected to an issue it evaporates swiftly. When these internal sensations are being experienced in the context of character and a narrative script, the actor will choose to call it sadness, connecting it to the character's dilemma. As they are working with *commitment to gesture*, they will be able to dismiss 'sadness' quickly because it is not anchored to the actor themselves. They do not get stuck in personal feeling linked to emotional memory. Feeling sensations are a consequence of the actor's process rather than the aim of this approach.

Challenge

Something must be said about tears. A frustration with the inability to produce them can often sabotage an actor's *commitment to action* and get in the way of believable crying. I have known actors who could produce tears as a party trick and others who will never produce them. In my experience, for an audience to respond empathetically to the gesture of crying, tears are irrelevant; if you are working on screen and there is a demand for the close-up tear running down the cheek, a tear blower will probably be available.

Task 3: E-monologues revealed

Now that performers are familiar with the task as a sound exercise, the next layer introduces an added degree of difficulty for the performer. They must marry their vocal composition with authentic physical gesture while being watched.

Split the ensemble into small groups of four to five performers. Make sure there is plenty of natural light or put on overhead lights. Visibility is important. Each group of performers sits closely together in a circle as far from the other groups as possible. One performer begins a crying monologue while their group observes. Either the trainer calls

SKILL FOCUS TASKS

'change' for the next to begin, or the group self-regulates, with the next person beginning when the monologue has clearly finished. Continue until all members of the group have executed an e-monologue.

Debrief: Bring all the performers together so the critique remains impersonal and offer the following provocations for them to reflect upon and to articulate their experience – as both performer and witness.

As an observer

- What impact did the addition of the visual image have?
- Could you identify when the performer was not *committing to the action*, either vocally or physically (i.e. did self-consciousness take their focus away from their action)?
- Was the action not believable because of this?
- Were there moments when what someone was doing looked totally genuine?
- What do you think contributed to this? How did that make *you* feel?

As a performer

- Did you stay focused on your composition or were you distracted by being watched?
- What happened when you lost faith in or judged yourself?
- Did you have intense sensations?
- Could you remain physically open to be seen?
- What did you discover?

Task 4: Four square emotions

In this task the ensemble adds the gestures of two other emotions – anger and fear – to their investigation. The notion of working technically, using the body and breath, remains the same. As we will be working with the gesture of anger, reiterate the need to work with respect and care for themselves, others and the space. If individuals lose sight of the aim of the exercise, ask them to come off the floor.

Allocate one of these four emotions to each corner of the room: joy, sadness, fear and anger. Divide the ensemble into four groups with each group beginning in one of the four corners. They are to work independently but they will be in proximity to others in their corner. The centre of the room is a neutral space where performers can go to release physical tension, or if they need time out. It must not be used as a viewing platform.

Having already explored crying and laughing, they will now investigate how anger and fear might be signified. As with crying and laughing, they should begin with a shape, then the breath and then experiment with vocal sound. For example, in the anger corner; tighten your jaw, clench and unclench your fists, open your eyes wide, rock or pace back and forth, accelerate the inhale and exhale, push the air out and suck the air in, make guttural noises and try different sounds. In the fear corner; contract physically against a wall or in the corner, hold onto your body and squeeze tightly, shake your knees together but work against the movement trying to stay as still as you can, hold your breath for as long as you can, then very slowly and quietly release it; try whimpering, muffled squealing or silent crying.

The trainer is the timekeeper in the room. Call 'change' every five minutes so the performers have a sense of how long they have been working. Their aim is to visit all four corners. After twenty minutes, call 'time'.

Debrief

- What did you discover about the gestures of fear and anger? Were they similar?
- Did your actions evoke a feeling response? Did you find it easy to drop the sensations and move to another corner?
- Talk about breath patterns and sounds that evolved for fear and for anger?
- What did you notice about the *juxtapositions*, for example, fear to crying or laughing to anger or crying?

Extensions

- Begin with only two people in each corner and the rest of the ensemble watching. Individuals may leave a corner and go to another or leave the space to watch. There must always be at least two people but only two, in a corner. Observers will enter to fill a vacant space and performers working in the corners will leave to go elsewhere when there are more than two in that corner.

- Two performers in each corner may work with each other in a duet. It is best that they do not face each other but *work in parallel* facing the audience but being affected by what they hear, sense and see peripherally. They may work physically and vocally in unison or experiment with the signifiers in dialogue form.

By now the performers have moved past their fear of being watched and the energy in the room might become playful. The physiological changes brought on by physical gesturing have kicked in; endorphins have been released and stress levels have dropped. There may be euphoria in the room, which is a wonderful note to leave the session on; however, it is important to stress that believability is what they are aiming for. They may have achieved a certain fluency (ability to enter the gestures and move from one to another quickly), but reiterate the Pulse working concept that truth is *commitment to action*. The performer must pay attention to detail, be energetically focused and connected through intention of action to be committed and therefore believable.

Task 5: Emo-choir

The following is a good preparation task for a Pulse Sketch after emotion has been introduced to the Canvas or as a reminder of the emotional gesture work if it loses detail, or becomes generalized and non-specific.

The ensemble stands in a choir formation and the trainer, or an ensemble member, takes the conductor role. Instead of singing, the ensemble will laugh or cry. Looking at an individual with a smile or a sad face the conductor indicates which sound to produce. A hand gesture brings the sounds in and takes them out. Invent hand signals to indicate the following:

- reduce volume
- all silent
- all sound
- *development to climax*
- *repeat* – isolate an individual or a small group to laugh or cry on a loop
- *juxtapose* – a laugh and a cry working in duet, allow both to be heard
- *sustain* sound – one person keeps the base note, while others are added and removed.

Words, silence and emotional gesture

It is rare to see actors voluntarily express intense emotion in an improvised scene. It is generally thought that rehearsal and preparation are necessary to achieve this. Therefore, comedy lends itself most commonly to improvised scenarios. The following tasks will draw on the new vocabulary of emotional gestures and invite the actor to improvise with them while relating to another actor.

Task 1: Come here

Set up the space with half the group sitting on chairs in a line across the space, with as much room between the chairs as possible. The rest of the group finds a seated partner and stands opposite them, at least two to three metres away. They are not allowed to come closer to their partner or touch them.

When the task begins, the performer standing works through a range of emotions using gestures in a sequence from any of the following: joy, sadness, fear, anger and perhaps even disgust, pride, desire or surprise, if they want to explore others. Within each separate emotional gesture sequence, they may use the phrase 'come here', but only once. Their intention is to get their partner to come to them. The seated observer sits with open body language giving their playing partner their full attention. During this journey, the observer counts to themselves, three moments where they were affected. With the third moment the seated partner comes off the chair, the pair hug quietly and pull away to observe the rest of the group working until all have finished. The partners then swap over and the group repeats the task.

The aim of those working is to create an empathetic response in the observer. This will only happen if each emotional sequence is believable. The observer may be affected by their partner's authenticity or imaginative capacity, or they may be surprised by genuine empathy.

Tendency

Many of the performers will tend to stare at the seated person, as if they feel they can only affect someone through intense eye contact. Continuous eye contact (especially when expressing emotion) is unnatural; it limits the ability to reveal 'inner life' and might turn the observer away. If you see this happening, softly side coach the actors during the process. Ask them to let their seated partner be a witness to an unfolding process. Encourage them to draw their partner in through transparent vulnerability rather than demanding attention through locked-in eye contact. As with all these tasks, it is for them to *investigate* how their objective might be achieved.

Debrief: When everyone in the group has completed the task, ask each pair to exchange what happened for them both as performer and observer. Which moments moved them and why? Then come together in the large group and share their discoveries.

- When was the performer most effective?
- What response did this create for you?
- When were they most believable? Why?
- Did you observe them allowing each sequence to unfold?
- Did they take you on a journey?
- Which emotions did they appear to be most comfortable working with?
- What happened when, through frustration, they yielded and let go of trying to force it?

Extension

- Set up this task the same as above. Beginning with the phrase 'come here', they will compose a monologue incorporating words, pausing and emotional gestures. Don't forget that physical gesture, action and especially silence are important parts of the composition.

Task 2: Emo-transformations

The purpose of this task is to play with emotional gestures while relating to another person within an improvised scene. Set up the space with a few chairs or a bench. The setting rests in the 'real world' but no 'given circumstances' are provided. The actors play themselves in an imaginary place. There is no speaking, but the audience must believe there is a reason they are not talking to each other, for example, they are strangers, or they are too emotional to talk. This context must be communicated by the actions of the actors.

Two performers, each expressing contrasting feelings, play a scene with the same objective: to do something to the other person that will allow that actor to transform their emotional state. Each can only be changed by something the other person does. They cannot pre-plan this engagement. They can only look for possibilities to act and take the opportunity to change when it arises.

The framework of the task

One actor begins in the space in a feeling state. After several minutes the second actor enters in a different state. They play the scene. After they have transitioned into another state, the actor who began in the space finds their exit. The other actor is left in the space. Before commencing the scene, give an emotional state to each performer to begin. They are free to transition during the scene into whichever state they choose.

For example: Person A sits in the space crying. Person B enters laughing. They become aware of the state the other is in, and both try to stop showing it, but can't. Person B sits beside the seated actor. The crying actor puts their head in the other's lap. This action allows person B to change. Person B stops laughing and strokes A's hair. This action allows A to change. A begins to tremble and with anger gets up and leaves the space. B is left sitting, softly crying. Alternatively, A could have begun to laugh, and B could have become angry. If the actor allows the change to evolve slowly without rushing, the transition will feel justified to an observer and the scene will be believable.

Extension

- Both the beginning and final emotional states are given to both players before they enter the scene. For example, Actor 1: begin crying and end laughing, Actor 2: begin angry and end fearful.

Task 3: Punctuations

In the following tasks we investigate the use of emotional gesture as a compositional tool during improvised speaking. The group splits into pairs. Sitting together on chairs dotted around the space, one performer works while the other is their interviewer. The working performer begins quietly evolving an emotional gesture. Once established, the interviewer asks them questions of an intimate and confronting nature, one by one, encouraging the working actor to slowly respond. They must not rush. The premise is that the working actor finds it difficult to speak (this is their obstacle) but they know they must confess.

Performers

To slow down the 'stream of consciousness' response, and give it shape and an unpredictable rhythmic dynamic, the performer experiments with three punctuating tools which offer opportunities for pausing:

- Searching for the thoughts, trying to remember
- Finding the words difficult to speak
- Any emotional gestures.

Using these tools will create time and space for the 'composer' and slow everything down but keep the tale connected. This allows the performer to invest in the story they are inventing instead of speaking in a rush and then 'blanking' – having nothing to say. Be sure to give the tools priority. Don't get lost in the enjoyment of weaving a coherent story. It should be fragmented and not easy for the interviewer to follow.

Interviewers

Some initiating interview questions could be:

- When did you realize they were dead?
- Did he leave when he found out you/they had failed/lied or were pregnant?
- How hard was it to face the truth?
- Do you regret what you did?
- How could you stay with them after that?

Once the story is underway the interviewer should tread carefully and only ask follow-up questions if the performer needs to be prompted. Their role is to support the speaker, not to catch them out.

Extensions

- A performer does the above task as a performed monologue without help from an interviewer in front of the ensemble.
- Do the above task but also work with the Principles of *repetition, recurring motif, development to climax, dynamic tension, denouement* and *finding the ending*. The interviewer can suggest them and/or the performer can work independently, applying them.

Task 4: Emo-juxtapositions

One way to avoid banal and predictable content when improvising 'real world' scenarios is to use *juxtaposition* as a structural tool. As one is always in the unknown when improvising, taking even further risk is not easy. This task shows performers that unusual and unpredictable choices can be believable and more exciting, even though they seem psychologically incongruent. In this task two performers will improvise a scene with emotional high stakes working from turning-point to turning-point by transforming direction into action.

SKILL FOCUS TASKS

Set up the space so ensemble members are scattered loosely around the room. It is better not to form a bank of audience but to keep the space fluid. Two performers improvise a duet in the space while the observers move around to accommodate the working pair.

Trainer

- The trainer or an ensemble member takes the role of conductor.
- Once the scene is underway, the conductor watches and anticipates. Their role is to step into the scene and make a whispered offer to a performer that will radically change the direction of the scene.

Performers

- They begin the scene by offering a bold physical shape and emotional attitude to the space, for example, one lying on the floor in foetal position and the other standing above them.
- When an actor receives the whispered direction, they continue to preserve the reality of the scene whilst looking for the moment to execute the direction.
- The other performer must be changed by the action or words. They are not to continue with the momentum of the previous moment.

For example, they begin with one actor dancing by themselves and the other sitting with their head in their hands: conductor whispers an opening line to the performer with their head in their hands – 'when did you start using again?' or 'I wish I'd never met you'. From this first line the pair begin to improvise the scene. The conductor will continue to whisper offers of action and/or language. For example, the two actors are close dancing: conductor whispers to one – pull away and say, 'There's something I never told you'. If the actors are having an argument: conductor whispers to one – go over and kiss their feet or say, 'is there anything to eat in the fridge?'

Ultimately this task is a three-way collaboration. The conductor is improvising with the performers to compose a scene. Due to the emotional high stakes and the focus demanded from all three improvisors, this task takes a lot of emotional energy to set-up and execute. It demands a high level of verbal, emotional and imaginal fluency. I rarely debrief this task. If five couples do the task back-to-back the experience for everyone in the room is intense. I generally call a break and let the learning be in the impact of the work itself.

Extension

- The conductor may also side coach either player or both by suggesting Principles to incorporate, for example, *repetition, development to climax, dynamic tension* and *finding the ending*.

Improvised speaking and yielding

Below are six tasks which involve structuring improvised speaking. The first three tasks focus on an individual performer's ability to compose while improvising a monologue, helping them to transfer this skill to speaking on the Canvas. Tasks 5 and 6 involve speaking in collaboration with others, Pulsing soundscapes together and serving the score.

Task 1: Compulsive monologues

This task reassures a performer that if they have nothing prepared and they open their mouth, something will come out. When working in a duet it is important to know you can trust each other to deliver when the time comes, and the other will build on your idea and support you imaginatively.

Split the group into pairs and ask them to find a place in the space to work. They decide between them who will begin. When a topic is announced, they must open their mouth and begin speaking. Give them a topic to begin with, so they can freely associate and go off on unexpected tangents. The less literal and more poetic the better, for example, the topic: swimming in honey.

The point of the task is for the speaker to speak faster than they can think, so the continuous flow of words just spills out. Their partner is listening and watching attentively. When there are signs from the speaker that they are 'running dry' (repetition of thoughts, ums becoming prolific, hesitancy or getting physically agitated) the partner takes over speaking. They try to pick up where the speaker left off, building on their partner's idea, beginning with the words, 'yes and'. They speak continuously until exhibiting the same signs of 'running dry'. This pattern is repeated back and forth until you call 'time', approximately five minutes.

Challenges

There may be a tendency to dialogue instead of speaking monologues back and forth. Participants may interrupt their partner and 'jump in' when they have something to say, instead of waiting until the other is in trouble and then picking up where the speaker left off. Participants may be too cautious or polite and leave their partner gasping for air until they are silent. They may store an idea until it is their turn to speak. Encourage them to take the risk to be in the moment. If they say, 'yes and' and nothing else comes, their partner will say 'yes and'. This may go back and forth until one person takes off.

Extension

- Use 'yes but' instead of 'yes and' and see the difference in performance energy and content. There will be a tendency to argue and be competitive. It will be difficult for them not to interrupt and talk over their partner.

SKILL FOCUS TASKS

Task 2: Pausing in unison

While working in the micro, composing a verbal monologue, the performer remains aware of and open to the macro picking up signals and responding to them. The aim is to work with a compositional objective while freely improvising with language.

Three performers sit in chairs, a hip-width apart, facing the ensemble who are observing. Give a topic to the players, for example, unrequited love, suggesting they are free to use fact and/or fiction. Ask them to breathe and connect. When one player begins to speak, they all speak, addressing the observers, in their own performance 'reality', as if the others are not there. Their intention is to engage their audience by delivering a story full of revelation and emotion. While they do this, the objective for all three players is to find moments of unified silence. We want them to find this through investigation, but if they don't, suggest that if one player pauses long enough and the other two respond immediately there will be a significant silence. While in this pause, all players try to stay in their own 'reality' and justify the silence, for example, pausing to remember or being overcome by emotion or struggling with the next thing to say. When someone begins speaking again, they all begin to speak. This is repeated until they have found at least four silences, experimenting with varying lengths.

Extension

- While speaking or in silence, performers can move in space. They might get up and stretch, hide under the chair, stand on the chair, move the chair somewhere else in the space, sit on someone's lap or another chair if it is empty. This must not compromise the unison pausing and speaking of the task but making bold offers will encourage all three to stretch the threads of connection.

Task 3: Run/Stop/Speak

In this task the performer elicits a theme to speak about from a physical source. As they create a body shape, they become aware of the sensations, images or thoughts it has evoked. This becomes the generative source for speaking.

Half the group stand against one wall and the other half against the opposite wall, lined up so each performer is facing a partner. On a signal, one half of the group runs to the centre of the room, throws their bodies into a shape, and then freezes. From this physical shape they find an imaginative impulse, and begin to move and speak. The moving is not abstract and separate from the speaking, but it is behavioural and congruent with what is being said. Their partner shadows them, listening, careful not to disturb their process. They are composing a reality for themselves. Perhaps they are alone and thinking out loud or they may be talking to an invisible person recalling the past. When the imaginative stream stops, their partner whispers to them, giving them another source, for example, where are you now? why do you care? Perhaps just a word (seaside, jasmine or death). They try to weave the answers or the words into the monologue.

Challenge

While improvising, the tendency to stop moving when speaking or being unable to speak while moving is common and understandable. If this is happening, encourage the performers to bring attention to one then to the other and fluidly bounce between the two. If the ensemble finds it challenging to initiate speaking during a Sketch on the Canvas, try doing this task as a preparation before a session.

Task 4: Applying Principles to verbal monologues

Just as we worked with the Principles to create structure for an e-monologue, the following task outlines the same approach but instead of laughing or crying the performer is speaking. You may wish to decode each of the Principles in a group discussion before doing this task (see below – Translating the Principles to Speaking on the Canvas), or wait until debrief or leave it until they are speaking on the Canvas and it is clear they need some support.

The framework of the task

Split the group into pairs and ask them to spread out into the space. One person will improvise a monologue while the other will be their coach. If you are doing this as a solo task, an individual performer works in front of the group, and you will be their coach. It is also a good idea to work with a solo performer before doing the group task to set the tone for the exercise. By now, the Principles will be embedded as compositional tools, and both the speaker and coach share the same shorthand. Give a topic, a first line, show an image or they can decide for themselves what to speak about. The speaker commences the monologue, and the coach guides them towards structure by whispering a Principle, helping them to move forward. The following Principles will be the most useful as shorthand:

- *repetition*
- *recurring motif*
- *juxtaposition*
- *dynamic tension*
- *development to climax*
- *finding the ending*.

If they are gushing, help them punctuate with *dynamic tension;* if they are struggling, suggest *repetition*.

Extensions

- Working without a coach, the speaker's aim is to improvise a spoken monologue composing a structure with the Principles. Give the player a generative source

SKILL FOCUS TASKS

to initiate the speaking, for example: ask them what they are afraid of, what they miss most or to recount a significant childhood memory.

For example, as the speaker you could find a way to *commence* speaking; try to '*smell*' *the dramatic potential* and once you find it, use *repetition. Sustain* speaking as you *develop the intensity to a climax*. Before it reaches the peak, abruptly stop, and build the *dynamic tension* through an emotional silence which then explodes by *shattering the space*. Begin the new *jo, ha, kyu,* with a *recurring motif* from the early *repetition*. Use *juxtaposition* with emotional gesture or content or speaking style, bring back the *motif* in the *denouement* towards *finding the ending*.

- The suggestion above can be learnt as a score to be applied to any improvised speaking on the Canvas.

Task 5: Vocal (sound) Pulse

Be affected by a source, make associations, and then transform them into performative actions. This is the process of making new work. This task helps the performer develop the capacity to do this, spontaneously, on the Canvas.

In a darkened space, if you can, use an overhead or digital projector to throw an image on the wall (you can also use a hard copy and a torch, but it won't be immersive). The ensemble sit huddled in a bunch and view the image for about five seconds. Then they close their eyes, the focus is on listening and from the silence begin to make sound. Group members make offers initially inspired by the image and then respond to the soundscape that is being built by the group. The compositional imperative organizing the Pulse soundscape is *what does it need?* Participants make vocal associations and layer the sound using any of the following:

- the sound of breath
- vocally produced sound effects
- emotional gestures
- song (no lyrics)
- *repetition* and *recurring motifs.*

Extensions

- There may be too many people in the larger ensemble to create detail in the soundscape so split the ensemble into small groups of five performers who sit in a circle, cross-legged, working with their eyes closed. Show a different image to each group. While one group works the rest of the ensemble listens.
- The same task but introduce different types of sensorial generative sources for them to respond to, for example play a soundtrack or with their eyes closed give them something to smell or taste or an object to touch.

Task 6: Verbal Pulse

Four or five performers stand in a circle. Someone initiates a solo which can combine any of the gestures (vocal, verbal, emotional). It must not be only words/speaking. The group listens and takes in this initial source material, trying to identify themes to associate with. Working in a clockwise direction around the circle, the next person speaks when they sense an opportunity. Their offer will layer, build upon or perhaps *juxtapose* the initiated 'story'. The offers may last just moments or be lengthy. It is a Pulse, meaning a group creation, so focus on *what does it need?*

Extensions

- Same as above, but not working one by one around the circle. Anyone can jump in and 'pick up the ball'. This is a Pulse without moving in space, the focus is totally on listening and making sound, so attention to detail is possible.

- Same as above, but the performers are standing in a line against a wall with a small space between each other. They can use the wall to work against physically (slide down, squat against, turn to or lean on) but not move away from the wall. Try this as a verbal pulse, working along the line, one by one. Then try it again, as with the extension above, where any of the performers can make an offer.

Translating the Principles to speaking on the Canvas

In only one of the tasks above have we applied Principles to continuous speaking, so you might find, now you have moved back onto the Canvas and the actors are trying to integrate spontaneous monologues, there is a need to decode the shorthand. Below is a translation of each Principle and how the actor might apply it to improvising a spoken monologue. I have described them in the context of speaking in a Pulse Sketch where the rest of the group will be looking for signals to join or take over or support. Note: those concerning space – *geometry of space, architecture of space* and *depth of field* – do not apply to speaking.

Concerning rhythm

- **KEY CONCEPT –** ***COMMITMENT TO ACTION***
  Whatever you are saying, do it with conviction. Commitment is the key to evolving a strong offer or letting an offer go. As insignificant as the offer may be, if done with performative intent it will be engaging.

- **SUSTAINING ACTION**
  Once you have begun to speak, continue speaking without rushing. There will be pauses, but don't abandon speaking until there is a compositional rationale to do so.

- **DEVELOPMENT TO CLIMAX**
  As the monologue continues, build the delivery of it; the pace, the intensity and the volume until you reach a peak, then explode, running into the space or fall. Sometimes because the other players are 'reading' the score, they will be ready to intervene when you have peaked.

- **DYNAMIC TENSION**
  Use the idea of silence to build the tension. During the monologue suddenly stop speaking; to recall something or collect your thoughts, because you are overwhelmed by emotion and trying to contain it, or because you said something you realize you shouldn't have, etc. Make sure you signal physically that you are still 'speaking' so your fellow players don't rush in to support and take over when they hear silence.

Concerning content

- **KEY CONCEPT – 'SMELL' THE DRAMATIC POTENTIAL**
  The performer is holding a performative reality – essentially bluffing, to maintain their presence while speaking. Their 'composer' uses this concept to identify the first spoken thought with the most storytelling potential. It is this idea that the performer picks up and starts to develop.

- **REPETITION**
  This is an essential tool to use when you 'blank' or get stuck. If no more words come, repeat what you just said, altering some aspect of it, or bring different emotional attitudes to it. For example, you've just said, 'He told me to go away … so I bit him'. Repeat it, dreamily, as a memory, then as if you are horrified, then humiliated, then angry; yell 'go away, go away, go away', then say proudly 'I bit him … (softly) bit him'. By then someone will probably be biting your ankle, pissing in the corner or barking. You can 'pass the ball' by joining in with them.

- **RECURRING MOTIFS**
  When the performer begins to speak, their 'composer' is alert to recognizing spoken thoughts and images that have the potential to give the monologue a poetic structure if they are sprinkled throughout. They may also come about from using *repetition* (see above).

- **JUXTAPOSITION**
  The performer was introduced to this Principle using laughing and crying when they responded to each other's actions on the Canvas. When using *juxtaposition* in a speaking monologue, the performer 'composer' is associating off themselves; one spoken thought leads them to the next thought or sound, emotional gesture

or action. There is a diversity of ways to use *juxtaposition* when speaking, limited only by your imagination. Here are some examples:

- *Tone* – speaking softly or excitedly then suddenly yelling.
- *Emotional gestures* – speaking in sadness then laughing, talking about a happy memory then crying.
- *Style of language* – using everyday speech (idioms and clichés) then drop into heightened verse (intelligible but not the way people speak). Perhaps you'll become a persona that speaks street slang but quotes Shakespeare.
- *Form of interaction* – speaking an interior monologue facing the fourth wall which turns into a direct address to the audience, or a monologue turns into a dialogue (conversation between two performers) then back to a monologue.

Juxtaposition is a tool, like *repetition*, that you can use when you get stuck. Just jump into the opposite of what you were saying. It is liberating to explore improvised speaking where you are not considering emotional congruence, psychological logic or intellectual rationale. If you work with *juxtaposition* rather than the rational mind (what you say must make grammatical 'sense'), you are likely to create a fascinating persona for that moment in the Pulse and because you are *committing to action* the persona will be believable. It is very human to leap abruptly from one extreme emotion to its opposite. *Juxtaposition* also undermines audience expectations, creating surprise and engagement.

Concerning structure

- **COMMENCEMENT**
  Entering the action of speaking should *seem* deliberate to an audience. The performer and their 'composer' will be associating off each other to find a starting point, or you might have the first line in your head. In any case, you will need to 'fake it till you make it', so begin slowly to give yourself thinking time and be attentive to what is coming out of your mouth. It may be perfect as a *recurring motif*.

- **DENOUEMENT**
  Bring back any repeated phrases or ideas (that may have become *motifs*) before you finish.

- **FIND THE ENDING**
  You will either be finishing at a peak of intensity or you will need to create a sense of closure with content, tone and rhythm. If it is the latter, make sure you slow down towards your ending, pausing rhythmically before delivering the final line. It should have gravitas as this is the message and the sentiment the audience is left with. Often the last line is the final *recurring motif*. Your fellow players will be able to 'read' the score and prepare for what's next.

SKILL FOCUS TASKS

- ***JO, HA, KYU***
  This is a compositional reminder to give the monologue shape. There may be one *jo, ha, kyu* or several; *commence* tentatively, as you get more understanding of what you are saying, build it in pace and confidence, let there be a turning point in rhythm and/or content, observe the hiatus before beginning again, or the pause before *finding the ending*.

5
INTEGRATING DESIGN ELEMENTS AND AUDIENCE

The design elements I work with in a training context are music, light, objects and costume. They have at least two functions in the Pulse. For the performers they can be a generative source for the development of themes in a Sketch, and for the audience they create theatrical mood and atmosphere as well as contributing to meaning through 'story' signals, for example costuming can shed light on persona, location and era. Each element, however, varies as to what it brings to the Canvas and as much as I am trying to organize their introduction, we know this is not a linear process. You might use them separately, layer them over time or introduce them at the end of the Canvas training in quick succession. This also depends on the resources at hand. In Masterclass situations I have found myself teaching in a theatre space where speakers and a lighting board were available. At those times I have integrated light and sound earlier in the process. There have been situations where I had no access to theatrical resources at all, so I asked the performers to bring in lamps from their lounge rooms and they used the torches on their phones with which to improvise. When working with natural light or in an outside environment you will want to lean towards objects and costumes.

Working with objects

The performance nature of Pulse draws on the 'poor theatre' tradition – actors making 'magic' in an empty space. The aesthetic is stripped back and bare, so whatever is brought onto the Canvas (action, gesture or object) has impact, meaning and resonance. The only objects that I introduce during training are multi-functional pieces of furniture. Chairs, benches or stools are useful to create different levels, can be transformed imaginatively, are usually available in a studio space and light enough for a performer to carry on their own. Line furniture pieces up against both side walls and invite performers to bring them into the space and use them. It might take them a while, but eventually they will become integrated into the action. For example, seven performers speaking simultaneously standing on a line of chairs or two chairs held high while actors 'dance' a duet or hiding under and crawling over them.

As an integration task, try starting Sketches by setting chairs in a shape on the Canvas. I would think that somewhere during Phase Six or Seven of the Canvas work they will become useful.

Extension

- Bring one set element into the space for the performers to integrate. It will also serve as a generative source (e.g. a large coil of rope, a long stretch of fake grass, a pile of umbrellas or a basket of lemons).

Working with costume

Any design element that enters the empty Canvas holds meaning and serves as a generative source. Wearing a t-shirt with writing on it cannot be ignored as it has brought words onto the Canvas and therefore must be referred to. Until Phase Six, encourage performers to wear only black; after that, you could introduce costume to generate themes for a Pulse Sketch.

Extensions

- Invent different categories of costume and use them as a generative source, for example the group all wear red, wedding dresses, underwear, suit jackets or rehearsal skirts.
- Ask the performers to come dressed in a way that gives off signals about a particular persona (e.g. chef, swimmer, gardener, stripper). Put them all in a Sketch together or make one persona the generative source for the Sketch. Also play with signals of eras, cultures and locations.
- Have a 'dress-up' basket in the space where performers can leave the Canvas put something on and find their way back into the Sketch.

Working with music

As we know, music is seductive and can overpower anything else operating in the space, so be careful and selective with how and when you introduce music as another element. I use 'music as a soundscape' in the Canvas work, Phase Two: Making Connections, when the performers are working in the macro and searching for patterns. You can segue into it from 'Singing from outside the Sketch' which works in the same way. This will give the ensemble a reprieve from their focus on juggling the Principles and injects a different energy and dynamic. I introduce 'Music as a Playing Partner' in Phase Seven: Adding Sound to the Physical World.

INTEGRATING DESIGN ELEMENTS AND AUDIENCE

Just as the performers juggled the Principles and the physical and vocal vocabularies, they will be juggling to incorporate this new element when it is introduced. Do some brief Canvas tasks, based on the strategies below where they can work with total attention with this new playing partner, and then try integrating sourced sound into the Pulse Sketch. If the Pulse Sketch struggles, go back to working in silence. Learning to Pulse with music can only be accomplished while keeping the Pulse 'alive'.

I operate the sound (and light) when introducing this element to the Sketch. As soon as it becomes familiar to the players, I hand the operation over to an ensemble member and side coach them while they experiment. Pulsing (with sound) from outside the Canvas gives the performer a dramaturgical view of the Sketch and operational agency, to affect the action and storytelling – an essential perspective for each player to have. When using sourced sound, you will need a sound system with enough speaker capacity to fill the space you are working in. If you are in a large studio space a small speaker won't give the volume or intensity needed to affect the performers.

Music as soundscape

While the performers are warming up their bodies in preparation for the Canvas, put on instrumental music to fill the space. Use very long tracks of five to ten minutes which organically build in rhythm. I find the artists Sigur Rós, The Necks, Philip Glass and Arvo Pärt useful, as well as some movie soundtracks, but you will have your own preferences so experiment and see what works. Through side coaching segue from warming up into doing Pulse Scales. The majestic insistence of the sound always carries the ensemble into another zone, and you will notice heightened sensibility of the shapes, patterns and rhythms they employ. This task is meditative by nature and can be very addictive so don't over-use it, or performers will feel there is something missing when they work in silence.

Using music in this phase serves several functions. The performers become familiar with an external generative influence as well as being affected sensually. Till this point they were predominantly using sight when responding to patterns and shapes in the space. The music now helps them find connections and patterns through rhythm. They will initially go with the rhythm of the music as they are used to dancing to music. The Scales, however, have inbuilt rhythmic variations from running to standing still. Encourage them to experiment working *with* and *against* the rhythm of the music rather than having it dominate their impulses. If they manage this, the use of music will feel liberating rather than controlling and their offers in future Sketches, in response to music, will be enjoyably unpredictable.

Once an ensemble is working on original material or rehearsing a play there will be a collated play list of themed instrumental music developed and used during rehearsals. The ensemble will often Pulse with the playlist to warm up before rehearsal and then use it when Pulsing as preparation before performing the show. In those two contexts, the actors don't speak in the Pulse, so a soundscape is generally used. Improvised speaking generally only happens in a Pulse Sketch. In that context music becomes a playing partner.

Music as playing partner

The live musician or operator of the sourced sound improvises with the ensemble working from outside the Canvas. They have an 'outside-eye' perspective and can support the Pulse dramaturgically by making offers and initiating themes as well as enhancing and layering already established motifs with sound. Whether you are using a live musician/s, singer, or pre-recorded sourced sound the same concepts apply, so for simplicity, I will be referring to sourced sound.

THE PLAYLIST

Thirty years ago, when I began this journey, I compiled several playlists and burnt them onto CDs. I operated the sound from a ghetto blaster, and it was easy to fade in, out and to rewind whilst watching the playing of the Pulse. If you have no idea what a CD or a ghetto blaster is ... Google it. These days we have playlists on our phones or computers. I find it harder to keep my eyes on the Pulse when I operate from a touch screen, but I have faith that you will find your own way.

Put together a playlist that is varied in genre, content and rhythmic possibilities, with lyrics and without. These are some categories you might like to include:

- Rhythm – up-beat, intense, fast paced/ slow, delicate, gentle
- Theme (Lyrics) – evocative of era, place and/or culture: Judy Garland, Bob Dylan, Vera Lynn, Jacques Brel, Billie Holiday
- Mood – classical, jazz, opera, world music, soul, seventies disco, Argentinian Tango
- Atmosphere – spooky, war, playful, elegance, childhood
- Sound Effects – baby crying, gun shots, water dripping, applause, breathing, church bells.

It will be useful to put a brief description beside each one so you can identify them immediately. This serves two functions: ease is essential, because you will have to work very fast when associating off the Canvas, and anyone in the ensemble can then use your list to operate the sound. For example, some descriptions I had on my list were fifties lounge, Polish melancholy, angry rap, eerie/sparce, delicate piano, grand strings, speedy sitar, psycho violin or first line/title of songs: What a Wonderful World, Cry me a River, Strange Fruit, Hallelujah.

WHAT TO OFFER

A Sketch is like a short moving poem. It can only aesthetically support one musical offer, which will become a *recurring motif*. That means music from one genre (opera, jazz, hip hop) or one ballad with lyrics. Just as you did when you began with physical gestures,

INTEGRATING DESIGN ELEMENTS AND AUDIENCE

your 'composer' will be looking for the many ways you can use the same musical motif. You can, however, layer the sonic landscape of the Sketch. For example: add to the musical motif – 'How can you mend a broken heart?' a sound effect (baby crying or glass breaking), or the performers may layer it by incorporating a line from the musical motif into a monologue or singing the song if they know it.

Lyrics operate in the same way as speaking does on the Canvas. They are a generative source for players to associate off and help build the theme of the Sketch. For example: if you played *'Non, Je ne regrette rien'* (No, I don't regret anything), sung by Edith Piaf, someone might describe a memory of their time in Paris, talk about regret, do a monologue in French or a group might cancan in a line in the background on the Canvas. As with speaking on the Canvas, one phrase is not enough but a whole verse or chorus would be too much. To become a musical motif, it would need to be repeated (same but different) at least three times. Ballads are the best way to start as it is easy in operation to separate a few poetic lines and easier for the performers to clearly hear and identify the source. Avoid current popular music as it is less likely to evoke associations for the players or tap into memories and life experiences of an audience. Ballads that are classics and have survived through time are the most evocative.

HOW AND WHEN TO MAKE OFFERS

Music is not played behind the action as if it were a music clip. You as the operator are using the Principles whilst Pulsing with the other players. When operating you will find yourself serving two functions: supporting the action already established on the Canvas (serving) and making thematic and rhythmic offers (initiating). You will be fading the offer in and out or fading it in and cutting it out abruptly – it will depend upon the rhythm of each Pulse Sketch. Think of the sound blueprint as silence and your musical offers as compositional extras. Our aim is always to achieve a balance with the addition of another performance language; less is more. Needing to 'read' the score of the Sketch and anticipate what the performers might do next, means keeping your eyes on the Canvas. You will have to practise this to master the technical requirements.

Serving: thematic and rhythmic support

- From the *commencement* of the Sketch, you are searching just like the players, to pick up a theme from a physical or verbal gesture. Once found, having made a sound selection to support or juxtapose, you are looking for the right time to play it. That will always come down to the rhythm of the Pulse. The fading in of a musical motif generally works best at the beginning or end of a *jo, ha, kyu,* in the pause before the next action.
- If the group is *developing to climax,* your musical offer would accompany the action and build in volume cutting out at the end of the *jo, ha, kyu.*

- During *dynamic tension* your musical offer could play for the duration of the stillness building in volume, or you could observe the silence and cut in with volume when the tension breaks into action.
- Be ready to fade sound when you see a performer about to speak and play it softly under speaking, or if there are lyrics take it right out. Bring sound in when the players are struggling, or as soon as they have finished a sequence to help them move to the next action.
- Observe the sonic symmetry of the overall Sketch. Whatever lyric and sound motifs have been introduced, bring them back during the *denouement*. As the action slows down to stillness in *finding the ending*, fade out the musical gesture with it.
- When working with the addition of light; at the end of the Sketch, action, music and light fade together.

Initiation: thematic and rhythmic intervention

- During the *commencement* of the Pulse make a sound offer and then fade it out. This will introduce a theme to the Sketch. Whether it is a sound effect, an atmospheric fragment, or lyrics, from now on you are searching for moments to repeat it. It will become your *recurring motif*. Sometimes it becomes attached to a group physical motif and then needs to be played whenever you see that recur; alternatively, the players may associate their motif with the music you played and go into action whenever they hear it. It happens both ways.
- During the Sketch, try using *juxtaposition* with a sound offer. For example, if a physical fight has become a motif you might play 'when I fall in love … it will be forever' or classical or the sound of children playing.
- If the action comes to a *plateau,* or expectations need to be subverted, create chaos by *shattering the space*. An offer that is brash, bold or rhythmically insistent will give the performers the permission to respond – *with it* (all run) or *against it* (dropping what they are doing and fall or stand still).

Draw on two guiding concepts for operating the sound: *'smell' the dramatic potential* and *what does it need?* Follow your intuition and learn what works in the doing. As Miles Davis said, 'Do not fear mistakes. There are none' (cited in Nachmanovitch 1990, 88).

Working with light

If you have been working in a studio already set up with theatrical light, make sure that the operational board is in the space and close enough to see the Pulse. If you haven't had access to light, you will need to black out the space, find some lamps and a small board. If

INTEGRATING DESIGN ELEMENTS AND AUDIENCE

you have no access to equipment, then apply the following ideas to whatever imaginative solutions you come up with (e.g. blacked out space and torches).

Light as landscape

Pulsing in theatrical light, as mentioned previously, is part of the Pulse culture and working style. Performers respond to the sense of safety it provides. It is an unconscious reminder of the artificial world they are building, allowing them to be vulnerable and take more risk. The atmospheric 'bubble' helps them stay submerged imaginatively.

Light as playing partner

When Pulsing with light, you or an ensemble member will change states, working with compositional consciousness. If you are in a small studio, it would be good to have at least a four-channel manual board. This will allow for a total 'wash' of the space as well as the ability to create four separate playing spaces with circles of light. Become familiar with the board and the areas of light. Make sure you can manually work the board without looking. You will need to keep your eyes on the Canvas. Like Pulsing with music, when Pulsing with light you will be balancing *serving* and *initiating*.

Serving: visual support

- Think of yourself as painting the Canvas with light. You make it beautiful.
- It is you that *makes seen* what the players are doing. Follow where the action moves and keep it lit. There will be simultaneous imagery, so try to juggle that.
- Highlight a solo if it is in the right place and dim or take out the rest of the space. When the solo is finished, bring the space back to low light waiting for the next action to take over.
- Be aware of balancing the space and *what the Pulse needs*.
- The Sketch begins and ends with a blackout. The sound and lighting operators work together with the performers to *find the ending*. The fading of sound or light or both might sometimes be made as an offer to the performers.

Initiating: conducting with light

- You can 'save' a moment by highlighting it or 'release' a moment by fading the light on it.
- As if you are working with film, you can direct the observer's eye, by lighting an image and not another. In this way you are *'smelling'* what images/gestures have the most potential. The players pick up this signal and work with that as a focus.

- At the end of a *jo, ha, kyu* or after a *shattering of the space,* experiment with fading the whole Canvas to black and bringing up only one playing space. To be seen the performers know that all action must take place in it. For example, a duet might enter the light, and the others remain in darkness, or the whole ensemble could squeeze into it. You can dictate where action takes place on the Canvas by which light or lights you bring up.

The performers need to feel 'held' with this new changing element. It will take some time before they can respond and adjust to such an impactful influence. They must be able to trust that if they start a solo in a light, the light won't suddenly disappear. Whoever is operating needs to build trust so they should focus on *serving* and hold off *initiating* until later in the process. If you have a larger space and more equipment, you could light the three bands of the *depth of field* and rig specials to highlight interesting architectural playing features (nooks, crannies, ledges) and a pin spot for the centre. If you have a digital board, you could experiment with fade times and pre-programme some states. This takes everything to the next performance level. When I direct a show and the ensemble do a pre-show Pulse in the performance space it is the lighting operator, who knows the board well, that Pulses with the performers.

With design elements integrated, the Sketch becomes a three-way improvisation; offers come from the Canvas, from sound and from light. At the beginning and end of the Sketch all three search for cohesion. Eventually conducting with sound and light takes the place of a trainer's side coaching as these technical signals complete the compositional process.

Extensions

- With everyone sitting in the audience, take the ensemble through the lighting states one by one, showing them the possibilities that exist. Then go through it again with the ensemble on the Canvas as they enter each state and find the light. Put tape on the floor in the centre of light circles and anywhere else that helps mark up the space. This understanding will give the performers more agency to play compositionally with the light. They will be able to give the operator cues.
- As above, take the ensemble through the playlist so they know what may be offered musically. Focus on the sources with lyrics so they can listen to them without distractions and identify their themes.
- Give/show a generative source for about five seconds to the players before they enter the Canvas to *commence*. For each Sketch, all the players in the group will be associating off a common source. For example: fade up a light, play a fragment of song or show them an image.

Working with an audience

The last layer of the training experience is the introduction of an audience. As the ensemble has been playing to an audience of peers throughout the development of their skills on the Canvas; there is nothing formalistic to add to the compositional structure. There are two things, however, to consider if introducing an audience to the work. First, there is the increased stress level that kicks in for the performer. To become used to the adrenalin surge that an audience evokes and to learn how to work with it effectively, means practising regularly in front of observers who are not initiated in Pulse.

Secondly, there is the lack of methodological knowledge that such an audience brings to their viewing experience. When presenting a series of Sketches to an outside audience, I have usually prefaced the work with a brief description of Pulse. This can be done in a programme format or spoken to the audience beforehand. Of course, this is not essential, but if the Pulse is successful and effective, audience members often think that it is rehearsed – they cannot comprehend that it is improvised. When this is the case, the audience and players miss the opportunity for an extraordinary connection. When an audience knows that what they are viewing is improvised, they go on an empathetically charged journey with the performer. The stakes are high if the observer knows that, at any moment, the performer could fail and when they succeed the reward is heightened. The viewing of improvised performance shares this feature with watching sport. Similarly, when you know the rules, the viewing experience is enhanced. As with sport, the rhythm of the *jo, ha, kyu* melds the performer and the observer. 'The audience experiences a sense of organic "rightness" when actors use this rhythm. The bodies of the actors and the bodies of the watchers become connected, and it feels as if they are sharing the same journey' (Oida and Marshall 1997, 32).

> The best performances of Pulse are performances of Pulse. They can be a knock-out. I watch and can't believe that these trainee actors are capable of such sophisticated work. They have a total kinaesthetic intelligence and make decisions that are extraordinarily creative. Pulse can be just miraculous.
>
> Richard Murphet

6
ALTERNATIVE APPLICATIONS

As previously mentioned, Pulse is a way of working rather than a technique. It is a conceptual approach to improvised activity and is fluid and adaptable to any environment. The size of the group can range from two to thirty, the shape and nature of the space can be reduced or expanded accordingly, and a generative element can be anything that stimulates the imagination. You can observe any improvised activity through the lens of Pulse such as sport, dance, music and even conversation, and then 'read' the score to identify which Principles are at play. Below I have outlined a series of contexts in which I use Pulse.

Independent practice

Free Pulse

Free Pulse is where a group of people Pulse with no intention to execute a Sketch. A Sketch is a performance form – there is a beginning, middle and end. Free Pulse is open-ended. It is like a free improvisation, but it draws upon the embedded notions of Pulse Principles and working concepts. With Free Pulsing composition is not the focus of a group's intention (trying to create a coherent piece of performance). A group's focus is on their context and purpose.

What is the purpose of free pulse?

Pulse begins with Scales – running, walking, standing and falling – and moves on from there. It is loose, fluid and generally remains physical with no speaking. It may or may not be accompanied by a soundscape. The following are some reasons to Free Pulse:

- Ensemble connection – for a group to meet each other on the floor through action rather than sitting and talking.
- Rehearsal ritual – beginning each session with Pulse to build a rehearsal room culture where daily work begins with ensemble imaginative physical action, not coffee and chatting.
- Performance fitness – a twenty-minute session at the beginning of every rehearsal so the ensemble develops readiness for performance.
- Research and script analysis – energetic preparation to connect with physical imagination and stimulate a group's connection to the material before doing a sedentary session.

- Creating material – as a preparation for performance making sessions. The research and themes being focused upon will generally emerge in this preparatory Free Pulse.
- Before the show – once a project has opened to an audience, the ensemble may Pulse for ten to fifteen minutes directly before the show starts, creating ensemble focus and readiness to perform.

> I meet up and have group practice sessions with an ensemble of Pulse graduates. For some of the others this comes of a desire to make work. I find Pulse is a good way to stay in my practice. Training is evolutionary and continuous. You never stop learning … I see Pulse as a means of continuing my training and as a theatre-making and readiness tool. It's a way to stay performance fit.
>
> Zahra Newman

Pulsing solo

A painter facing an empty canvas, or a writer facing a blank page, knows how daunting it is to be a performer sitting alone in a studio working on a solo piece. Many solo artists find the transition from the 'real' world to an immersed creative state difficult to negotiate. If you are working alone, you can make the transition to a creative state without a director or trainer facilitating your entry. All you need to do is enter an empty space, fall to the ground, stand, then run, then fall, then walk, then run and run and run. If you are doing this, you are doing the Scales, making patterns, and using *repetition, contrast* and *sustaining action*. You have made the transition.

Pulse is an ensemble practice, so how can you pulse solo?

Once performers have experienced most of the training phases of Pulse, it is up to the performer or director using Pulse to choose which tools, concepts and Principles serve the context and purpose of the work, as mentioned above. If you are doing a solo, you will not be working in duets or a chorus, but you can work with any of the Principles. Instead of using *contrast* or *juxtaposition* in relation to others, the soloist uses these tools in relation to what they themselves are doing. For example, running then standing still, laughing then crying, silence then speaking.

To experiment working Solo, begin with Scales and allow other physical gestures to evolve. Establish two repeatable units of action (a unit of action has three or more gestures, for example slapping yourself, falling, crawling) that may become *recurring motifs*. Add vocal sound to the units. The gestures become the content while the Scales serve to move them around the space. Create a physical score by yielding to whatever emerges

ALTERNATIVE APPLICATIONS

based on *'smell' the dramatic potential*. Once a fundamental physical score exists, bring in speaking (monologues or fragments) and singing. Play rhythmically with *sustaining action, development to climax* and *dynamic tension*. Explore the space with *architecture of space, geometry of space* and *depth of field*. Investigate the potency of moments of change.

Pulse jamming

> You know the scales and you start riffing ... You could join the Pulse band without knowing the other members and still riff together and make music. For me, Pulse represents a musical composition in a visual form.
>
> Darren Natale

A Pulse jam is simply a group of performers coming together to Pulse, like a group of jamming musicians. You may not have trained with or know anyone else on the Canvas, but if you all share the Pulse 'language', you can make art. You might be in an ensemble making a show and want to jam once a week during rehearsal for performance fitness. You may be one of a disparate group of performers, not currently working, who want to keep skills up or re-skill. Whatever the context it is useful to have a simple framework for the session.

A jam session would typically last an hour. The idea is that individuals can come to a space and find people to play with. The size of the working groups will depend upon how many people are jamming. It is useful if someone volunteers to be the timekeeper. Decide on the length of the Sketches (start with five minutes and a warning bell at four). If it is a small group, play with two or three performers Sketching. There may even be some solo Pulses. Whatever is decided, make sure there are a few observers, and that all Sketches are applauded afterwards. It is not a training session unless a trainer is running it, so critical diagnostic debriefing of any individual's work is not appropriate. Making positive comments about great moments is important, however, and making observations around structure will, I'm sure, be welcomed.

> The mix of people changed all the time and there was always such anticipation and excitement in those sessions. If you were open to the session and breathing deeply you could experience both total release as a performer and the sophistication of an inner composer of body and space.
>
> Grant Cartwright

Frameworks for Pulsing

The framework of seven people on the floor doing a Sketch is a fundamental way of moving through Canvas phases. However, there are many ways to facilitate a Pulse session. Below are some frameworks to try. The Pulsing will be mainly free (open-ended), rather than Sketching (beginning, middle, end), as these alternative frameworks now determine structure.

Numbers

Experiment with different numbers of players on the Canvas from a solo, a simple duet or five on the floor to the entire ensemble (perhaps fifteen to twenty). The performers will experience how differently they must work in each context. With only a few, players must make many more offers and will be initiating most of the time. With a large group, players will need to minimize their offers and actions, be prepared to mainly serve and support and pay more attention to the balance and coherence of the Canvas.

Entrances and exits

Whenever a player enters or exits the Canvas, they must find their way into the image, group pattern or motif and when they leave, their exit must be performatively justified (have intention). You need to nominate, on the Canvas, where the entrances and exits can happen. If entering is from the fourth wall – the observers can be actively watching the action and then leap in spontaneously. Players could exit down a middle aisle through the audience or at a diagonal. If they are entering and exiting from the sides (the concept of 'wings'), they are in the audience's sight line – you could formalize this with lines of chairs on both sides of the Canvas where the actors sit before entering or when they have left.

Extensions

- The Sketch begins and ends with an empty Canvas. Suggest that players enter the space (one by one) until an agreed number has been reached. Instead of *finding the ending* they are to *find their exit* (one by one). This happens organically without side coaching.

- While a group is Pulsing, observers may enter the Sketch (one by one) to add to the size of the group (e.g. the Pulse starts with two players and ends with ten). Similarly, you could start with ten and end with one. This happens organically, or the trainer can call players by name to enter and exit.

- An observer may enter a Sketch, tap a player and take their place on the floor. The original player finds their exit.

- Half the group can be sitting on chairs along the side walls. The other half is Pulsing. When you call 'change' the group on the chairs morph onto the floor and the group working make their way to the chairs.

ALTERNATIVE APPLICATIONS

- During a long Free Pulse session, whoever is playing in the space may enter and exit at any time. This creates contraction and expansion, rhythmically and spatially. It also facilitates bringing objects and costume into the Pulse. They may leave or enter with a chair or bring in several to set in the space.

Duration

Play with different durations, like the experimentation with the number of players contracting and expanding. To execute a one-minute Pulse players will find they need to focus quickly on the first offer and there will only be one *development to climax* if any. They may work on *finding their ending* from the outset. A fifteen-minute Pulse (a bell at thirteen minutes) shouldn't mean they work slower, but they can work with more depth and detail. Every altered Pulse framework and context challenges performers to work spontaneously with the changed circumstances and adjust swiftly in the action.

Content

Utilizing any of the above you can suggest themes to work with or actions to include within that framework. For example, while working in small teams of three or five:

- Each member of the team has a different source to bring into the Pulse – a song, a line of text, an action. They will be looking for their moment to say it, sing it or do it.
- Each member of the team has a different task to execute whilst in the Pulse – tell a story/make action/sing: about your father, what you hate about the world, what is most important to you, what makes you angry, what gives you pleasure.
- Each team is given a familiar story to draw from in the Pulse – *Macbeth* or *Little Red Riding Hood* or *The Titanic*. They can work from whatever they remember if they know it, or they can have time to investigate it before the session.
- If a group is working on a particular play in rehearsal, their strong familiarity with the characters, ideas and lines will make it fun to deconstruct the narrative in a Pulse. If they are in the last section of rehearsal, it will be like working on a themed Pulse.

Making new work: Strategies

Themed Pulse

Themed Pulse is a Free Pulse (open-ended) where performers bring ideas from rehearsal discussion and research, percolating within them, onto the Canvas. The American painter Brian Rutenberg notes that 'cognition comes in before and after but when you are painting there is no thinking, just doing' (Rutenberg 2013). This is also true of using Pulse to make performance material. Immersing yourself in research, images, music and ideas is essential before coming to the floor. I call this 'filling up'. But you must let it all go and enter the Canvas with no expectations to force the creation of anything. Your job is to be open to any connections that may occur. You are pouncing on opportunities rather than trying to construct an idea that you have previously thought of. Be 'in the doing' and trust your 'composer'. You and your fellow Pulsers, who have also 'filled up', have no idea what will trigger each other on the floor. If you work with Pulse in this way, there will be unpremeditated and unpredictable moments that you could never have created knowingly. Once the group is off the floor you can debrief the Pulse, make notes and plan what's next. As performer or director, you may have noted a solo or *recurring motif* that will be useful to build on later. You may want to use an aspect of relationship that emerged during a duet or a fragment of a chorus moment that could become an extended piece. There will be times however, when the entire five-minute Pulse needs to be captured as it was played. It might be a Pulse that worked moment-to-moment, and you want it as a section in the piece. This happens more often than you might think. But the intricate rhythms and interweaving of actions of multiple performers were created in a state of spontaneous creative flow. If you don't immediately do something to 'imprint', it will be lost.

Recall

How do you capture a Pulse to repeat it? If you have access to a camera (often people use their phones) and can film it, you can study the replay and try to reconstruct it. I often did this before I developed the 'recall', and believe me, it is painstaking and time-consuming. The footage is very useful as a record or a reminder, but I have found it to be an inefficient retrieval tool for Pulse developed work.

Immediately after the Pulse is finished, the performers should not discuss anything or speak. Ask the performers to individually (they are working concurrently in the space together) retrace their physical/action journey through the playing space. They may need to do this a few times. They should do this in silence, being aware of the other players but focusing on their own journey. They now have their own personal score. The group then replays the Pulse, with the *attitude* of Pulse as they will need to adjust placement and shift to accommodate changes in timing. In a sense they are re-composing. Adjust then enact the Pulse again. What should now exist is a rough map of the Pulse. All the elements and layers of material have been retained even if the spontaneous essence of the Pulse is no longer there. This map can now be rehearsed and directed either to articulate certain aspects and/or to develop performance definition.

Challenge

I found that if performers repeated the 'recalled' Pulse more than a few times at this point in the process, it fell apart because they tried to fix it in time. The rhythm became ironed out – they didn't allow for simultaneous action because they began to wait for others to finish. Losing sense of composition, they began to instinctively structure the piece according to theatrical convention. The lesson here is to tread lightly with the 'recall'. Don't try to tie the Pulse down. It is ephemeral. Be satisfied with a rough approximation that can be etched when deconstructed in rehearsal.

Modular construction

When I make a new work using Pulse, the process consists of creating a series of modules (group Pulses, duets, solos, written fragments, scenes) that are dramaturgically constructed or woven together to make the piece. Each module, as well as overall construction has a *jo, ha, kyu* and all the other Pulse Principles and working concepts serve as compositional parameters for the piece. Once the modules have been made and an order has evolved, I will use Pulse to create transitions between each module. There are always difficult staging issues, so rather than trying to 'think it out', I let Pulse do the problem solving. When curating the composition, I don't start with an overall intended framework of meaning for the piece. The accumulation of the modules, which are nonlinear but associative, creates a prism effect whereby themes are refracted. Curation choices are dictated by the Principles specifically, *juxtaposition, repetition, jo, ha, kyu* and all the parameters concerning rhythm. The witness gives it meaning. The imagery will pose unexpected questions and usually does not propose solutions. The audience interprets the work through the lens of their own experience. They are integral to its meaning.

Figure 3 Matt Furlani, Nikki Shiels and Kyle Baxter, *Invisible Stains,* October 2009.
Credit: Photo © Jeff Busby.

Figure 4 Mike Steel, Joshua Ryan, Kevin Fa'asitua Hofbauer and Emily Thomas, *Invisible Stains*, October 2009.
Credit: Photo © Jeff Busby.

Figure 5 Hannah Liddeaux and company, *Invisible Stains*, October 2009.
Credit: Photo © Jeff Busby.

Figure 6 Emily Thomas, Alice Sainsbury, Lia Davies and Maj Thomsen, *Invisible Stains*, October 2009.

Credit: Photo © Jeff Busby.

Towards an original performance text

Case Study: *Invisible Stains*

... a fast paced, allusion filled, highly intelligent theatrical essay on the conflicted 20th century. A chock-a-block Einstein on the Beach, *speeded-up, but 400 times more interesting.*

(Reviewer/Green 2009)

Conception

In 2009 I devised a new piece of work at the Victorian College of the Arts (VCA) with students in their final year of training, twenty-three acting and three design students (light, set and costume) and a production crew of fourteen. That meant an ensemble of forty artists. All twenty-three actors had trained extensively in Pulse in their first year of actor training and I had directed half the group using Pulse in a production of *Macbeth* the previous year. We would have ten weeks of twenty-four hours a week to build the piece which would be performed eleven times. It was going to be a challenge to create an original work with so many actors within the constraints of an acting curriculum, but I was confident that our shared 'language' would facilitate the process.

The actors were about to go on mid-year break and would begin rehearsals when they returned. I needed to come up with a concept for the show so they could do research and come back prepared. An idea had been floating in my mind for a few days. In relation to some work being done, a first-year student had asked, 'what's the Holocaust?' I was floored and horrified. I couldn't believe that someone had reached adulthood in this country, without knowing about the Holocaust. I started to wonder what other atrocities of the twentieth-century Generation Y might not be aware of. I thought about cultural amnesia and the danger of its unfolding. I wanted to know what they understood about our collective global traumas. How had they absorbed the knowledge – films, photos, family, oral histories? I thought that this creative experience might be an opportunity for them as artists to speak to man's inhumanity to man. I gave the actors the following provocations with which to wrestle over their mid-year break.

FRAGMENTS FROM A CENTURY PAST

- Trauma sites of the twentieth century, some examples include: Hiroshima, Maralinga, Holocaust, Killing Fields, The Troubles, ethnic cleansing, war on drugs
- Memory – personal, cultural, political
- Amnesia – personal, cultural, political
- Tools of remembrance and forgetting: photography (images), mementoes (objects).

ALTERNATIVE APPLICATIONS

I asked the actors to begin an investigation of something on the list that resonated with them and then follow that path down the 'rabbit hole', to eventually frame it performatively and share with the ensemble on their return. I asked them to consider whether, through film and the power of image, collective memory can traverse generations? Is history no longer tied to time, tied to personal experience? I gave them the following framework for the project and suggested they begin collecting texts.

WORKING THEME – thinking globally about ordinary people caught in extraordinary circumstances.

Scope of project

- Space – global
- Time – twentieth century
- Content – political, cultural, personal
- Narrative – nonlinear, character driven
- Form – collage with linear threads
- Texts – in the first person – to be written and sources gathered. Sources could include philosophical essays, novels, non-fiction, journalism, testimonials, documentaries, film scenes, dramatic text, song lyrics, scientific papers.

One of the actors recalled: 'The actors took responsibility for writing fragments or scripting vignettes, creating storylines and characters and appropriating verbatim quotes from films, documentaries and other sources. As a process I thought *Invisible Stains* was constructed much like a film' (Woods 2013).

Process

It took the first two weeks of rehearsal for the twenty-three ensemble members to performatively share their research. From the plethora of ideas and ingenuity, I distilled it down to around eight areas of interest. I commenced the development process using two types of material generation: Free Pulsing, and the creation of brief vignettes to be inserted when the larger frame for the show became apparent to me. I did not know how the work would come together, but I trusted that if we kept developing material the answer to that question would show itself. We worked with these two approaches in parallel. The ensemble divided into pairs or small groups according to their areas of interest and worked on small compositions responding to my provocations. These were many and varied and as they accumulated, each actor found a character that began to take form. At the end of week four, the actors presented five-minute performance vignettes based on their areas of interest. The events encompassed were:

- The Troubles – Belfast
- Bosnian conflict – Kosovo
- Holocaust and dismantling of the Berlin Wall – Germany

- Vietnam War – in the jungle and the United States
- Middle Eastern Conflict – Golan Heights
- Stolen Generation – Northern NSW
- 9/11 – New York.

Most of these compositions found their way into the final show.

> As a spectator you travelled from two American GI's joking in the Vietnam jungle, to a German couple fleeing over the Berlin Wall, to soldiers in Northern Ireland, to Egyptian lovers playing Romeo and Juliet and a couple on a park bench being showered with dust and ash from the Twin Towers on 9/11.
>
> (Woods 2013)

In the past, I had only worked with Pulse to develop and extract material, so I was proposing to do that and then make a piece out of those ingredients. We started every session with Free Pulse, as an ensemble ritual and to prepare for the day's work, intending to do some Themed Pulses (based upon specific research) later in rehearsal. I soon found that it was impossible to separate these rehearsal functions. Characters that had emerged in vignettes composed by small groups, in separate areas of interest, entered the Pulse 'world' and created mutual relationships. Every Pulse that happened, regardless of purpose, became a Themed Pulse. This is how the nature of the piece gradually and organically evolved.

During each Pulse the actors were not only working from their own investigative research, but it became clear they had absorbed the entire ensemble's research material. This meant that every group member could facilitate another performer's exploration by transforming into characters and creating environments that would assist that performer to tell their story. Consequently, group imagery and text possibilities 'spilled out', but due to the application of Pulse Principles they had coherence. The chaos of such varied information absorption now had its expression in structure and form. The ensemble began building on repeated imagery with each Pulse; and motifs became shared ensemble vocabulary which were developed and given depth and detail each time they were repeated. The daily accumulation of shared materials enabled performers to devise possible through-lines for their personal narrative.

> To aid the Pulse improvisations the costume designers brought along two long racks of costumes and placed them either side of the stage so we could play with costumes and character. There were also props to play with – I remember a suitcase stuffed full of possessions. I remember a moment when someone threw a jacket over an imagined wall before they escaped. The costumes and props meant the possibilities for transformation increased and its potential was even greater.
>
> (Woods 2013)

These Themed Pulses were a magic alchemy of research, the developing text material, evolving characters and the atmospheric 'world' of the piece that was emerging. With such a large group of individuals entering and leaving each Pulse, however, I did not expect the rhythm and structure of the Pulse to be a finished Sketch of improvised performance standard. This ensemble had not Pulsed together for two years and had only renewed Pulsing over the previous couple of weeks. As individual actors they were at different stages in their personal performance process. Some had already established through-lines of possible action while others were yet to find their place within this evolving nonlinear narrative. Then a miracle happened. I had asked the stage management team to source old newspapers with the idea that they may serve at some point as props. The day before, they had tied them into large, heavy bundles and left on the side of the performance space. As I watched the morning's Pulse unfold, several actors dragged these bundles onto the floor. One of the actors describes it like this:

> I remember that there were piles of newspapers which had been delivered to the rehearsal space and somehow, they got kicked into the playing space and we began to improvise with them. They became bricks and weapons, or a baby ripped out of my arms. They became props in a war zone. There was a moment when a performer was delivering a monologue on a scaffold and below, the rest of us were hurling these rolls of newspaper at each other. Those rolls of newspaper became a means of constructing and deconstructing a war zone … you create moments in Pulse improvisation that you could never create through one authorial, traditional directorial approach.
>
> (Liddeaux 2013)

Every performance moment was watchable. Each offer involving a pair, a small group or an individual actor was spontaneously woven into a visual and aural tapestry that had total structural coherence. The imagery was layered and simultaneous with metaphoric resonance. The use of horizontal space and depth of field was compositionally sophisticated with structural clarity and aesthetic symmetry. The piles of newspapers were pushed, opened, scattered, built into structures, balanced on heads, given birth to, carried as babies and fought over during a ten-minute Sketch. All twenty-three of the actors came on and off the Canvas in a fluid motion and the piece had a relentless, pulsating, rhythmic momentum. Straight away we did a physical 'recall'. It was then that I saw the potential to build the entire piece through Themed Pulse Sketches. From that session onward, that is how we made the show.

By week five of the rehearsal process (half-way through), I had not found an overriding concept. In every session I was searching for the idea – for a performative framework – that could hold the material and glue it all together. Experience informed me that a framework usually emerges from the early part of rehearsal – but nothing had materialized for me, and time was marching on. Having gone down the road of trauma sites and experienced the performance responses of the first two weeks, I had become uncomfortable about the idea of performing other people's suffering in snapshots, not contextualized within a narrative. We were actors/artists – and that's the job – to create moments of impact to affect an audience empathetically. But we, ourselves, represented white privilege. The ensemble was young, with little lived experience, safe and free. I knew I had to state this position up front, so that our intentions weren't construed as arrogant and ill-informed. I later wrote in the programme: 'As I watched this group from the "post-military, laptop generation" investigate the past, unencumbered by moral baggage, I could see that they were changed by what they were experiencing, but I wondered, had they earned the right to "pretend" other people's suffering' (Message from the Director 2009).

In the Monday rehearsal at week five, a few cast members revealed to me that the ensemble had come together for a party on the previous weekend. They giggled and whispered accounts of wild behaviour that had taken place. Dropping all previous rehearsal plans, I proposed that the actors set-up the rehearsal space like a loungeroom with a few break-out spaces and construct some lavish costumes to replay their weekend party in 'real-time'. It became a marathon improvisation of four hours' duration. Tic Tac candy was used as ecstasy tablets and much of the weekend behaviour, I am informed, was re-enacted. I had finally found the framework. As I watched the party unfold, I realized the potential of a dramaturgical juxtaposition, a play within a play within a play. These young actors could play the part of self that was entitled, hedonistic, self-absorbed and vain as a frame through which the sufferings of others could emerge. In the space between that juxtaposition, we could examine generational residue – memory and forgetting – the invisible stains. 'One thread of narrative took place in the present: it was a crazy, decadent, self-referential group of actors throwing a bacchanalian party. This narrative would suddenly plunge into a dark, historical moment somewhere else' (Woods 2013). Not only did it serve the function of acknowledging this generation's privilege, but it dramaturgically served as a joyful, anarchic, ecstatic and ebullient contrast to the darker material.

Outcome

'We as humans, to survive and to fulfill our potential, must be able to forget, and yet to survive, we must be changed by the past. We are compelled to remember. We live with this paradox. We must remember and forget at the same time. We all carry invisible stains' (Message from the Director 2009).

Having made their way past 'border control', the audience enters the darkened performance space to the searching of torch lights. The instrumental sound of Led Zeppelin's *Stairway to Heaven* can be heard as the first words are spoken.

'The things I remember are not the things I wrote about ... The Hopi, an Indian tribe, have a language as sophisticated as ours but no tenses for past, present and future. The division does not exist. What does this say about time?' (Prompt Copy Script 2009).

The character who speaks wears a First World War army cap and large, white, angel wings. She talks into an old, audio device. Later, we meet a London journalist standing on the Berlin Wall during its collapse, and we find out that the angel, her grandmother, was an Australian war correspondent.

All the actors created a first-generation character, for example: Sean O'Connell – born 1947, Belfast; Nadia Andropova – born 1919, Stalingrad; Jana Capek – born 1920, Rotterdam; Ruth Jones – born 1928, Moree. Many actors had contemporary characters that were the sons, daughters or grandchildren of their first-generation character, for example: David Abrahams (photographer) – born 1965, Chicago, was the son of Gideon Abrahams – born 1928, New York; Sabine Cohen (writer) – born 1975, London, was the granddaughter of Sabine Rosenbaum – born 1915, Berlin. It was through these second-generation characters, travelling the world, that performance fragments set in Kashmir (part of the hippy trail), modern-day Hiroshima, at the 'fall' of the Berlin Wall and in an Alzheimer's nursing home evolved. For some actors this meant their individual through-line involved several characters and crossed two or three generations. At least sixty characters came and went throughout the piece. The second-generation characters represented interwoven investigation of memory and forgetting. There was a journalist, photographer, neurologist, radio interviewer, writer and translator. 'Another thread running through *Invisible Stains* explored questions of memory and how through the generations, histories are rewritten or excised. I'd seen a documentary in which a white male had suffered inexplicable amnesia, and he slowly rediscovered everything about his life. I created a character based on this idea' (Woods 2013).

In the acting company there were three European students from the Netherlands, Sweden and Denmark as well as other company members who fluently spoke languages other than English – German, French and Arabic. The verbal texture of the piece included all these languages as well as other English dialects – Irish, Scottish, Australian, Southern and Northern American. Members of the company sang, individually and together, and one of the actors played a bass guitar 'live', moving throughout the playing space. He composed a soundscape that wove its way, together with the sourced sound, through the entire show. Monologues and dialogues were written by the actors. A memorable one was a scene written and played by two actors. They were a couple of friends (the journalist and the war photographer), finally declaring their love to each other, while standing on top of the Berlin Wall only days after it had fallen. 'The words heard in *Invisible Stains* were composed by the creators with occasional assistance from: Emily Bronte, Marguerite Duras, Adolf Eichmann, Anna Funder, Milan Kundera, Robert Lepage and actors of Ex Machina, Simon McBurney and actors of Complicité, William Shakespeare, Susan Sontag, Jeanette Winterson and Led Zeppelin' (Programme Note 2009).

There were choreographed Pulse fragments that emerged and disappeared and would 'bleed together in a dizzying fashion' (Reviewer/John Bailey 2009). For example, an actor shouting: 'They are taking me. I am Yana Capek. Yana Capek' or 'Yasmina, they are taking me' as they were dragged away or individuals being searched and arrested, or others being interrogated; '*Wo sind deine papiere*?' or '*Où sont vos papiers*?' (Where are your papers?). These were *recurring motifs* that had emerged through Pulse. The playing space (where we also rehearsed) was huge, perhaps twenty metres in width, depth and height. The only set piece apart from large, black theatre wings on either side of the space was a three-storey scaffold tower on huge casters that could be moved by the actors in and out of the empty space. 'It was another playing space – a tower, a wall, a viewing platform, a clothesline, a kitchen. It became anything we needed it to be, and it allowed for a degree of interesting physical work and acrobatics. The scaffold was there from early in rehearsal, so we had plenty of time to improvise with it' (Woods 2013).

Apart from small objects and costume pieces coming in and out of the space, the major use of suitcases in multiple contexts and recurring sequences spoke of impermanence and escape. Actors were hidden inside them, and possessions emerged from them. One audience member experienced the suitcases as a kind of connection.

Invisible Stains had many suitcases – the image of the displaced person – which has such resonance in Australia. The objects had a life of their own and were used in multiple ways. So often objects are extraneous in physical theatre and are not used to keep the flow, but in *Stains,* they really acted as a bridge between performer and audience.

(Lawton 2013)

'The show was practically all side-lit so that you couldn't really see the performers' feet clearly. It gave us the appearance of seeming to float' (Woods 2009). Every sequence looked like a painting that moved and melted, then another would take its place. The fragility of the show's form seemed to metaphorically echo the developing of a photograph (pre-digital era) and its layered imagery, the palimpsest of history.

Invisible Stains has formed itself into three episodes, each separated by a moment of 'negative space'. The first is **The Shoot**; images of collective and personal memory are embedded, moments are captured in time, they shift and slide, they dance together as the past becomes a layer of the present. The second is **In the Dark Room** where narratives develop, snap-shots of personal story collide and the 'invisible stains' of inter-generational trauma are fleetingly revealed. The third episode is **(Im)print**. Damage to the mind and loss of memory has impact upon identity – the notion of self and who we are. Is our identity the collection of what we remember?

(Director's Note 2009)

The final image of the show was comprised of the actors in their own clothes, entering the space (one by one) with the object (memento) most closely associated with their character's through-line, and placing it in a pile. For example, a bicycle for the Irish lad, a model of a brain for the neurologist, a suitcase for the refugee, a gun for the soldier, a camera for the photographer and a ukelele for the troubadour. 'An empty theatre space, referred to as a "black box", was also an early photographic camera. The black box of the mind is our memory and just as the re-telling of narratives through performance plays with history and truth, memory is known to be slippery and deceptive' (Message from the Director 2009).

Congruence of content and form

The precarity of an artist's existence is magnified when they practise theatrical art. It involves breathing life into something that doesn't exist, and then when it's over, extinguishing it so it no longer does. I have spent most of my professional life in the realm of improvisation – the most impermanent aspect of an ephemeral art form. It is not a coincidence that the style of a Pulse-made piece is fluid, fragmentary, transient and represents the temporariness of everything.

In *Invisible Stains* the images appeared and dissolved like the illusive imagery of dreams. This form might have challenged an audience's search for cohesive meaning, but on an instinctive level it reiterated the themes of the piece. The image of a refugee escaping from a suitcase dissolves into one of soldiers in the jungle, balancing life and death, to a ghostly figure in a business suit covered in ash, wandering past an indigenous mother wailing for her stolen child. These fleeting fragments echo the shape of memories, the snapshot of a photograph and the thematic notion that 'impermanence governs all things' (Baird 2020, 110). It's the ephemeral nature of 'live' performance that is a large part of its identity and allure for an audience, because they *must* pay attention. Unlike the re-reading of a book or re-watching a favourite film or hearing music again and again, the inability to experience the 'live' act repeatedly, heightens our appreciation. It sharpens our perceptions. And if we witness something good, we are invisibly stained. It will remain with us forever.

The viewing experience

During the final week of rehearsal, we created a pathway for the audience to enter the space.

> Reworking establishment of the opening sequence as audience are walking in behind seating bank – Mike and Kev, in uniform, as bouncers at a club, Beck in a solo spot dancing to *Stairway to Heaven*, Alex and Lachy checking tickets (passport papers), as indiscriminate eastern-European border guards. Actors behind seating bank in Decadence costumes, looking at themselves in wall mirrors. Behind them is the first-generation character history and photo board. Audience enters a darkened space (as much as houselights will allow), actors with torches roaming through the space and behind the scrim.
>
> (Rehearsal Process Report, Kissane 2009)

'By the time the show opened, the audience and actors had already shared a common space so the segregation between playing area and audience had a different quality to it' (Woods 2013). It was important to me to reveal to the audience they would be watching actors putting on a show, so that when they bought into the 'world' that we'd created, we could go on that journey together.

> The resulting style of the piece looked like a Fellini film; it had an ambiguity which meant that individual spectators each had their own experience ... After *Invisible Stains* a woman came up to me and said that she'd recently been widowed and hadn't been out very much. She'd been sent a ticket for the show but came out reluctantly and anxiously. During the show she found herself literally reaching forward to try and touch one of the performers. The power of that encounter is what Pulse is about. For the first time in months that woman wanted to reach out to another and communicate something about what she was feeling.
>
> (Liddeaux 2013)

Even though watching is a communal activity, the perceiving of meaning is an intimate one. But here too, as co-collaborators, the audience and actors are again in the same slippery, undefined space. The nature of a Pulse event means that all actors are mostly on stage together, and if not, they are off stage hastily changing to come back on. There is no possibility to watch scenes. If they are not acting, they are probably moving chairs, suitcases or a huge tower. The complexity of layered imagery and simultaneous moments means actors can't possibly know what it looks like. 'The performers often don't fully understand what they're in until they've talked to audience members and asked them about the show. For performers, I think there's a certain pleasure and safety in not knowing how the show will be received' (Woods 2013).

Pulse actors are accustomed to performing in the unknown, they have trained for this, but it still involves a great deal of trust in the director and the structure of the process and its resultant form. For me, it feels a bit like high-wire walking; when you get to the other side the sense of achievement is euphoric. It is particularly satisfying knowing that it has been achieved through ensemble practice. A director remarked, 'They worked as a genuine ensemble. Most theatre now is based on stars, leaders. There were so many people on stage and any of them, at any point, could become a leader. Everyone was equal – that is remarkable' (Lawton 2013).

Invisible Stains had been a brave endeavour in terms of size and scope, and a risky venture in terms of social/cultural and politically charged content, but I was enormously relieved when a reviewer summarized his understanding of the project:

> When some kids try to waterboard one legless party member and film it on their phones so they can post it to YouTube, you realize how this terrifying political and historical blindness is being held up against real instances of torture (and much else). It also makes a lot of sense when you read director Tanya Gerstle's program notes, in which she wondered whether this generation really had the right to 'pretend' the suffering of others (especially in comfortable, often clueless Australia). Given the level of rigour and self-scrutiny with which the cast and crew clearly took to *Invisible Stains*, I'd say they've earned that right.
>
> (Bailey 2009)

PART TWO
DIRECTING WORKBOOK

Figure 7 Meredith Penman, Grant Cartwright, Terry Yeboah, Carl Nilsson-Polias and Tim Potter, *Yes*, October 2007.
Credit: Photo © Jeff Busby.

7
INNER LIFE REVEALED THROUGH ACTION

How to use this workbook

This workbook offers instructions and advice for directors on how to prepare for, execute and use the outcomes from a layered Pulse rehearsal process. When working with Pulse on a script, the director leads the actors through several weeks of physical improvisation using the text of the play as an imaginary 'world' evolves. Relationships between characters emerge, hidden aspects of character are discovered and through the actor's ingenuity, design and staging challenges are solved. This type of improvisation produces a heightened physicality which informs the nature of acting and dynamic of staging. The ethical framework and performance aesthetic and style of this staging approach emerged from the Pulse training culture. Consequently, as I've already mentioned, the Training and Directing Workbooks are inextricably linked. I will be referring to directorial shorthand, performance and compositional Principles and key working concepts that Pulse trained actors will understand, so even if your interest is only in directing, you will need to look at the Training Workbook to prepare yourself conceptually for working with Pulse on a script.

This chapter refers to the fundamental premise behind the approach to rehearsal. The hidden story of a character's inner life is physicalized. Many scripted texts, especially dramatic theatre texts, from Shakespeare to Chekhov to screenplays, and much contemporary writing contain restrained emotional landscapes and unspoken feelings. What is *not* said and what is *implied* by what is said become fertile grounds for physical exploration. The Pulse rehearsal environment allows an actor to drop self-consciousness and immerse themselves deeply and quickly in the process, encouraging access to the inner life of the character. In Pulse-generated productions, an audience sees what drives the character through their physicality. Before you begin to improvise in rehearsal, make sure you read the case studies in Chapter 8 which refer to each layer. There I explain how I have worked with each layer and why the outcome was useful. Although you will have your own context and curate your own material, the case studies will alert you to the possibilities that can emerge.

In the section in this chapter 'Rehearsal Practice', I discuss the attitude that is necessary to create a conducive rehearsal culture, what the structure entails, how to set-up a stage design framework, prepare the ensemble for the journey and conduct the experience.

I am addressing my comments directly to the director, who in turn, will brief the actors on how to approach each layer. The above-mentioned section details each rehearsal layer: Intuitive Investigation, Immersion, Mapping and Rendering, which involves working through the script horizontally – moving chronologically through the material four times as the actor builds upon the kinaesthetic experience of each layer from the one before. I describe the setting up of each layer, what the actors will be attempting to do when improvising and what your role as the director will be in the space. In the section 'Advice for the Director', I've made suggestions on how to approach the rehearsal, particularly if you are an inexperienced director. The tools you will need to conduct the process are explained in 'Rehearsal Concepts' – how to direct through side coaching, how to support the actor who is speaking, feeding text into the improvisation and recording the discoveries made. How the fusing of emotion and action happens as well as the emergence of a character is also outlined here. As you work through each layer, I have indicated where you will need to jump ahead and read about a particular concept. Advice on the integration of sound and light during the layered process as well as in the technical rehearsal is addressed.

In Chapter 8 you will find case studies, citing productions I have directed using Pulse. I wanted to illuminate a moment of discovery that happened during each of the rehearsal layers and describe how I translated these moments into the final staging. By looking at the layer of Immersion during the rehearsal of *The Mill on the Floss* after George Eliot, adapted by Helen Edmundson, I explain how the emergence of recurring motifs created metaphoric resonance for the final staging. For *Pericles Punished* after William Shakespeare, Immersion produced action sequences of non-scripted narrative which drove the complex plot forward. The layer of Mapping helped solve issues around working with and depicting confronting content in *Five Kinds of Silence* by Shelagh Stephenson and *Stage Beauty* by Jeffrey Hatcher illustrates how a story set in the sixteenth century with wigs and corsets became physically energized. The Rendered outcome of *Manbeth: Macbeth Amplified* after Shakespeare shows how the fluid use of space, place and character was discovered. At the beginning of Chapter 8 the section called 'Using Pulse as a Rehearsal Device' explains how you can use the layers flexibly to serve your own context, and there is a section on time management and how to take advantage of staging solutions when they magically appear. If you haven't already looked at the filmed extracts from *The Mill on the Floss* rehearsal process with my accompanying commentary, do that before you embark on this workbook. It will help you visualize the physicality involved. It is hosted on the Bloomsbury companion website https://www.bloomsburyonlineresources.com/the-pulse-approach.

This workbook is not about acting or directing in general but about using a specific approach to work with the body (image) and a script (words). I am not proposing to tell an actor or director how to work on their script. They will need to prepare the language for rehearsal, and each will have their own way of doing that. This rehearsal context prioritizes Pulse as an ensemble and directorial process for staging and realizing a production where the development of the character emerges as an outcome of the improvisational process. Directing is a curatorial process in and of itself. Working in ensemble practice with Pulse does not escape this aspect of theatre-making, even though the structures built into the process create more of a horizontal hierarchy than many other rehearsal practices. The Pulse approach itself produces a style of 'physical acting', but it is largely my personal curatorial choices (often implicit), that create heightened physicality when staging my work. In this workbook, I will be talking about the curatorial selection and shaping of material from my point of view, based on the choices I make and have made. Running your own four layered Pulse rehearsal will require you to make your own curatorial choices. I am hoping the demystification of my process will encourage others to take a leap of faith and enjoy working in the unknown.

Directing a play through improvisation is like diving into water without land in sight. It can be frightening, but what you come across on your way to safety is remarkable and exhilarating. I do believe that the product reflects its process, so the eventual telling of the staged story will be unexpected and leave an audience breathless until they are deposited upon the shore. This way of working demands much of you. For both the actor and director, every moment of the imaginative exploration engages your whole being (body, mind, emotions and psychic energy). When you come off the floor, you are exhausted. There is no holding back, and the more you give the more you receive. The nature of the work may be taxing, but it is incredibly rewarding.

Rehearsal practice

Culture

Many directors design a rehearsal process where individual actors make their own issues with character and language paramount. This workbook, however, details a rehearsal process for an ensemble to realize and stage the performance text. A director will guide and help the actor where necessary, but the actor's personal preparation, which is extensive, is their own responsibility. If the actor brings that preparation to the floor, each rehearsal layer will unearth what the attentive actor needs.

All members of the ensemble have their role to play; actors perform, designers design, technicians operate and the director curates throughout making ultimate staging choices. Along the way, everyone involved contributes at appropriate times to the conception of the piece. It is important that the whole company invests in the shaping of the 'world' that is emerging. This style of group collaboration is my version of ensemble practice. Ideas emerge in an improvising process and they are developed and extended by others, regardless of the size of the role they play. To use this process, there needs to be a perceptual shift before rehearsal begins. Encourage the ensemble to see themselves as maker/actors and maker/designers. They need a dramaturgical consciousness as well as a directorial eye.

Improvising horizontally through the play (moving chronologically through the script) involves a great deal of support. Actors who are not in a scene are still necessary in the room, as they facilitate the journey of other actors. Sound artists need to be at most rehearsals, as they feed sound sources into the Pulse. Costume and lighting designers also take their inspiration from what is happening on the floor. It is an all-consuming and immersive experience from beginning to end. It requires discipline, a strong work ethic and a collaborative spirit. Actors need an open heart and the ability to let go of their ego. Their priority is to work for the ensemble, for the piece of art and for the audience. Not all actors enjoy such selfless intensity, but those who do gain a lot of satisfaction and become dedicated to working in this way.

It is important to set up a physical practice to begin all rehearsal sessions. Whether individuals do their own preparation, or group warm-ups together; stretching and preparing the body for athletic expression in Immersion and Mapping is essential. You will find that once an actor's physical imagination activates, their 'creative will' takes hold and pushes them to execute actions without 'thinking'. Of course, they will work safely regarding others, but if they are not physically warmed up, they can pull muscles and hurt themselves. If they are nursing injuries, they need to be mindful and be reminded to pull back. As with all group physical work it is essential that all cast members have given their consent to be touched. You may already have protocols in place, but as I mentioned previously in the Training Workbook (How to Approach the Work), make sure that you have a conversation before commencing the two central layers of improvisation. If individuals declare certain boundaries, those need to be respected, and you might have to adjust their participation accordingly. Make it clear that if anyone feels unsafe, they must leave the floor, and you will need to deal with it after the session. Physical intimacy is inevitable when doing this work, so make sure that you are transparent from the beginning about the rehearsal process, and the actors understand what will be involved.

Attitude

I often experience scepticism about using half of an allotted rehearsal time for improvisation; and I have noticed that observers who view Pulse rehearsal are unable to decipher its value. It is difficult to interpret its utilitarian function. There is no exercise or game structure within which to judge the work's success, and if you don't speak the 'language' of the process you will miss the images, connections and associations that can be transformed for later use. Although not explicit, there are detailed parameters, goals and outcomes built into the four layers of Pulse. By reading this chapter, an apprentice director will be able to 'read' the rehearsal work and recognize the strategies.

Using Pulse with a script is both a theatre-making exercise and a scripted play rehearsal in one. What I mean here is that the theatre-making aspect of the process involves the physical revelation of form and stage composition, while the scripted rehearsal aspect deals with language in the play and its subtext. These two functions are usually separated in a text-based rehearsal, but in the improvisational layer of Mapping, both functions are served. An actor who has done their script work and engaged with the meaning of their lines, goes onto the Pulse floor to find their character (what they do), discover subtext (how they do it) and develop relationships (who they do it with/to). As they are doing all that, the director supports their experience while absorbing what takes place, so they can do the 'recall' and later construct the play's overall form and stage action. Both director and actor work with the script's narrative through the lens of what each is trying

INNER LIFE REVEALED THROUGH ACTION

to achieve. It is always a process of 'hit and miss', that's what makes it so much fun, but it saves rehearsal time and allows for deep penetration of the material.

The director's role during Pulse rehearsal is to create an environment that facilitates the revelation of how a story 'wants' to be told. Their focus during these improvisational layers is on receiving rather than instructing. The actor's aim is to resist all assumptions about their character and improvise with a willingness to discover 'who they are' through 'what they do'. They will eventually understand their character's motivations and intentions, not by mentally working them out beforehand, but by having an improvised lived experience of that character's context and relationships. I have worked with actors who discover extraordinary physical, emotional and relational moments during Pulse, but because those discoveries appear illogical or irrational, they get scared and retreat, ultimately replacing their discoveries with intellectualized motivations that make their character's journey predictable and unengaging. You will need to encourage your actors to trust that discoveries made via instinct create authentic action.

> I saw *Yes* and *Anna Karenina* and was struck by the wonderful economy of the storytelling and how the physicality of the actors could shortcut the narrative. I most admired the physical commitment of the actors. They were all in the same world and they all told a story through their physicality.
>
> Sam Strong

Structure

A typical Pulse rehearsal structure, compared to traditional systems, will seem back to front. Conventionally, a play's movement design or 'blocking' usually takes place early on, after which characters and relationships evolve through repetition of the 'blocked' scenes. During Pulse rehearsals, the exploration of character and relationships is done through improvisation in the first few weeks and the movement design or 'blocking' happens later on where directorial curation becomes very active.

If you are working half time, perhaps four hours a day, five weeks is a comfortable timeframe when rehearsing with the four-layered process. If you have full rehearsal days, a traditional four-week rehearsal process is sufficient. Depending on the length of the project, the following provides a general timeframe for the structure:

- Two days Intuitive Investigation
- Three days Immersion
- One week Mapping
- One week Rendering
- One week detailing, running and technical rehearsal.

What is distinctive about this structure?

Every day for the first two weeks of rehearsal, the ensemble of actors, designers and director come to a space that resonates with shared experiences from previous days: motifs and images, character discoveries, emotional connections and relational understandings. They are physically, spatially and experientially immersed within an evolving narrative world. Improvising for four to six hours a day for eight straight days is like a marathon of the imagination. I think of it as 'deep diving', where the actors are submerged in an alternative world in which they are searching for something, only surfacing when they 'need air'. The durational aspect serves to imprint experience profoundly upon the actor's body and psyche.

By the third week, when the director needs to pull all the elements together and create a movement design, the actors have collated their character's actions, developed relationships and experienced an emotional through-line. They instinctively have a strong idea of how, and often where, to move in the space, so they can collaborate with the director's perspective as the 'outside-eye'. (See 'Rehearsal Concepts: Directing Though Side Coaching' to get a sense of actor/director interaction, and 'Emergence of Character' to gain insight into how the character finds the actor.) Most importantly 'the creature' that will become this unique theatrical event has revealed itself. From what they have witnessed, the director has drawn a strong curatorial sense of the staging aesthetic and vision for the storytelling. By this point, the actors have absorbed their lines – they have experienced them, not learnt them by rote, soundscapes have been tried out so a playlist exists and furniture and costume choices have been explored on the floor during the process. All of this has been achieved in two weeks through an organic, improvisational structure. What is left by the third week of rehearsal is for the director to select and assemble these elements.

Most conventional processes concerning text-based staging rely on verbal discussion, reflection and decision-making where intellectualized precepts result in a particular outcome. The level of control one has over this kind of process can be reassuring when working within limited timeframes. The Pulse rehearsal paradigm does not seek to reject the intellect in favour of the non-calculable benefits of feeling and sensing. It seeks to re-define the entry point for prioritizing intuitive and imaginative release. The intellect is deeply engaged during the first layer – Intuitive Investigation – as the ensemble negotiates dramaturgy, research and text analysis. The intellect is also accessed and balanced with physical memory during the fourth layer – Rendering – as distilling, editing and selecting of material for the staged piece takes place. However, during the middle two layers – Immersion and Mapping – the actors enter a sensory, imaginative realm, where logical assumptions must 'take a back seat'. Conversations and questions regarding motivation and character do not take place during these layers. As director, you want to keep actors in a subjective state and not bring them out of it through initiating reflective verbal dialogue. 'Allowing people to operate without having to explain themselves constantly ... enables rapid cognition. Insight is not a lightbulb that goes off inside our heads. It is a flickering candle that can easily be snuffed out' (Gladwell 2006, 119–43).

Design and pulse structure

There are many models for approaching the rehearsal of a scripted text. A familiar one is where the director serves the writer's intention, the actors serve the director's vision and creative technicians serve the context which holds them both. In each case, the written text is the generative idea and many decisions pertaining to each have been confirmed before rehearsals begin.

Pulse, as an actor-driven process, means the form and style of the staged piece evolves from what emerges during the improvisation. Designers collaborate by investigating and enhancing what is taking shape. During Immersion and Mapping, the sound designer tries out sound sources, the lighting designer observes the rehearsal and experiments with equipment, if available, and the costume designer experiences the physicality of the work and brings sourced costumes into rehearsal to try out. All design creatives make offers concurrently to facilitate the emerging performance text. Unless you are working with an empty space, because of production timelines the only design aspect that needs to be confirmed before rehearsals begin might be the set.

Three case studies in Chapter 8 – *The Mill on the Floss, Pericles Punished* and *Stage Beauty* – involve the following two-stage set design strategy. First, I talk with the designer about the nature of the landscape in which we are telling the story: multiple locations, wood or metal, access points to audience, entrances and exits on and off stage; and they watch the actors Pulse to understand the physicality of the aesthetic and the spatial expanse and fluidity that is needed. We agree upon an unadorned, sculptural shape offering different levels, which is then built and 'bumped-in' to the rehearsal/performance space, ideally before Mapping begins. It functions like a 'playground' with open potential for the actors to explore. While the actors improvise and play in, on, under and around this structure, the staging ideas for the director begin to emerge. The fundamental design of the piece becomes this basic structure, transformed through the way it functions for the shapes and actions of the actors. The second stage of the design strategy allows for the designer to observe this transformation. While I consolidate the staging in the last week of rehearsal, they will be adding objects and decorative features to the basic framework; they often do this right up until the show opens.

Rehearsal process

Intuitive Investigation

Anticipating the rehearsal period, actors work on their scripts in the way they would normally prepare, which should involve many read-throughs and their own text analysis.[1] Intuitive Investigation begins rehearsal with the ensemble. It gives the director and actors an opportunity to agree upon a 'score', allowing everyone to embark on the journey together. It involves making a visual map (using a white board) to collaboratively make lists. Begin by doing a 'first read', and then read each scene again as you work through the play. Depending on its length and complexity, it will take one or two days to work through the script. The 'score' should include notes on action (what is happening), content (themes, preoccupations), time, place (given circumstances), who (characters involved and their functions in the scene) and the function of the scene within the narrative. From this map, patterns will emerge for the company to share and discuss. Be careful, however, to only discuss the telling of the narrative, not how individual characters behave. That is a matter for discovery on the Pulse floor.

This would also be the time to break the script into beats or units for rehearsal, identify rhythmic shifts and turning points and share sensory research each actor has been working on. Sensory research, which is about feeding the senses, is a vital aspect of this layer. Exploring tastes, sounds, textures, smells and images of place and time in the script's story 'world' will feed the actor's imagination and physical responses during the layers of Immersion and Mapping. You should encourage the actors to continue sensory research throughout the rehearsal process as actors need to be imaginatively 'full' before going on the Pulse floor. This is an essential part of each actor's personal preparation for rehearsal.

At the end of this layer, I ask each actor to prepare a performance response: a five-minute solo based on any aspect of the text that has sparked their imagination. It is an immersive exercise, so light, sound or audio-visual tools are encouraged. I have found that ideas from these responses inform immersive layers, and many have made their way into my productions. Some examples: an actor in his underwear throwing a bucket of water over himself; an actor barking like a drill sergeant, coercing others to do push-ups; an actor doing a striptease, another singing a torch song and another playing an electric guitar solo; as well as lighting ideas (torches and phones), soundscapes and audio compilations.

Immersion

Having viewed the company's performance responses, I initiate the next layer of rehearsal: Immersion. This is where, without having to speak the text, the actors get very familiar with the story by physically sharing it with one another. As the director, I read the script as if I were slowly and deliberately reading a book aloud. Ensemble members respond individually and collectively to thoughts, images and story moments they hear, by improvising in the space. It is not like 'free improvisation' where actors might individually follow an imaginative experiment without a working intention. The focus of this 'rolling' improvisation is upon a group objective, which is to respond physically (no speaking), in the abstract, to the literal story. I speak the text of the script in the order it is written, which gives the improvisation its working structure. This is called working through the text horizontally and this is explained in 'Rehearsal Concepts: Feeding in the Text'.

If you have an empty space, set up several floor lights that throw shadows on the walls. This creates a creative bubble and a sense of otherworldliness. Try to avoid working with fluorescent or overhead lights. I have used lamps from home and candles when theatrical light was unavailable. Place a few objects, such as a table or several benches, stools, or chairs randomly in the space. If there are rehearsal costumes available, make a pile somewhere to the side and have access to sound equipment and a playlist. Instrumental

INNER LIFE REVEALED THROUGH ACTION

tracks can be played during Immersion by the director, sound designer/operator or some of the actors that intermittently come off the space. During this layer, an instrumental 'wall of sound' played softly is useful for building the immersive environment.

Often, I will place objects in the space encouraging the actors to play with them. They are my instinctive choices, based on what is available. The objects might be seized upon by the actors and transformed, or left to the side and not explored. If they prove useful for the telling of the story they will remain on the floor and be carried forward into Mapping. For example, during rehearsals for *Anna Karenina* I brought a huge bucket of pearls and a large suitcase, for *Five Kinds of Silence* a microphone and three red coats, and for *Manbeth: Macbeth Amplified* ten benches. Ultimately, these objects were incorporated into the staging of each piece. They had become intricately woven into the fabric of the storytelling and were laden with meaning; they had become the only set objects necessary.

It usually takes about three days of rehearsal to slowly make our way through the script. The nature of the reading is not unlike a 'talking book', except that I continually stop, slow or quicken the pace to implicitly affect what is happening. If something complex emerges or an image is being physically built and needs time to evolve, I will wait. If a section of text is not sparking the actors' imagination, I will race through it. You need to work instinctively. Don't be precious or pedantic. What is not explored in this layer will be picked up in the next. At times, during the reading of the narrative script, I may diverge from the linear structure to break the rhythm and bring the earlier cognitive work onto the physical plane. Sometimes, after intense activity or when I perceive the actors to be stuck, I might read out significant quotes from research material or mention themes and other aspects of the 'score' that were found during Intuitive Investigation. You don't need to prepare for this; it happens in response to what is happening on the floor. As your choices are intuitive and instinctive, whatever you choose gives you information about your own curatorial priorities and simmering visions. In a sense, this is where implicit directing begins. It serves to imprint your preferences, kinaesthetically, onto the actor's psyche. You might also emphasize shifts in the rhythm of the text (by the way you read it) and literally, state turning points and the beginning and ending of beats. Often, I mention the function of a scene within the overall narrative or function of a character in a particular scene – I don't talk about objectives or intentions, only functions. All the while, actors are immersed in the imaginary 'world' and responding physically to whatever is spoken into the space. In this way they experience a kind of 'kinaesthetic script analysis'. They are physically experiencing the dramatic structure. This taps into the actor's intuitive intelligence, instead of entering the text through the intellect and analysing it through seated discussion.

As directors/readers we need to be fluid and adaptable, responding to the rhythms and actions in the space. We are influencing the space through the way we read as well as when and how we change the light and soundscapes. Macro and micro awareness is key to keeping the momentum flowing and to supporting the actors submerged in this evolving 'world'. If they are exhausted, you need to 'rest the action' by speaking gently, leaving silence or introducing soft music. You are the one that 'holds the space' and the emotions that emerge. You will also be taking notes or making a sketch or instructing an assistant to do so. It may seem like an overwhelming task, but when the ensemble is 'jamming' in the room together, if you remain present and in-the-moment, it will flow. It is important not to be precious but to enjoy the chaos. Trust that whatever has impact will stay with you.

An Immersion session may take one to two hours. You will notice when the energy flags: the imagination stalls, the offers seem tired and the actors lose focus. Bring the actors back to the 'surface' gently and suggest a break while they write notes about their discoveries during the experience (see 'Rehearsal Concepts: The Recall'). This is the point where you might quietly suggest to individuals (one on one) that they record certain moments and remember certain images or actions that had impact. Mention impactful group images or scenarios to the ensemble only after actors have finished their individual recall. This is part of the director's ongoing curation. It is also a way of training the actors in 'the ways of recall'. A rehearsal day may consist of four or five Immersion sessions. Discourage any general discussion about what happened on the floor until the ensemble has worked through the whole script in this layer.

Advice for the director

- I have described *what* to do to set up the space and get the actors improvising. As I've mentioned before, you can only understand *how* to do it by doing it. This goes for all the layers. If the above description seems complex or intimidating, it is only because I have proposed what *might* happen and how you can respond to it, but the actual execution in the room begins very simply.

- When you are trying this for the first time, all you need to do is set-up the space, feed in the text and observe what the actors do. Once you commence feeding in, commit to working through the whole script. Don't back out halfway through. You know exactly what to do in each session because the script gives you the rehearsal structure. Simply pick up feeding in where you left off. If you have an assistant or a stage manager, get them to feed in the text when you need a break or need to watch and absorb for a while.

- As a director, you may be accustomed to instructing the actors or leading the exercise knowing the outcome you desire. You may have doubts or be insecure about the quality of what is happening in the *doing* of Immersion. It will not be organized, logical or even cohesive. It will be messy and sometimes chaotic, which may be new and unfamiliar to you. But in this layer, your job is simply to stimulate the actors' imaginative responses (by reading the script), and to absorb what they give you. The key is to let go of any attachment to what you think should happen. In the surrender, the mind lets go and only then will associative connections appear and ideas bubble to the surface.

- Like anything new, you and the actors will take a few sessions to negotiate how to do this. Be patient and don't lose faith. Questioning mid-process will only get in the way of the work revealing itself. Revelation happens through the quality of

INNER LIFE REVEALED THROUGH ACTION

your watching and listening with no judgement. It is when the layer has finished that you will be able to collate your thoughts about associated images and symbols that emerged.

- If you are working with an ensemble trained in Pulse, you and the actors will be able to activate the shared 'language' and even work with the training Principles. For example, if you feed in a dialogue of two characters arguing, the actors playing those characters might begin to physically fight (safely). This could be picked up by the group as a motif and consequently other actors form duets and fight (*recurring motif*); alternatively the group may surround the couple and stir them on, like a *chorus* in *juxtaposition*. The fighting will *develop to climax* and then disperse. This rhythmic pattern – a shared notion – helps them move from image to image.

> Pulse has taught me that creating theatre is about discovery, and as a director I create the space and bring the tools to allow that discovery to take place. It takes away the fear of having to know. It is the opposite of knowing. That is powerful, freeing and a great equalizer.
>
> Gary Abrahams

Outcomes for the actor

- Bonding with the ensemble through sharing an immersive, durational experience.
- Experiencing a 'shared history' of improvised backstories and memories.
- Physical aspects of character begin to emerge.
- Relationships increase in substance and understanding by the end of the layer.
- Not having to speak the text, the actor is free to experience their character's function in the overall narrative, which helps them to feel the emerging dynamics between characters.
- By the end of this layer, an improvisational approach/style has evolved that is unique to this ensemble of individuals.

Outcomes for the director

- Physical solutions to transitions between scenes appear.
- Prospective and retrospective images and scenarios from the story line are created.
- Recurring physical motifs and the imaginative solving of staging challenges occur.

- The pace and fluency of the Pulse increase as the story accelerates through the layer increasing the efficiency of the exploration.
- During rehearsal the director is Pulsing with the actors, feeding in the text and conducting other elements in the space. But durational improvising also gives the director space and time to watch, absorb and dream.
- The physical and scenic 'world' of the play begins to emerge. (In Chapter 8, I describe in detail how this layer can create physical and visual storytelling for the Rendering layer.)

Mapping

This second layer of improvisation involves starting from the beginning of the script, and again, working horizontally through it. The set-up of the space (sound, light, objects and costume) is the same as for Immersion, and once again, the lines are read into the space, predominantly by the director, but this time the task is often shared with some of the actors. In this layer the actors are speaking their text. The director reads each thought or line and waits for the actor whose line it is to physically experience the language *before* they speak the line. How they do this is described below. Feeding in, line-by-line is referred to as working in 'extended time' (see 'Rehearsal Concepts: Feeding in the Text'). 'You mine every moment; you do not gloss over anything, and this is how you make important discoveries' (Abrahams 2013).

All the other actors in the scene improvise to help facilitate the speaking actor's experience (see 'Rehearsal Concepts: Serving the Speaking Actor'). It is like a baton relay. When that actor has accomplished their moment, the reader feeds in the next thought and either the speaking actor moves to their next line or a different actor whose line it is next picks up the baton and begins to Pulse. Don't be in a rush. Allow each actor the time they need to find what they are searching for. What Rutenberg (2016, 85) says about painting could equally apply to Pulse: 'Art is carefully orchestrated wandering. If you are in a hurry, you will miss everything.'

Actors remain working in the space until they have finished their beat or scene, and then they come off the floor to write notes, the 'recall'. If that actor is not in the next scene, Mapping can continue. The momentum of feeding in the narrative rarely stops. I keep the actors 'submerged' for as long as practical, taking breaks when the imagery has accumulated to the point of saturation and needs to be 'recalled'.

> Pulse requires all the performers to immerse themselves and not to come up for air until they have found what they are searching for.
>
> Grant Cartwright

I think of Mapping as 'kinaesthetic dramaturgy' – a non-literal translation of the spoken text through an actor's spontaneous actions. Rutenberg (2016, 30) talks about abstraction as a process not a style: 'to abstract means to remove, which implies it must be removed from something'. Mapping is an *abstract* process, where the actor, inspired by a line of text, searches to create an action giving them a bodily experience (sensorial/emotional), which is 'removed' from its literal context or meaning. For example, responding to the line 'I love you', an actor might repeatedly kiss the feet of another actor, or run around the space tearing at their clothes breathless, or curl up in a foetal position crying and slapping the wall in anger or laughter. Their response may also be more internal and less expressionistic, like gently and slowly caressing a window frame. When they are at the peak of whatever physical/sensorial experience they are having, they say their line, fusing thought, emotion and action together. In this way, spontaneous actions will unearth subtextual associations. For example, an actor might be surprised when saying 'I love you' that they find themselves breathless, suffocating and running away because when they initially read the script, they thought of the line as tender. Note, that only the actor themselves can really evaluate the depth of their kinaesthetic connection; the process teaches them to self-evaluate, but you will know if they are skimming over lines and not investing in the task, because if you are not affected by that moment, then they have not been 'changed'.

> Something occurs vocally when you are ready to embody the words, and they resonate in you in an extraordinary way. Part of the process of Pulse is the burning-off of excess energy: when you've done that the physical and verbal offers become simpler and more streamlined.
>
> Meredith Penman

As the director you might decide not to use this action when the actor eventually speaks the line in the play, but the actor can use this visceral experience as subtext for the relationship. As an actor accumulates action/experience while going through the whole play, it becomes apparent from an instinctive point of view how that relationship must be played out. A different actor playing that role will have different responses, therefore the character will be different, and their relationships will present differently. Do not decide before rehearsal, or discuss with an actor, what a character's objectives, actions or reactions should be. Wait to see the inner life of a character develop and the subtext for a line as it reveals itself through the actions of that actor on the Pulse floor.

> I might have been punching Brett in the guts when I spoke the line in the Pulse rehearsal but for the final version, I may just be standing in front of him – there is still a body memory of violence, or betrayal or lust.
>
> Luisa Hastings Edge

Advice for the director

- Depending on the length of the play, Mapping will take at least a full week to complete, so mentally prepare yourself. The actors may be on and off the space, but you will need to have focused attention all the time. You are not controlling what happens in the room, but you are conducting the external elements (text, music and light) and watching keenly. After a week of focused attention, you will be exhausted, so make sure you eat and sleep well.

- If you only have time to do Mapping, set up the space as I have described at the beginning of Immersion above. If using Mapping as an isolated rehearsal task, you can do it in an empty space with no objects; but if the actors are new to this, it is easier for them to develop imaginative responses if they have things to play with.

- Put on instrumental music appropriate to the 'world' of the play. (There will be pieces that recurred during Immersion, so make sure that you use them again.) Read the initial stage directions, then begin with the first line and follow your instinct from there. If you are a novice director, be gentle and don't try to do too much or overpower the actor's process. When you feed in the line, watch and observe what the actors do with it. Their response might be miraculous, or it might be banal. Until you gain more confidence let it all pass and just take note of the miraculous.

- Your main task in the early stages of experimenting with this process is to keep the working rhythm alive in the room by encouraging momentum through the way you feed in the text. The group energy will stall if actors get stuck on a thought, are judgemental of their response or become self-absorbed, losing sight of the purpose of the task. When this happens just feed in the next line which will be an indication to move on. While the ensemble is learning how to do this layer the improvising can be very hit and miss. Even after the ensemble gains experience, where they 'drop deeper' and work faster, there will still be individual actors who do not have a visceral relationship with each line. Depending on the skill level of your actors this is to be expected, so be more concerned with momentum and the group experience than the detail of *every* line. If it's the first time for the ensemble, the actors should be aiming to experience strong responses to most, but not all their text.

- If the actor is too focused on the text, their body will default to behavioural gesture, and if they are too focused on creating heightened physicality, the meaning of the line will suffer. Finding the balance only comes with practice. You can assist them through side coaching by gently drawing their attention to one or the other in that moment while they are in the Pulse. This gives them the opportunity to immediately try an action or a line again.

- When the nature of this kind of Pulsing has been established and you have gained the trust of the actors, see 'Rehearsal Concepts: Directing through side coaching'. There you will find suggestions on how to interact with the speaking actor during Pulse as well as advice for dealing with what often happens to the spoken line when actors improvise with physical intensity.

There are opposing forces working within a director in any creative process, especially this one. It will take time to find the balance between the 'dreamer' and the 'pragmatist'. 'The 'dreamer' is searching for metaphors and poetic symbols and is constantly surprised by the associations that they make, and the 'pragmatist' is working to timelines and the need to deliver an outcome' (C.Wood 2021, 29). As with any artistic discipline, sustained practice is the only way to find artistic fusion.

Outcomes for the actor

- Verbalizing lines during the experience weds them to actions, emotions and sensations, giving the actor a map for their emotional journey.
- Working in 'extended time' allows space between thoughts so they can be profoundly impacted by their experience.
- 'Your imagination drops into your body, and you are physically doing what you would normally just be imagining' (Cartwright 2013).
- Improvising back stories and memories, spoken of in the written script, will give actors in character relationships a shared 'lived' history to draw upon.
- Physical imagination is stimulated to respond in a non-literal way, producing unexpected and exciting physical possibilities.
- Absorbing lines connected to image and action usually makes line learning redundant.
- Autonomy and freedom of experience: the actor drives Pulse with the intention to find out who their character is. They initiate all action.
- They do not consciously 'build' a character. At the end of this layer, they reflect upon the accumulation of their instinctive responses and surrender to the character that has emerged. We are what we do. The character has found the actor.

> I could be self-sufficient as an actor. I knew where to position myself in a shot, how to balance the stage picture, where to stand and what I needed to do.
>
> Lachlan Woods

Outcomes for the director

- Actors thinking (with their bodies) and not calculating (with their minds) allows for surprise meetings on a rehearsal floor. There is continual astonishment at the unpredictable and poetic associations that are created unintentionally by the actors.

- The predictable, logical, physical and emotional response to meaning is subverted and the attachment to behavioural gesture is broken, producing heightened responses and physicality.
- Unspoken feelings in the narrative are physicalized; the character's inner life is actualized, facilitating the physical staging of subtext and emotion.
- A character's inner turmoil may be juxtaposed with the spoken text, either reinforcing the verbal meaning or casting doubt upon it. This ambiguity can be used in Rendering.
- When characters are spoken of and/or remembered in the text, the actor playing that character appears on the floor to interact, even though they may not be in the scene. This conjures the possibility of past and present colliding: making memories visual.
- A coherent vision for the practical integration of the verbal and heightened physical 'world' emerges.
- Visual imagery for the physical map is created, becoming the framework for the staged outcome.
- The pace, depth and momentum of the evolving story increases during the layer making rehearsal efficient and streamlined.

Rendering

Two weeks of rehearsal have passed. Being 'submerged' in this imaginary 'world' for that period of time has had enormous impact on each member of the team. The ensemble is now saturated in shared experiences of character histories and relationships. Each actor/character understands who they are because of what they have done. Everyone knows the sweep of the narrative intimately and the actors know their lines (if they don't, they will have to learn them before Rendering begins). As director, you have a strong sense of which images and physical engagements from Immersion/Mapping you could use. Even though this last layer is focused upon construction; I think of it as improvisation, as the pieces of the puzzle are put together organically, unit by unit, moving chronologically through the play. When I curate, I work in detail, not knowing where I'm going exactly, adding one scene to the next. I don't have an overarching agenda for the entire staged piece. But what I always have is secure knowledge that the play's 'world' is complex, unpredictable, heightened, visceral and beautiful because I have already experienced it with the ensemble.

This layer can be a shock for the actor who has fallen in love with 'diving deep' and doesn't want to come back to the surface. Rendering is like walking a tightrope. The actor must serve the practical demands of the construction process (by accessing their composer), and yet stay connected to the inspiration of their original response. 'As a performer, you can feel you lose the magic in the Rendering process, but actually you don't; it's merely the contradiction of rendering improvisation' (Liddeaux 2013). Rendering

INNER LIFE REVEALED THROUGH ACTION

is the most difficult layer. Both actors and director must snap back to reality out of a wonderful dream. The trance-like state of 'flow' that the ensemble has experienced for two weeks has been creatively freeing, deeply impactful and addictive. But it is during Rendering that the previous two weeks of improvisation pays off. There will be much physical and imagistic material to choose from, so directorially, it is a matter of selecting, editing and shaping. Referring to the 'recall' (notes, sketches or filmed fragments), mine and the actor's, from both Immersion and Mapping, we move from scene to scene. I converse with the actors during this phase, recalling actions that happened, images that had impact and spatial dynamics that expressed meaning.

> I've found Pulse work very useful because it generates lateral staging possibilities from the actors, which are always more visually dynamic and physically arresting than anything imposed top-down by a director.
>
> Sam Strong

As director you will have your own vision and aesthetic, so your choices will be different to mine. But regardless, the priority for selecting physical actions that accompany the text rests on the clarity of the storytelling from the perspective of an audience. You will be attempting to juggle the physical and verbal language equally, so one is not favoured over the other, but both performance languages dance together to enhance meaning. Be mindful of becoming attached to physical images that distract from the flow of the verbal story. That is when you must 'kill your darlings' – you will need to let go of some of what you love.

Advice for the director

- In preparation for commencing the last layer, it is important to renegotiate your role and your relationship with the actors. Remind them that you are moving from provocateur using implied direction to curator and decision-maker. If Rendering is the phase in the dark room, you are the alchemist transforming the material and fixing the elements.
- It is ideal to have the shape of the set or a physical substitute in the space before you begin Rendering. This is the only way to integrate the movement design with the physical environment as you construct the piece (see 'Rehearsal Practice: Design and Pulse structure').
- Make sure the actors know their lines before they begin their scenes. If you want to incorporate the physicality that was discovered in Mapping, the actors will need to be free of scripts in hand.
- Work out how many scenes you must Render in each session to get through the whole play in your allotted time. This will give you an idea of the pace at which

you need to work. Some sections will be complex and take longer, you probably already have a sense of which ones, so schedule more time for those. I have often been surprised, however, that what I thought would be simple becomes complicated, and those sections I feared, basically Rendered themselves.

- The night before, have a look through your 'recall' of the scenes you want to get through the next day. Let your subconscious work on them while you sleep. I often wake in the morning with a general shape and sense of what I want to include.

- Start by 'sketching' a rough shape of the scene with the actors in the space so you can share bits of 'recall' and propose a physical design. Then go back to the beginning and 'colour it in' moment-by-moment with the actors speaking the scripted text. Search for a balance between the physical life and verbal life of the text. By now, you know the story well and how you want an audience to receive it, so don't let the heightened physicality get in the way of an audience understanding the narrative. It must enhance not distract from the meaning.

- If you get lost in a scene and can't solve it, turn off the lights, put on some music, and encourage the actors to enter the 'submerged' state again. They know their lines now so they can play the scene, but they are released from the constraints of staging and can re-connect with their imaginative impulses. I will often do this when I need to re-find a moment that we knew had impact, but can't remember what happened in Mapping, or to re-construct a scene that we just can't solve. I will always go back into Pulse, using music to find transitions between scenes.[2]

- This layer is exciting but demands a lot from the director. Having to make choices every minute for a week can be emotionally and psychically challenging. Try to limit the decisions you must make daily in other areas (what to wear, eat and do) to alleviate the pressure.

> Pulse enables the creation of non-figurative gestures which an audience accepts as the language of that stage world. The audience accepts the style and form unquestionably.
>
> Sam Strong

Outcomes for the actor

- Having worked from the 'inside-out' (responding by impulse to external stimulus – a line of text) during Mapping, as the script is Rendered, the intention behind each thought is already married to action.

- Sometimes a physical sequence is dislodged from its original source and rather than drop it, is placed with different text (a curatorial choice because the image is exceptional). In this case, the actor will need to work from the 'outside-in' (from action to intention) to find the bridge for the character.

- The actor's sensory recall from Mapping becomes the Rendered plot of the character's emotional through-line.
- Physical embodiment of the verbal language has been achieved.
- 'The way the audience perceives the moment is the way you made it' (Liddeaux 2013).
- The actor now has a sense of the entire staged story and understands the 'picture they are in'. They can independently run through their physical map, work on the rhythms and detail their character's journey.

> Pulse made me a natural dramaturg in the room ... I found that as a Pulse trained actor, I had also become a directorial problem-solver. I could make suggestions to the director about how to trouble-shoot difficult transitions.
>
> Meredith Penman

Outcomes for the director

- Improvised sequences that emerged in previous layers have solved complex staging demands.
- Actors are occasionally guided back into a submerged Pulse state to find transitions (moving of objects and actors between scenes with no blackouts).
- The physical landscape has not become more important than the text; the viewer must hear and comprehend the verbal narrative, but it bears equal weight of expression in the space. It is not just an underscoring of the verbal meaning.
- The director has carefully curated the balance of physical imagery against the verbal text, making sure that at no point is the viewer's comprehension of the story compromised.
- Compositional Principles such as *architecture of space*, *depth of field*, simultaneous imagery, *recurring motifs*, and *juxtaposition* have been employed in the shaping of the whole.
- As design elements have been experimented with from the beginning of rehearsal, they can now be selected and synthesized into the staging of the action (costume, objects and set).
- Sonic themes and motifs that were used in previous layers are distilled and made into a sound score.

Once the script is Rendered, rehearsal will consist of running the piece, working on rhythm, delivery and detailing moments through note sessions.

Sound, light and rhythm

In this process sound and light are not cosmetic; they are the tools assisting transition, and along with the actors, they create the flow from scene to scene. Rhythm is very important in 'sculpting' the piece. I don't use blackouts, as I find they disconnect the viewer from their experience, but this can present logistical challenges. Indicating changed locations and time, the 'striking' and setting up of the next scene with furniture and props and costume changes, all need to happen in front of the audience as part of the story being told. During Rendering, I can sense if a transition needs to be slow, fast, abrupt or dissolving. I have a musical palette to choose from and the ensemble knows what must come on and off the space. Moving through the story, putting each scene alongside the next, the actors Pulse the transitions to solve these challenges. What eventuates and is consolidated with sound and light during technical rehearsals is a choreographic swirl of objects, furniture and clothing coming on and off the space. It may contain a relationship revelation, give plot information or represent a dynamic interlude out of which the next scene explodes. Whatever its frame, it must hold the viewer's attention and progress the story.

I usually plot and tech the sound and light together rather than in separate sessions as they are intricately interwoven with the actions of actors. You will find that most of the technical shifts needed will be from visual cues rather than line cues, as the actions of actors drive rhythm and pace, not spoken language. Technical rehearsal is experimental in the sense that you must play with the rhythms of each transition to find out what is needed. Try to allow time for this exploration. Does sound, light and action all go together? Rarely. Sometimes the actors move, then sound, then light fades (fast or, perhaps, slow). There might be one actor moving, then sound fades, then another actor moves and light snaps off. You must feel the musicality in the rhythmic changes because this is what keeps the audience suspended and the storytelling all in 'one breath'. You are 'painting' with sound and light. I cannot emphasize enough how important this is. If there is pressure from technicians to get on with it and just press a button with the fade time computerized on a word cue, try to resist this pressure. Sometimes I have tried four different versions of a transition before it felt right.

Rehearsal concepts

Physical acting

I am often asked how the actors in my productions achieve such a physical dynamic in the telling of the theatrical narrative. Three conditions conspire to create this. First, Pulse actors are athletic. They prioritize physical stamina and embrace the notion of physical effort and duration. They have trained their physical imagination and are drawn to expressing

INNER LIFE REVEALED THROUGH ACTION

inner life through action. Secondly, in the Immersion and Mapping layers, the actors work with physical extremity to produce heightened gesture and action, which means their verbal and physical dexterity is enhanced, and thirdly, it is my directorial selection of that heightened action, placed together with behavioural gesture in the outcome that gives the 'world' of the play a raw, physical dynamic. It is my aesthetic, politics and obsession to energize stage performance that lies behind my curatorial choices, as you will see from the case studies.

> When I watch Pulse performers, I see a beautiful, fully embodied, fully inhabited, vital and unself-conscious world. Every atom of the performer is alert, every hair on their body raised in awareness.
>
> Graham Abrahams

It is entirely possible, however, to work with the layers of Immersion and/or Mapping to give the actors a visceral, sensory and embodied experience of the text (which can translate into embodied performance) and not include heightened/non-behavioural action when Rendering the scripted outcome.

Language

Regardless of the style or genre of the scripted material – heightened text (Shakespeare, Howard Barker), contemporary speech (Chekhov, Churchill) or everyday language (screenplays) – searching for the most engaging way to tell the story is the lens through which to work. In the first layer, Intuitive Investigation, when the intellect is active, you will be discussing the language and its impact. If it is heightened text, the literal meaning must be examined before entering the Pulse; therefore, the actors will need to paraphrase their lines for meaning in their own time. You may also need to do this after reading each scene during Intuitive Investigation. If the piece involves learning an accent, they should do that ahead of time, so that when they reach Mapping, they can speak the lines on accent. It helps them to embed the sounds if they speak only on accent during the rehearsal day.

The middle layers of improvisation are approached by the actors in the same way, whatever the style of text. The emphasis is on image-making and experiencing the thought. What does shift when working with heightened text is the way you and the ensemble might prepare for Mapping and the way you feed in the text. Literal clarity is paramount regardless of an individual's interpretation. If you are not sure the actors have done their own preparation, gather those who are going on the floor before the session and paraphrase the lines. Be aware of the added degree of difficulty for the actor on the Mapping floor. They may be translating the Shakespeare line in their head before acting upon it. When you are feeding in the text, be mindful not to rush, and you may need to repeat each line two or three times (see 'Rehearsal Concepts: Feeding in the Text').

When actors come out of the improvisational middle layers the language and rhythm must be attended to. If it is Shakespeare, the actors will be working on the pentameter and the other language principles, bringing that to the Rendering phase. It is after Rendering, when I am detailing scene by scene and then running the show, that I will give attention to the language, focusing on shaping the speech and dialogue rhythms.

> There is no anxiety about the cultural heritage of doing Shakespeare hanging over you … the language becomes robust and physical. You are full of the experience and the direction you need to go in is clear to you: the meaning is clear to you … You simply have no choice but to act, to do it.
>
> Zahra Newman

I have often been asked about applying Pulse to the direction of Musicals or Comedy. My response is simple. Practice follows purpose. If your aim is to physically energize the actors speaking their text or you want to create a non-behavioural physical world or you need an ensemble process to blend disparate energies and focus everyone on telling the same story, then try commencing with Immersion. Using Immersion with any genre of text will enrich the character's relationships and create staging solutions. There will also be unexpected discoveries. I would feed in the song lyrics for actors to respond to and play instrumental music evocative of the era in which it is set, not the actual songs from the musical. Using Mapping will depend on your rehearsal timeframe and what you want to achieve. Both the above genres have specific technical requirements so you will need to allocate time for song rehearsal and/or detailing rhythm and timing.

Directing through side coaching

Directing does happen during the Mapping layer, but it is implicit through side coaching rather than explicit through conversation. When the actors are 'deep diving' the director helps them stay submerged. I don't want them to come out of a subjective state by discussing meaning or answering questions about motivations and intentions. If they continually shift from subjective to objective, they cannot drop deeply into the imaginative 'world' in which they are being inspired. Conscious interaction will break the spell and bring them to the surface. The actors and director are having their own experience of the unfolding action and should only compare notes conversationally at the end of the day. During the eight days of improvisation the director's priority is to support the actors to *do* and to *sense* and *feel* without activating their 'rational' mind.

I side coach the actors during the Mapping Pulse in many ways: I might whisper verbal suggestions to them ('involve your wife in this action') or catch their eye and gesture (to draw their attention to an image), or through physical intervention (by literally moving their body in the space because I want to see their action in relation to another). I might send an actor, who is not on the floor, into the space with an instruction to change what is

INNER LIFE REVEALED THROUGH ACTION

happening. Or I side coach in the rhythm, pace and volume of the way I feed in the text. This does not involve directorial preparation as in conventional rehearsal, but it requires the director to strategize on their feet. The director is free to work intuitively and from impulse. Fundamentally, you are Pulsing with the actors. If this seems too daunting, take it slowly and experiment. The above are guidelines only, you will develop your own style.

> Tanya comes in very close to whisper specific instructions to individuals engaging with you in the energy and rhythm of the moment or she will vocally shatter it, if that is what the moment calls for ... She is Pulsing with you as a director; she must, otherwise the 'spell' will be lost.
>
> Grant Cartwright

By the time we get to Mapping, I have a strong idea of each actor's capacity for physical exploration. I might whisper suggestions or use hand signals to encourage an actor to take the action further; to physically commit and go deeper or higher, or to slow down the action and find the connection calmly, to feel it internally. I monitor the rhythm of what is happening in the space. I may need to create silence, to give the actors space to feel, sense and rest, or raise the energy in the room through the pace and volume of the soundscape. If they are Pulse trained, I might use Pulse shorthand to conduct their experience, whispering in the ear of an individual or calling out to the group *repetition, shatter the space, develop to climax* or *juxtaposition*, all of which will trigger their 'composer', and bring their awareness to the macro. For reference to Pulse shorthand, see Training Workbook, Chapter 2. Often, I will initiate feeding in the text but then pass it on to one of the actors not in that scene. As the process proceeds, feeding in the text becomes a group responsibility. This allows me to take notes and conduct elements in the room. When I need to 'direct' I will take the text feeding back again.

In Mapping, the line of text spoken by an actor is fused with their sensory experience through physical action. The fusion of the moment is dependent upon the vocal action of speaking; therefore, I am also listening to the quality of the spoken line. There are many challenges for the physical actor during Mapping. When working with physical intensity, 'patterning' (shouting or declaiming) commonly occurs. In this case I'll suggest that they embark on the action/image again by simply saying *'again'*. They know this means that they are to pay attention to the speaking of the line. Having discussed verbal tendencies and vocal habits, you might establish a shorthand with the group. For example, if an actor hears the word *washing*, they will realize they are blurring separate thoughts together, *washing* them with emotional expression rather than finding a connection to the meaning of each thought. By doing this, I try to prevent them from kinaesthetically imprinting a line that has no meaning. I have found the following tendencies to be the most common (words in italics could be used for shorthand):

- Using the wrong *stressing* which compromises meaning.
- Using *attitude* instead of the detail of the line to express meaning.

- If they are caught in the physicality of the action, they may be *declaiming* the text instead of finding the meaning of the line in the resonance of the action.
- *Emphasizing* the line instead of internally connecting to its meaning.
- *Playing the scene* – creating a literal context within which to say the line/s.
- Physically *illustrating* the line/s – acting out what is being said. This may often be a way into the exploration, but it is not the goal. Usually this means that the actor is narrating the line, removing themselves from the sensorial experience. Generally, this makes it devoid of connection, a 'dead' thought.

> If you stop investing in the imaginative world, the text can sink the boat … The burden of responsibility for staying inspired is on the actor; you are the fertile bed of imagination.
>
> Stephen Phillips

Through whispered side coaching you might at times encourage the actors to separate a heighted body state from their vocal delivery, for example, a contorted body with a calm voice. This will happen naturally if you are drawing their attention to the issues above. I often use this juxtaposition during Rendering as it allows for the physical text to be read by an audience as the character's internal state.

Serving the speaking actor

During Mapping, all ensemble actors are focused on serving the actor who is speaking and driving the action. Encourage the ensemble to read ahead and become familiar with the events and dynamics of each scene, so they can be improvisationally pro-active. If they are in the scene but have no lines, they will be serving in the Pulse. If they are in the scene and have lines, they will be shifting back and forth between serving the speaker and driving the action. If they are not in the scene they will be in the space, feeding in the lines or making music and sound offers as well as being available to enter the Pulse with their own offer or enacting a suggestion from the director. Serving actors may use sound but do not speak. Ensemble actors may find themselves serving the speaking actor in the following ways:

- When the speaking actor begins to improvise a situation the serving actor/s support(/s) that image/action.
- When the speaking actor accepts an offer made by a server, they build a situation together.
- When a serving actor's character name is mentioned, they improvise as that character, and if they are off the floor, they must enter the Pulse. In this way

memories and back-stories are played out, ghosts appear (characters who might be dead in the actual plot), time becomes fluid, and alternative versions of the scripted story become possibilities.

- If someone is being spoken about and they are not a character in the play, a serving actor will be endowed as that person and will interact accordingly. Similarly, if the actor playing a certain character is not available any serving actor can be endowed as them.
- The serving actor may initiate but must always accept and build upon whatever endowment the speaking actor places upon them, be it human, animal, object, or an aspect of nature.
- A serving actor might inhabit their own character (who is not in that scene) to interact with the speaking actor.
- If a serving actor is in a scene where a situation is being improvised and it is important for their own character to witness it (a backstory, memory or relationship), they might shift into a 'subjective state' and take in the experience from their own character's point of view.

The experiential outcome for the serving actor is 'objective' when they participate to support another actor, but also 'subjective' when they absorb the sensory world and witness moments that have impact for their character. When a thought is fed in for the speaking actor it gives the serving actors (who as their characters all have a relationship to some degree with that character) a chance to be affected in that moment as well as when the actor speaks. They will get to experience the content of the line twice.

Line learning

It is not necessary for an actor to have learnt their lines before embarking on Mapping, but it is their responsibility to be prepared and totally familiar with them. This means they recognize the line as their own (they have done their own analysis), and they know the literal meaning, especially when working with classical texts. Having commenced with two days of Intuitive Investigation, the actor knows their given circumstances, their character's function and, during Immersion, they have also had the experience of 'kinaesthetic script analysis'. The ensemble has already been immersed for several days; the intuitive part of this process has begun. As we don't want the actors drawn back into the mental activity of line learning, it is preferable that they only work outside of rehearsal on familiarity to expand possibilities when they reach Mapping.[3] Some actors are nervous about learning lines and feel more comfortable and able to be free; if they learn them before rehearsals start, so they should do that, but make them aware of the danger in rote learning, of making choices and closing off possibilities before they have begun. 'When you just learn text in your isolated bubble, it is not in your body ... with Pulse the text is absorbed kinaesthetically inside you' (Abrahams 2013). As they will not have scripts in their hands for Rendering, if they haven't absorbed their lines through Mapping (and you don't have an assistant to feed in the text) they will need to know them before Rendering begins.

> Performers can become anxious about speaking. Text is layered in after substantial physical work and it is fed in gradually; so, the event is not reduced to language. You make the whole work with all the elements, building a story slowly.
>
> Zahra Newman

An actor once told me that he gave a lot of attention to his lines before going on the Mapping floor. He felt that Pulse was like surfing. If he was under prepared, he struggled to take off, but if he prepared well, it was like 'riding the wave' and having the ultimate experience. Preparation can mean the difference between 'surfing the barrel' or being dumped on the sand. By entering Mapping well prepared, the moment-by-moment intensity of focus upon each thought means that, by the end of this layer, actors generally know their lines, and each line is inextricably linked to action and emotion, fused to the character's journey.

> I still use the Pulse method of learning my lines through the body – even if I'm being conventionally directed ... When I learn the lines physically I have a body memory of the words in different parts of my anatomy. It means I'm never searching for words in my head... My performing is lived in my body.
>
> Grant Cartwright

Feeding in the text

The benefit of feeding in the text is that actors don't work with scripts in their hands. Script holding inhibits movement; their eyes are on a page and their focus is on how they are saying the line. Feeding in the text is a tool to free the actor physically and mentally, and it takes the pressure off the actor having to learn their lines by rote before they can enter the work. For the director it means that the work is not held up by actors who haven't learnt their lines. 'There's no pressure to get the line right ... this keeps the actor's pathway open to their creative self' (Abrahams 2013). If the idea of feeding in the text for a two-hour Shakespeare play seems daunting, just begin with Immersion, and then make your own judgement call around how much of each layer you feel you have time to use (see Chapter 8).

Feeding in the text during Immersion constitutes reading the text loudly and clearly at moderate pace. Mention the character's name before the line so all the actors can become familiar with who says what and include all the stage directions to help the actors understand what might be literally happening. During Mapping you are feeding in a thought or line (one by one) and waiting for the actor to respond physically and verbally.

INNER LIFE REVEALED THROUGH ACTION

Keep mentioning stage directions as they help to anchor all the actors to the plot, but you can probably dispense with mentioning the character's name before the line. By this stage all actors should know who is speaking which line. Be careful not to give a 'line reading'. The delivery of the line should have sense and meaning, but devoid of interpretation.

There is a lot going on during Immersion and Mapping Pulse. Sourced sound is sometimes playing, actors might be making sound (breathing, crying, laughing, yelling, murmuring and more), and there will be actions and physical sequences emerging simultaneously. To the outside eye it can appear chaotic. This form of improvisation is robust, messy and not precious. That is why sometimes during Mapping I will be inside the Pulse feeding in text near the actor so they can hear me, while at other times I will remove myself to the sidelines so I can control the dynamics of the room. I conduct the experience in the room like a jazz artist. Improvised jazz is where Pulse began, and its origins can be most keenly felt during this phase. We can ramp it up energetically (through the pace and volume of text feeding and the volume and rhythm of sourced sound), or we can bring the energy of the room into quiet focus by creating silence and stillness. The juxtaposition of these atmospheres has resonant kinaesthetic impact on the actors.

> I think Pulse gets at something suggested by Stanislavski's late work and by Grotowski's experiments, but Pulse is less holy – it's dirtier, rougher and more lateral in its operations.
>
> Richard Murphet

This kind of heightened chaos is rarely sustained and usually only emerges during intense turning points of the storytelling action. For the most part during Mapping, the focus of the room is on the actor working to deliver their line/s. So, when feeding in a line, speak clearly, sometimes loudly, and often you will need to repeat the line. If you are keenly watching the actor, you will sense if they have taken it in or not. Your priority is that each line reaches and is absorbed by the speaking actor. It is also important that everyone in the room hears the line so they can all be focused on building that moment together. For this reason, feeding in the text needs to be used even when individual actors already know their lines. Familiarity with each moment of the narrative is paramount for the ensemble otherwise they can't build on group imagery and motifs. Feeding in the text is an important collaborative tool that engenders, in the actors, a sense of ownership of the whole, but ultimately, the best thing about it for a director is that for two weeks it creates a moment-to-moment rehearsal structure.

The Recall – for director and actor

I have found – through painful experience – that the 'recall' or recording of improvisation is often forgotten or taken for granted. I believe this is ultimately why improvisation gets a bad rap and why some practitioners might feel that it is not an efficient use of time. The experience for some actors can be overwhelming, or the discipline required to capture that experience is lacking. I allocate significant rehearsal time post each session to do the 'recall'. It is the thought-by-thought detail of what took place during Immersion and Mapping that becomes the physical blueprint for my staging.

When the actors come off the floor, they sit by themselves and write/sketch what *they did* and what others *did to them* during that session, making sure their action record is connected to the lines where it happened. Every actor will find their own system of notation. Make sure you allot a timeframe you can afford. Some actors will make incredibly detailed notes they have to finish after rehearsal. Others may only highlight the most impactful actions and moments experienced. They will also note what feelings arose and other discoveries, again connecting these to the lines in the text. As the director, I make a few notes during, and more after each session from my own perspective, capturing what physicality and images had impact, drawing connections and associations, and noting other epiphanies I've had along the way.

If I have time, I will do a review after a particularly fruitful day of Mapping. This is where the actors and I will go through our 'recalls' and compare notes. I will mention discoveries I found impactful. This serves as a curatorial tool encouraging actors to align their understanding with mine. Often a physical sequence involving two or more actors can be so complex and nuanced that I will ask actors, when they come off the floor, to do a physical 'recall' – physical re-enactment of the sequence. They need to create body memory by repeating several times what would be impossible to describe in words. When I directed *Vinegar Tom* by Caryl Churchill, about witch hunting in the seventeenth century, an assistant director took on the role of recording the Mapping layer. The result was a brilliant and useful document containing instant life drawings of as many physical moments (mainly duets) as she could manage to sketch. Like an alternative prompt copy, it was the record that we drew from to corroborate the actor's sense memory and my visual recall. It was this experience that prompted me to work with a video camera in the room during later productions.

As a solution to 'recall', there are pros and cons to filming rehearsal. What is great is that everything is captured, nothing is lost. During Rendering you and the actors can watch certain sections of both layers again. This can alleviate the need for you to take notes while conducting the room and feeding the text, and filming can be an effective tool to align the intentions of the ensemble. There is, however, a downside to using the filmed rehearsal. Firstly, the time it takes to go over the footage adds hours onto rehearsal as well as post-rehearsal time, and there may be too much material to consider, which can weigh down the process. Secondly, there is a lack of immediacy when you do this. Having explored both options, I prefer to receive the raw intensity and visceral nature of the work in real-time as I record my impressions in a chaotic instinctive manner. I trust that what stays with me is meant to and what doesn't didn't have the necessary impact.

Emergence of character

Writers often talk about characters having a 'life of their own', that when they are in a state of 'flow' the characters assert themselves, take control and drive their own actions. All the writers must do is get out of the way. This creative state of 'flow' is akin to the 'submerged' state of Mapping, and similarly, the actor aware of the character emerging needs to get out of the way. Deep immersion creates a fundamental platform for the actor's imaginative intelligence to take off, so they can respond from impulse to events and people in the newly created 'world'. The actor becomes the 'minder' of the character being channelled through them. This 'minder' has the detachment of a witness, enabling them to observe and imprint, not judge, censor or discard. This is where the notion of duality and split consciousness from Pulse training asserts itself. Activation on the floor and reflection during the 'recall' is a cycle that repeats itself whilst moving through the narrative. Instinctively, the actor absorbs what actions had impact. As the journey proceeds, the character gains confidence, becomes surer of themselves and takes greater risks. When this happens the edges of actor and character blur. They merge and become one.

Just as a couple might develop intimacy through experiencing a 'shared history' the actor and the character become intimate through the conditions set up for Mapping. Within the week of improvisation, the actor and character undergo a sustained durational experience where they feel 'supported' by each other. The actor/character takes emotional risks, shows their vulnerability, and interactions become truthful and authentic. Intimacy through 'shared history' has been created and the actor/character commits to a future together.

In real life, humans generally act and re-act to their circumstances spontaneously when they are triggered unconsciously by experience. Only afterwards might they reflect upon their behaviour (the therapeutic industry is built on this). When behaviour is thought out before hand, and then acted upon, it is intentional, planned and does not spring from spontaneous impulse. In some contexts, this behaviour might be viewed as inauthentic – manipulative or deceptive. This is an issue for actors who prioritize intellectual strategies to construct the behaviour of their character. Acting methodologies that ask the actor to think about actions and intentions before experiencing interactions try to 'make sense' of the character. This model doesn't broker unknowability. Experiential investigation, such as this process, means valuing experience in rehearsal above ideas and letting yourself be present, trusting your discoveries. Spontaneous actions show others who we are, they express our nature and when collated together reveal our 'character'. We become the choices we make. During Mapping the actor discovers the fusion of action and emotion that is the response to a thought. This response is then captured through Rendering, and if the actor *commits to that action* and does so whenever it is repeated, they will achieve authenticity.

If an actor enters Pulse rehearsal trying to control their environment and the outcome, wanting to etch out a character journey because they think they know how the character needs to be portrayed – what they would and wouldn't do – the actor will miss opportunities and reject spontaneous action that doesn't fit into 'their world view'. Here, the notion of surrender from the Pulse training is fundamental. If an actor rationalizes their responses during Mapping to create psychological continuity, they will inevitably minimize heightened physicality in favour of predictable behavioural tendencies. Characters may be devastated, ecstatic, unreasonable, passionate and vulnerable from moment-to-moment. They are fully alive because their physical life tells us so, not because the words do. Each moment has its own integrity, and the Rendering process is the 'scaffold' that accumulates them. It might not be until the running of the staged result that the actor experiences the character's complete emotional 'through-line'.

> You must know your function – a solo, a duet, a trio, or choral work. I have translated this idea into the whole of my acting career. I had a minor role, playing Catesby in Richard III, a role of about six lines … my function as Catesby was to follow Richard III and give him affirmation… mostly I was silent, but audience members spoke to me of 'my character' and how struck they were by it. I saw most scenes as Richard's solo, and I had a strong sense of how to position myself in relation to that.
>
> Zahra Newman

Function

I use the concept of function to instil the notion of ensemble practice – every actor has their role to play, their function – but also to suggest a utilitarian notion of storytelling. Only what is essential to make the narrative function will be included. It speaks to the mechanics of the drama. Also, if an actor establishes their character's function in the story/scene before they enter the improvisational layers, it can assist their search for relationship and meaning and give them a focus for their actions. Patterns will usually emerge, and the character's intentions will become clear. I discuss each character's function during the first layer of Intuitive Investigation.

> My function was to serve and affirm. Function is about physical action and communicating relationships to an audience … Directors always tell me that I never need to be told where to stand in a space or how to position myself – I know how to make shapes which create meaning. And meaning is physical not just language… My intention was to get Richard to fall in love with me.
>
> Zahra Newman

Character and physical acting

The notion of working towards character through physical means is an approach generally described as 'outside-in'. Either you do detailed observation of a prototype (animal or persona), or you select a concept (rhythm or dynamic) and alter your body accordingly. Laban analysis, Lecoq's process of using natural elements – wind, water and fire – and imitation are 'outside-in' strategies. In the case of Pulse physical acting, an actor changes their physicality not through observation or a concept but through a psycho-imaginal response to thought (line of text). Actions are created as an expression of interior impulse, so actors are working from the inside-out, yet their experience is 'written' on the body. It is not quite as simple as that though, because the Pulse actor also 'internalizes the witness'. They might adjust the image of the action – pace, shape, intensity – during execution because they understand what it needs to look like. Working with the dual consciousness of the actor/composer, they will work from inside-out and often simultaneously, outside-in.

The playing of character involves illusion. We may have seen an actor perform many times before in different stories playing many different roles. We may know about them as a person. But we come to the event in hope. We invest ourselves in make-believe and if the actor gets the signals right, we see the character in front of us, not the actor. Their actions executed with commitment are the signals we are searching for. We know how the character thinks and feels because of what we see them do.

Fusing emotion and action

The following section assumes the director and performers understand how emotion is signified within Pulse work. The expression of emotion is treated as a synthesized vocal and physical exercise, not as something psychologically motivated. In Pulse training, emotional gestures are brought onto the Canvas in Phase Seven. In preparation for this there is commentary, and a suit of tasks offered in Chapter 4: Committing to Emotional Gesture and more advanced tasks at 'Words, Silence and Emotional Gesture'. If your actors are not Pulse trained you may wish to take them through some of these tasks before Immersion.

Neuroscientists tell us that emotions can be induced in two situations (Damasio 2000). The first being when a person takes in a sight or smell, touches, sees or hears a familiar face, or place, and the second, when they conjure up from memory images in the thought process, for example, someone close who has died. 'Emotional or Affective Memory', a technique found in Method-based approaches, relies on the latter situation, in which the actor uses images from their own lives to induce emotions. By improvising scenarios with high emotional stakes within the Mapping 'imaginary world', the Pulse actor creates a visceral experience which they can use instead of conjuring images and emotions from their previous lived experience. Then, during Rendering, when they retrieve an action, it will bring with it the mental and emotional state of its creation. The actors can rely on images from the improvised scenario rather than from their own lives.

Often during Mapping, emotional response will be accompanied by physiological changes that we know as feelings. I call their associated externalized expressions 'emotional signifiers'. These can be both aural and visual (crying, yelling, muscle contraction, tears, breathing patterns). When feelings happen for an actor on the Pulse floor, due to the nature of working in 'extended time', it is an opportunity for their 'composer' to play with the emotional signifiers, extending, enlarging or diminishing them to experiment with range. Working with this duality helps an actor imprint the physical experience of the emotional signifiers without attaching themselves to genuine feeling.[4]

Thinking of emotion as e-motion or 'energy in motion' will help an actor work fluidly on the Mapping floor as they create their mercurial character. During any Mapping session a character might cry, laugh, be scared, angry, or hate, from one moment to the next. The actor's aim is to work in detail, thought-by-thought, being careful not to gloss over entire sections with one emotion. Because emotion will be fused with each action, or the action itself might be an emotional signifier, the actor needs to be able to 'drop out of it', to let it go once the experience of that line is finished. They will need to find emotional neutrality so they can move onto the next moment. This strategy of investigation allows for the expression of heightened emotional states that serve the creation of an unpredictable emotional through-line, but one that is also functionally coherent.

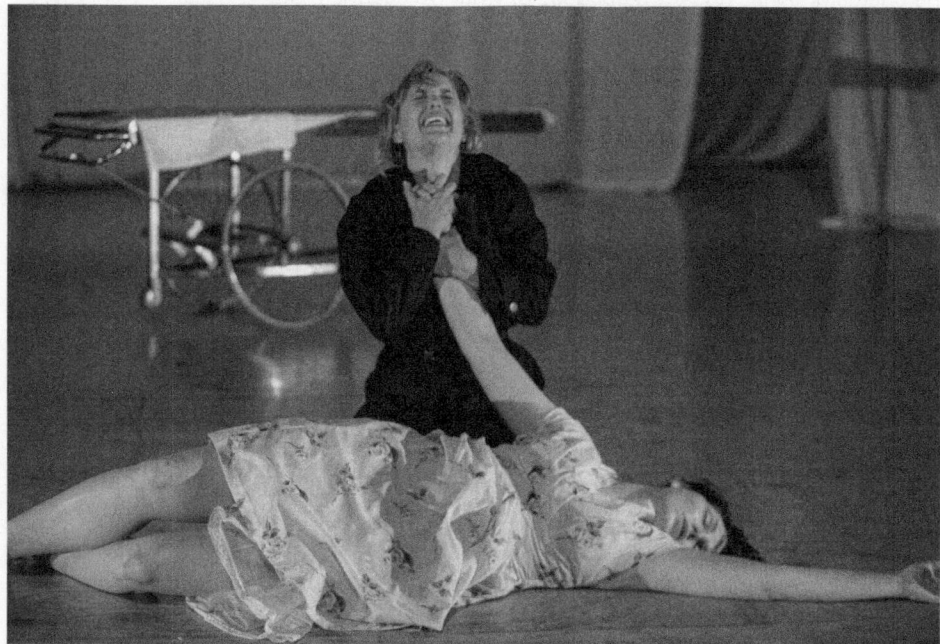

Figure 8 Meredith Penman and Anne Louise Sarks, *Yes*, October 2007.
Credit: Photo © Jeff Busby.

8
CASE STUDIES

Chapter 7 has given you the fundamentals of the four layers of rehearsal; their functions and how to use them. In this chapter, I offer examples of what each layer might provide toward the staging of a production.

Using Pulse as a rehearsal device

The notion of working horizontally through the script, once during each of the four layers, means that you and the actors interrogate each scene from a different perspective four times. Also, each time the actors enter a particular section they bring with them what they discovered in the previous layer/s. In this way, each moment accrues depth and detail. Your role, specifically in the middle two layers, is to anticipate this and help shape the experience for them. In the early days of working with scripts, I used Pulse *in* directing rather than directing *with* the four-layered process outlined in the previous chapter. The following experiments illustrate how to use Pulse as a rehearsal device rather than a layered process. It was the gradual accumulation of these experiences that led me to eventually commit to using all four layers in rehearsal.

When I directed *Angels in America Part One: Millennium Approaches* by Tony Kushner in 1999, I tentatively introduced my actors to the fundamentals of Pulse training, merely as a physical preparation for rehearsal. But as they knew the story well, the play's themes emerged through the physical imagery (I later called this a Themed Pulse). This gave me the idea to start the play with a devised prologue of image and sound based on Pulse which would lead us into the first spoken scene. It was then that I worked out how to 'recall' a Pulse so that it could be repeated later. The prologue introduced the performance style to the audience and had a significant impact upon the actors' approach to the material.[1] It was during *Angels* that I discovered how to dispense with blackouts between scenes. Even with the rudimentary skills these actors had developed, purely through Pulse warm-ups; they were able to Pulse the transitions between scenes, working to keep the audience visually connected. The story could now be rhythmically told in one continuous sweep. While I was 'blocking' the play using conventional rehearsal means, I drew many times upon Pulse to find staging solutions.

The following year when directing *Top Girls* by Caryl Churchill, I had no staging vision for Act One – a fantastical dinner party attended by mostly dead, famous and infamous women of the twentieth century. My challenge was to breathe physical stage life into a dense, wordy discussion involving ideas, beliefs and memories, whilst the characters consumed a three-course meal. For want of a plan I experimented with Mapping the first act. Using a four-metre length table and a huge swath of blue satin which I had placed in the space, the actors physically engaged with the images the language implied. Towards the end of the act, when the last character Gret tells her story about war and mayhem, the dinner table was up-ended, and chaos ensued. When the scene came to an end and there was no more text, Marlene, the only contemporary character, and host of the dinner party, was left in silence, alone, lying on the table. It was then that I realized that Act One could be presented as Marlene's dream. In the final staging of the production, the characters crowded on top of the table, hid underneath it, moved it around the space and wrapped themselves in the blue satin tablecloth; none of this bore any resemblance to the realism of the elegant dinner party on the scripted page. The heightened physicality visually implied an imaginary world, and at the end of the act the audience discovered it to be Marlene's dream.

In 2001 I did an adaptation of *Caucasian Chalk Circle* by Bertolt Brecht. It was titled *Zivot* (meaning 'light and life' in Serbian) and was set in a refugee camp in the Balkans. In preparation for rehearsal, the actors created backstories for characters who had been displaced by the Bosnian conflict. We rehearsed and were to perform in a huge warehouse where the actors/characters built their own improvised shelters, including a shower and camp kitchen through which the audience wandered before taking their seats around a fire pit at the camp's meeting place. The audience represented a United Nations delegation that had come to observe the camp's inmates perform Brecht's story. During the making of the piece, the ensemble of actors improvised as the group of refugees, 'the frame acted as a set of imaginative parentheses around the text ... it was always a kinaesthetic exercise, never a straightforward dramaturgical recontextualization' (Phillips 2013). As well as developing refugee characters for the 'play within a play', Pulse sessions (I had trained the twenty-three actors in Pulse the previous year) created the physical storytelling necessary to facilitate Grusha's epic journey. With their bodies, the ensemble created mountainous terrain and deep ravines on which she travelled, as well as the crowds of disaffected revolutionaries sacking the city.

When I directed *Cassa de Alba* after *The House of Bernarda Alba* by Garcia Lorca, I set up one Immersion session focusing on hidden feelings and thoughts engendered by Alba's violent behaviour. I 'fed in' verbalized subtext while the actors, playing her daughters, Pulsed to create a disturbing dream sequence. This sequence became part of the final movement design. It progressed the story visually and revealed the fractured relationships created by Bernarda's inner turmoil. With *Vinegar Tom* by Caryl Churchill in 2004, I found using Mapping to be incredibly useful, as woven through the text of *Vinegar Tom* are the lyrics to seven songs. We did not have the original music, nor a musical director, but I knew some of the actors were musically talented. By Mapping the lyrics to the songs, I found the actors could freely improvise the tunes without the pressure of having to compose them in a separate process. As they were continuously immersed in the imaginary world of atmosphere and character they worked intuitively with rhythm, mood and emotion. As soon as I heard the first improvised song, I began recording them. Ultimately, most of the songs retained their originally improvised tunes for the production. I would say that this saved at least a week of rehearsal time. It began to dawn on me that instead of this process taking more time than conventional rehearsal, it could possibly be more efficient.

Pulse allows for the creation of a visual, physical world outside the scripted text. So even if you do not use it as a layered process, using it as a rehearsal device allows you and the ensemble to invent non-scripted moments (wordless action to progress the story). This is what I mean by Pulse being a way to combine theatre-making and script directing.

Time management and magical solutions

As you can see from the examples above, when I began directing using Pulse, I used it as a device, and later, only used either Immersion or Mapping. Working towards an opening night deadline was always stressful, but doing it while trying to apply an evolving, untried rehearsal process was terrifying. Time was the major issue for me. It was difficult to see how I could move improvisationally through the narrative twice, then stage it, and trust there would be enough time left to do the necessary detailing before technical rehearsals began.

Every time I used Mapping, however, I found the results so inspiring it compelled me to find a way of bringing them to the staged outcome. Eventually, this became Rendering. I had always begun rehearsal with a version of Intuitive Investigation, but I had not included the horizontal layer of Immersion if I intended to use Mapping. I thought it would absorb a week of rehearsal, which I couldn't afford. But to my surprise, it took only a couple of days, and its value was incalculable. I knew it would create a visceral world of relationships before the actors knew their lines; however, their ability to present staging solutions for often-complex choreographic demands of the script whilst improvising imaginary landscapes totally amazed me. Although both Immersion and Mapping are improvisational layers, they stimulate an actor's imagination in different ways. Immersion facilitates the freedom to play in a child-like state, whereas Mapping involves a psycho-linguistic relationship to action.

Without faith that the process will deliver valuable outcomes within your timeframe, it will not be easy to improvise in-the-moment with the actors in 'extended time', as days and days of rehearsal pass. At first it will be nerve wracking. So having faith and trusting the process is essential if you want to lead a group through this process. After many trials I am completely relaxed about it now, because I've experienced so many times how discoveries from Immersion merge with those in Mapping, resulting in deep transformation for the actors and a staging outline for me, making rehearsal more, not less, time efficient.

Figure 9 Ella Watson-Russell, *New Anatomies*, June 2005.
Credit: Photo © Jeff Busby.

Immersion

Immersion facilitates the conjuring of physical and visual storytelling. In *The Mill on the Floss,* physical metaphors created through recurring motifs framed the movement design of the piece, and in *Pericles Punished,* non-scripted action sequences progressed the story and solved complicated staging challenges. I used all four layers of Pulse rehearsal in the production of these two shows, but the following case studies specifically demonstrate how to recognize and apply outcomes that emerged from Immersion.

The Mill on the Floss – Recurring motifs and metaphoric resonance

The darkened space ripples with blue light as the audience enters. Once seated, a piercing Gregorian chant is sung acapella, and a woman is dragged through the space to a chair. A man sits, pulls the woman onto his lap, violently grabbing her hair, and doubles her over, pushing her between her legs. As he pulls her up, she gasps for breath before she is pushed down again and again until her body becomes limp. As she is carried from the space, chatting actors enter to commence the first scene. This is the first image of *The Mill on the Floss* by George Eliot, adapted by Helen Edmundson, which I directed with my company OpticNerve at Theatre Works, Melbourne, in 2016. The story is set in nineteenth-century England where the protagonist, Maggie Tulliver, is fighting for the right to express her full humanity while being excluded from every opportunity. The story spans fifteen years and begins when Maggie is nine years old, ending when she and her brother die in a flood. The adaptation stipulates that each five-year period is to be played by a different actress; in my version the company of eight actors also played seventeen characters.

Having finished Intuitive Investigation with the knowledge that water was a pervading theme, I commenced the Immersion phase, curious to see what it would throw up. I had no preconceived ideas or objectives other than being alert to the creation of non-verbal, physical storytelling. As soon as I fed in the text from the first stage directions, 'First Maggie is standing with book in hand, staring at the river. The air is full of the sound of water rushing through the mill wheel' (Edmundson 1994, 1), the actors became water. They fluidly explored the different rhythms and properties of water and the physicality of being drowned by water. As each actor found a strong image, they kept working with it until it became a group motif. I didn't stop and wait too long before continuing, because I knew there were continuous references to water throughout the text – the action being set on the river Floss – where the actors could continue exploring and building upon these evolving motifs. When I fed in Maggie's first lines, 'bringing those things called witches or conjurors to justice; this is first to know if a woman be a witch, throw her into the pond; and if she be a witch, she will swim' (Edmundson 1994, 1), the actor, who eventually plays Second Maggie and the actor playing her cruel brother Tom, began to explore the physicality of witch drowning; he the oppressor and she the witch. A bit later, as the stage directions describe a threatening crowd and a disturbed nine-year-old Maggie watching the drowning of a witch, these two actors repeated the water imagery and developed it. The actor playing Second Maggie had risen instinctively to serve the story (there is no witch in the cast list) by continuing to develop the witch imagery throughout Immersion – sometimes singing hauntingly, sometimes floating, often drowning. Immersion had enabled this actor to develop a through-line of action for an invented character. See Bloomsbury companion website for rehearsal footage: https://www.bloomsburyonlineresources.com/the-pulse-approach.

When it came to Rendering the play, I wove the witch's physical journey through the story. Often when water was mentioned, the witch appeared as a drowning apparition in the background of the action (unless she was playing Maggie). 'In one particularly effective recurring motif, Zahra Newman – as the drowned witch – appears as if dancing under water, highlighted in a narrow column of light' (Reviewer/Fuhrman 2016). Different recurring motifs of bodies in water, often gasping for air, served to make transitions between scenes fluid. 'Again, and again, performers are lifted off the floor, held briefly in the light, then pushed down and sent sprawling. The context is always different, but the ultimate trajectory is the same' (Fuhrman 2016).

For the last scene we needed to create a vast flood in our bare space – with only an upturned table as a boat – so at the end of the Rendering week, we went back into an Immersion session to bring up all the drowning, suffocating and rolling body imagery that had been created. Instead of feeding in text, the actors worked with the sound of crashing water, pulsating music and the knowledge that the end must incorporate the drowning of Maggie and her brother. One reviewer described the outcome like this: 'gestural movements that evoke images of drowning, of sexual longing or emotional distress ... Here it forms a powerful, churning undercurrent beneath the surface of the play, achieving its apotheosis in the stunning final scenes on the river' (Byrne 2016).

What emerged from Immersion not only became the central movement design of the piece but its metaphoric through-line. 'Gerstle projects the image of the drowned siblings backwards onto the narrative, as if it were an organizing metaphor. Thus, Maggie and Tom are drowning from the beginning, and their lives are only a futile struggle toward a surface that they can never reach. It's a melancholy vision, but it makes for fascinating theatre' (Fuhrman 2016). The metaphoric resonance that Fuhrman suggests was created by the repetition of a motif which afforded me staging solutions. The decision to repeat this image during scene transitions related more to form than symbolism. I did not choose it intentionally, as a metaphoric message – although my Rendering choices will always reveal poetic association. It was only after I read that review that I remembered an early imaginative impulse – having no idea how I would achieve it. I had wanted to give the audience a continuous reminder of the river flowing through the space.

In narrative terms, when Rendering the play I wanted the women's struggle and oppression to be the focus. I didn't want any decorative distractions, so I chose to have no distinguishing design features (set or costume) speaking to an audience of the era or location of the story. It took place in an empty, black space with a raised platform, and all the actors wore the same flexible, calico outfits, evoking the idea of olden-day underwear. The playwright's use of language, the content of the narrative and the actor's Yorkshire accents were all that anchored the story to nineteenth-century England.[2]

Figure 10 Grant Cartwright and Zahra Newman, *The Mill on the Floss*, August 2016.
Photo by: Pia Johnson.

Pericles Punished – Non-scripted physical storytelling

> Our Pericles inhabits the dark side of a contemporary world. He is a freedom fighter amongst displaced people searching for asylum. One king he encounters is a power-hungry warlord and another an underground bar entrepreneur. Murder is common and death is an everyday reality. War zones and rough seas are traversed, and sexual slavery is a vulnerable woman's destiny. When our hero finally breaks, he is lost with nowhere to go.
>
> (Director's note 2013)

Such was my directorial vision for *Pericles Punished* after *Pericles, Prince of Tyre* by Shakespeare, at the Victorian College of the Arts. It was 2013 and the middle of a Melbourne winter. We were rehearsing in a vast warehouse space painted black with a concrete floor and high ceilings. The space was dissected across the middle by a floor to ceiling wire fence with a gate in the middle (it used to be a storage space). The content and rehearsal circumstances were bleak to say the least.[3]

The production crew and set designer had constructed a series of layered and connected platforms before we began rehearsal. They were to act much like a playground upon which the actors could improvise and on which I could imagine the spaces for each scene as we progressed through Immersion and Mapping. The costume designer brought in piles of old clothing (pants, shirts, jackets, dresses, coats and headscarves) from which the actors selected, and I asked for suitcases, a long piece of thick rope and a few large pieces of material to be brought into the space. Sound equipment was in place, and low light threw shadows onto the black walls. Our research for the piece had centred on Syria's civil war and the thousands of refugees crossing daily over borders. During Intuitive Investigation we traced the 'hero's journey' of Shakespeare's Pericles, re-inventing the 'given circumstances' of each scene for our freedom fighter: Pericles. We called them Units, for example, Unit Four – *Pericles Leaves Tyre*, Unit Five – *Pericles Crosses the Border*, Unit Six – *The Gypsy Camp*. There were seven actors playing fourteen speaking characters, with the potential for them to create a multitude of others. So, only having a rough idea of the landscape Pericles might move through, we embarked upon Immersion.

I fed in the text of Units One to Four where Pericles was imprisoned (tied up by rope and wrapped in material) by the warlord Antiochus and now he was escaping from Tyre with the help of his best friend Helicanus in search of asylum. At the end of Unit Four – *Pericles Leaves Tyre*, Helicanus farewells Pericles with the lines, 'We'll mingle our bloods together in the earth – From whence we had our being and our birth' (1.2.121–2).

The next section in our score, Unit Five – *Pericles Crosses the Border* had no text. It was to act as a transition to the next scene where Cleon and Dionyza his wife (in Shakespeare's version, the Governor of Tarsus who rules over a land gripped by famine), speak of their sorrows before Pericles arrives at their court. In our version, the Governor and his wife are now refugees on the run, so somehow, Pericles had to meet them on the road. During Intuitive Investigation we had discussed the possibility of different types of border crossings, by sea, by mountain, by river and by rail. After the break, the actors having done their 'recall' for Unit Four came back into the space ready to begin again. I put on some music in anticipation and said, 'Unit Five – *Pericles Crosses the Border*'. This is what happened next.

The actor playing Pericles grabbed a suitcase, hurriedly putting whatever he could find into it, then climbed the wire fence. He jumped through the open gate and began running and hiding in and across the platforms. The other actors, immediately inhabiting refugee personas, picked up suitcases and huddled somewhere in the space. Suddenly one of the actors stole another's suitcase and rushed towards a side wall. He ran on the spot for some time looking at a long, thin brick ledge jutting out from the wall (I didn't even know it was there) eventually jumping onto the ledge and sitting. Clasping the stolen suitcase to his chest, he began vibrating his body. In that moment we all understood that he had jumped onto a moving train.

I put on a train sound effect over the instrumental build of the music already playing and immediately the actor playing Pericles ran to the wall and jumped athletically onto the ledge. Soon the two actors playing Cleon and Dionyza (she with a baby in her arms, she'd made it from a rolled-up dress) and he (carrying two suitcases) ran alongside the wall. When Dionyza managed to hang onto the ledge with one hand, she sought help and offered her baby to the man already on the train. He put his suitcase aside and carefully received the baby. Finally, Dionyza made it onto the ledge with Cleon's help, but just as she stretched out her arms to take back her baby, the man leapt from the wall with the baby and ran. Screaming, Dionyza fell off the train, and with Cleon, gave chase across the platforms as the man with the baby (making crying baby noises) ran behind the fence

Figure 11 Oliver Coleman, Rachel Perks, Nicholas Kato and Tristan Barr, *Pericles Punished,* June 2013.
Credit: Photo © Jeff Busby.

CASE STUDIES

and climbed it one-handed. As the chase ensued, Pericles slipped from the train and hid in waiting. When the man with the baby ran through the open gate our hero grabbed the man from behind, brought him to the floor and broke his neck. When Dionyza, exhausted and hysterical catches up with them, Pericles hands her the baby. After she hugged him and kissed his feet (conveniently implying they don't speak the same language), he put the body of the man over his shoulder and left.

In the calm of the following moment, I fed in the title of the next Unit, *The Gypsy Camp*, and began with Cleon's lines,

> My Dionyza, shall we rest us here,
> And by relating tales of other's griefs,
> See if 'twill teach us to forget our own?
>
> (1.4.1–3)

They comforted each other and attended to their baby. Towards the end of the scene, on hearing the lines,

> Welcome is peace,
> If he on peace consists;
> If wars, we are unable to resist.
>
> (1.4.84–5)

Cleon suddenly becomes alert to danger and hides beside the gate, ready to pounce when Pericles appears. There is a scuffle, but soon Dionyza recognizes Pericles. I fed in his lines, the last of the scene and the last of Act One in our production.

> Nor come we to add sorrow to your tears,
> but to relieve them of their heavy load …
> Arise, I pray you, rise:
> We do not look for reverence, but for love, …
>
> (1.4.91–2,101)

Pericles takes a small Persian rug and a flask out of his suitcase. He spreads the rug for them to sit on, cuddles the baby and shares his flask as other refugees emerge from hiding. Recognizing an opportunity, I offered Greek dancing music – the actor playing Pericles was Greek and for his performance response earlier in the week, he had done a passionate dance. Hearing the music, Pericles dances for the crowd as they clap and laugh joyfully. To juxtapose this happy scene, I cross faded the Greek music with a war soundscape of planes flying overhead, bombs and machine-gun fire. When they realized what they were hearing, all the refugees scattered and hid amongst the platforms until the sound faded out. It was only then that Dionyza realized her baby had been hit by a bullet and was dead. When her wailing came to an end, I suggested we take a break.

This is only part of what took place on this rehearsal day, but it illustrates how Immersion can facilitate non-verbal storytelling. *Crossing the Border* and *The Gypsy Camp* were placed exactly as I have described, with virtually no adjustments, into the final Render. There is a reason I have chosen to highlight this Immersion session.

Figure 12 Rachel Perks, *Pericles Punished*, June 2013.
Credit: Photo © Jeff Busby.

My memory of it is visceral. I remember how astounded I was by the actors' imagination, by the offer of the train, a baby (crying), and then stealing the baby and the baby's death. The creation of a context in which our hero Pericles could be heroic, and then the reunion and celebration juxtaposed with despair. It took my breath away. This scenario did not unfold because we had decided upon events and turning points beforehand and then acted them out. We never discussed the framing of such a plot. The scene emerged from *group consciousness*. Each actor drew upon sensory research and the invention of our adapted, given circumstances. The actors were in 'flow' making inspired offers that I responded to spontaneously with sonic interventions. Such is the power of ensemble improvisation. If you are a theatre-maker/director needing to create physical storytelling, Immersion could be an essential rehearsal tool.

Mapping

Mapping was the only layer of improvisation used in the following two case studies. Consequently, these productions reflect the staging process from Mapping straight to Rendering. I focus here on how the actors responded to speaking the language in the social context of each narrative and demonstrate how Mapping can shape the physicality of the acting and staging. I describe how the confronting content of *Five Kinds of Silence*, a contemporary radio play, was realized physically, and how Pulse helped defy the physical constriction of period costuming in *Stage Beauty*, set in 1660.

Five Kinds of Silence – Depicting confronting content

> You come into the room. I can't see your face. It's dark. I'm lying on the bed and I've no clothes on. You kiss me a lover's kiss. You put your tongue inside my mouth, and you tell me that you love me. I say, I love you too. That's what lovers say, isn't it? I love you too, Dad.
>
> (Stephenson 1997, 125)

Five Kinds of Silence by Shelagh Stephenson was first broadcast on BBC Radio 4 on 29 July 1996. It was the winner of the 1996 Writer's Guild Award for Best Original Radio Play and the 1997 Sony Award for Best Original Drama. When I came across the radio script I was attracted to the evocative language and importance of telling that story, but also by the challenge of physically staging a script written for an aural experience. Stephenson eventually adapted her script to the stage, but when I directed it in 2005 at VCA with actors completing three years of training I stayed with the radio play for that challenge. The radio play was written for three male and three female actors doubling for eleven characters – four family members, a lawyer, a psychiatrist and three police officers. I had three female and one male actor to work with. Before rehearsals began, I edited out the incidental characters but left in the essential questions they asked the three women. These questions were important, as they represented 'official' voices disrupting the family's world from the outside. I hoped that Pulse would solve the dilemma of how these questions would be asked.

The narrative conjures a very dark world. Enclosed in a family bubble, a violent father abuses his wife and a daughter and rapes his other daughter. The play begins with the women shooting the father. The language driving the narrative is a set of monologues describing past events. There is no physical interaction between family members and the description of what happens is confronting. I knew that if we worked this material through the layers of Pulse, a visceral experience for an audience would emerge. It would be visual and physical. What I didn't know was how the actors would deal with the physical approach to the explicit nature of the material.[4]

As we had four weeks (including technical rehearsal) to bring the script to physical life, after two days of Intuitive Investigation, we began Mapping. I still had no idea how to stage this raw and difficult material about incest and domestic violence, and I knew I would need to have some difficult discussions with the actors. I prepared myself to negotiate a potential resistance to working physically with this material. What happened was the reverse. Once we hit the floor the actors felt safe in the 'womb' of the submerged Pulse, and they took emotional and physical risks that I could never have anticipated or asked for. Their commitment in turn inspired me and we worked fast, from moment-to-moment without sacrificing depth. I discovered that because the physical exploration of the language was non-literal and the actors were searching for metaphor, they had agency over how they physically expressed a thought. They were not illustrating the ideas and we were not concerned with what is traditionally seen as psychological realism, so the imagery that emerged was not explicit. For example, when Susan the daughter is explaining how she felt about having sex with her father, she says, 'You touch me. I want you to'. During Mapping the speaking actor was on her stomach on the floor, scrabbling to get away, dog like, while the actor playing the father stood very still straddling her body holding her back by one ankle.

Most of the narrative involved the mother and two daughters recounting the father's abusive behaviour. Although this character was dead, every time the father was mentioned the actor playing this character was present on the Pulse floor to serve the speaking actor. Because of this presence, the father's menacing, controlling behaviour was visually explicit as he physically manipulated them, shadowed them and witnessed everything. The Mapping layer had revealed to me how to stage the narrative. In the Rendered outcome, all actors remained in the space throughout and when the women spoke, the father lurked – a ghostly yet interactive figure only 'seen' by the audience. His indelible presence was imprinted on the psyches of the women and would be for the rest of their lives. Form had become content, creating psychological and metaphoric resonance.

Although we were Mapping in an empty space, there was a three-metre-high, cage-like trolley (usually holding platforms for the seating bank) stored in the corner of the room. Early in the process the actor playing the father pulled it into the space so he could tower over the women. After that he used it to climb on and leap from, he dragged it in circles around the space and imprisoned his family in it. Inevitably, it became the one piece of set for the production.[5] At the beginning of rehearsal, I had introduced a microphone to the space and when the script demanded questions be asked of the daughters (by the psychiatrist, the lawyer and the police) one of the other actors randomly used the mic to ask them. A dilemma was solved. When we Rendered these questions, the actor on

CASE STUDIES

Figure 13 Ella Watson-Russell and Grant Cartwright, *Five Kinds of Silence*, October 2005.
Credit: Photo © Jeff Busby.

the mic slipped unnoticed from the space to position themselves in the front row of the audience. Rather than playing a character, they became a disembodied voice, complicit with the inaction of the witnesses.

The actor playing the mother took on the responsibility of the sound design for the piece. When she wasn't needed on the floor, she used the Mapping layer to try out atmospheres, moods and musical motifs. The sound offers then became embedded in the action. With few adjustments, what was found in Mapping became the continuous soundscape of the piece. Similarly, that week of explosive improvisation was so dynamic that Rendering simply became a staging of the Mapping layer. It was the rehearsal of *Five Kinds of Silence* that finally convinced me of the efficiency and profundity possible when rehearsing with Pulse.

Reception

While training in Pulse at the VCA, acting students were concurrently watching its outcomes in productions I directed. Such a curriculum structure enhanced the training experience and gave them a practical frame within which to understand the merging of improvisation and script work. An actor in training, who eventually became an OpticNerve ensemble member, observed the following:

> You could see all the structures and rules, but it also contained an explosion of emotion and storytelling. To me the performers were like speaking dancers. It was visceral, electrifying and terrifying. I'd never seen anything like it and the performers seemed

Figure 14 Grant Cartwright and Alice Parkinson, *Five Kinds of Silence*, October 2005.
Credit: Photo © Jeff Busby.

> to have such freedom ... I could see that the improvisation came from meticulous preparation and shared understanding; every choice they made was exactly the right choice ... I'd never seen a piece of theatre which was so totally fluid.
>
> (Woods 2013)

When I began OpticNerve Performance Group in 2008, we re-mounted *Five Kinds of Silence* at fortyfivedownstairs, a theatre in Melbourne. One reviewer described their experience in the following way: 'Violence is written on the body and engraved on the mind. Gerstle's direction seamlessly entwines both aspects of performance. This production combines such urgent veracity and technical accomplishment that it is impossible to remain unmoved' (Woodhead 2008). And another: 'The company reminds us theatre is not just words spoken, but words made flesh' (Boyd 2008).

The audience did have a visceral experience of the savage material and I think two factors contributed to its physical presentation being palatable. First, the audience did not see a middle-aged man touching a teenage girl. The actor playing the father was athletic, attractive and the same age as the actors playing the daughters. Meaning was derived though poetic association. Secondly, it was shaped by the Pulse performance style – the staging involved abstraction from realistic circumstances. When the written word implied sexuality or violence, the action of the actors was interpretive and metaphoric. It was beautiful to watch and yet the verbal information was abhorrent. This juxtaposition was impactful giving an audience the space to think as well as feel.

Stage Beauty – Corsets, wigs and social norms

> Stage Beauty is about most of the ideas that interest me. It deals with the construction of identity and the way gender roles and sexuality are conditioned by the context and times in which we live. It's about the confusion and dislocation of self that happens when social paradigms shift rapidly ... It shows us how adaptation and the building of resilience is key to survival ... ultimately it reveals to us, that we are the actions we take and become the choices we made.
>
> (Director's Note 2012)

In 2012 I directed *Compleat Female Stage Beauty* (full title of the playscript) by Jeffrey Hatcher, a VCA project with eleven graduating acting students and eleven design students from the Production Department. Set in London in 1661 and based on real characters, it is about a male actor called Edward Kynaston who was famous for portraying Shakespeare's female roles – Ophelia, Cleopatra and particularly Desdemona. At this time, only men were permitted to act on the public stage. One night a woman named Margaret Hughes played Desdemona in an underground, illegal theatre, and 'instead of stopping the show, the ever-game King Charles II changes the law to allow women to act' (Playtext 2006). When Kynaston is told of the change in the law, he says, 'A woman playing a woman. Where's the trick in that?' (Act One, Scene Four):

> It is also a meditation on the art of acting ... It was a time when acting was obvious artifice, an intricate vocal and physical choreography involving gesture to signify the

feminine and the masculine ... This was an historical moment of transformation ... the notion of theatrical representation was questioned. If the portrayal of gender was no longer about vocal and physical signifiers, what would acting need to become?

(Director's Note 2012)

When I first came across this story – the film adaptation *Stage Beauty* directed by Richard Eyre – I saw how the form that Pulse could evoke would align with its content. I was eager to put it to the test. Preferring the pared back writing of the film version, during Intuitive Investigation, we dramaturgically spliced sections of the play script and screen play together.

Research into the clothing, customs, mores and social behaviour of the time informed the actors' imaginative 'world' early in rehearsal. Extravagant physical and emotional behaviour was not publicly expressed by the upper classes in the sixteenth century, and the clothing of the time served to reinforce this. In naturalistic representations of narratives set any time before the 1920s one generally observes only sitting, standing and walking. Physical acting involves embodiment and heightened action regardless of the era. Although the actors would eventually be performing in long skirts, corsets, tight jackets, boots and wigs, I didn't want the notion of such restriction to affect the actor's gestures and sense of physical abandon. Many scenes were set in the court of King Charles II, and I didn't want the social norms of the time and place to inhibit the actors' physical imagination. I hoped that Mapping would allow for the visceral, emotional and physical exchange I needed to happen between characters, and that it would generate heightened and extravagant character action. During Mapping the female actors worked in loose rehearsal skirts. They got used to holding them up while running, wrestling and simulating fornication. There were old jackets, boots and corsets lying around the space. The actors experimented putting them on, and taking them off and discovered how to use them as props as well as clothing. Once the show was in performance, the actors wore elaborate costumes and wigs but executed unusual, heightened actions, and moved deftly in an unrestricted way.

In the improvisational playground of Mapping, the actor playing King Charles II discovered his divine right to power; he could behave in any way he chose. Unhampered by any sense of decorum, the actor courageously committed himself to the experience of hedonistic extravagance. Magical images from Mapping, such as instigating orgiastic behaviour at court, to receiving ministers on business in his underwear and a wig, were accumulated and transferred to Rendering, creating the eccentricity of our King Charles II. He sounded like a responsible monarch, and yet, what was visually presented to the audience was his decadent underbelly.

As the days of Mapping wore on, I could 'smell the greasepaint, and the roar of the crowd'. It made me want to enter the emerging 'world' myself. This is when I decided to immerse the audience just as we were immersing ourselves in the process. My actors were in a theatre rehearsing a story about actors in a theatre rehearsing a story – *Othello*, during an extraordinary moment in time. Assisted by a perverse King, women who wanted to act, broke the 'thatched ceiling'. Although it happened shy of four hundred years ago, if it hadn't happened, I wouldn't be doing what I was doing. I

Figure 15 Rosie Lockhart, Tom Heath, Matt Whitty, Christian Grant, James Townsend and Sam Young, *Stage Beauty*, October 2012.

Credit: Photo © Jeff Busby.

wanted the audience to take part in this historic moment. When the audience entered the space, they were diverted to backstage set up as a seventeenth-century theatre, replete with actors doing pre-show rituals – getting dressed and threading each other's corsets, some rehearsing lines, a couple simulating sex. When they emerged into the auditorium actors were hawking oranges and others setting up the stage for the performance of *Othello* as the King's entourage entered the Royal box. A reviewer experienced what I had hoped: 'a true feeling of immersion and involvement ... during a bawdy tavern scene when Kynaston is at his lowest, and undergoing great torment from his "audience", my theatre companion had to stop herself from heckling back in his defense' (Moffat 2012).

Rendering

For Rendering I have chosen to discuss *Manbeth: Macbeth Amplified* after Shakespeare. Unlike the case studies above, this rehearsal process moved straight from Immersion to Rendering, without employing Mapping. The contingencies involved with Immersion had a fundamental impact upon the Rendering result and the nature of the staged 'world'. This case study illustrates how using improvisation in this way can facilitate fluidity in form, and in place, space and character.

Figure 16 Mike Steel, Lachlan Woods and Alexander England, *Manbeth: Macbeth Amplified*, August 2008.

Credit: Photo © Jeff Busby.

Manbeth: Macbeth Amplified – Fluidity of space, place and character

'If you like your theatre docile, pre-masticated and lifeless then it's probably not for you. However, if you want to be shaken by the scruff of the neck until it almost hurts, this is your show. *Manbeth* exceeded my expectations in every way' (Review/Captain's Blog 2010). *Manbeth: Macbeth Amplified* was remounted for a three-week season in July 2010 at fortyfivedownstairs, Melbourne. But it began its life called *Manbeth*, a version of *Macbeth*, as a second-year actor training project at VCA in 2008.

As actor trainers who also directed shows, we were committed to adjusting the production process to fulfil training demands, and as Shakespeare's tragedies generally have a few very large roles for male actors and only one decent-sized female role, we decided to split the year group along gender lines. The thirteen women in the year would rehearse *Julius Caesar*, giving most of them decent-sized speaking roles, and I would work with the ten men on *Macbeth*. My aim was to mount a physical and sensual attack on this classic text. I wanted to penetrate the artifice of the language by 'dragging out the guts' of what was really going on.

The production process began with several challenges. Rehearsal time was limited – four weeks half time, equalling two weeks full time – and to facilitate ensemble practice and train all the actors in speaking Shakespeare's text, the largest roles of Macbeth and Lady Macbeth needed to be split. The play was two hours and thirty minutes when read, and it needed to be half that. Whilst moving through the text in Intuitive Investigation I drove the dramaturgical process to remove the sub-plots and support characters. We distilled the scenes into one major plot line, Macbeth's drive towards power, leaving us with one hour fifteen minutes when read. I asked the actors to engage in sensory research involving male-dominant domains: the military, private boarding schools, elite competitive sport and prison systems. They shared this with the group, and from this research I decided we would focus on the hierarchy of the prison system. I could sense the potential impact of this landscape's implicit power games if the violent undercurrents were explored and expressed through the lens of Macbeth's ambition. During that first rehearsal week, I set up a durational improvisation with the actors playing prisoners and me, the warden. The result, as one actor describes it, set the tone for Immersion: 'tensions surfaced, the psychological game-playing increased, our frustrations and paranoia came to the surface, the gang mentality became apparent, and there were certain idiosyncrasies about how each of us moved around the space and how we functioned that emerged' (Woods 2013).

Rather than two actors playing the one role of Macbeth and two playing Lady Macbeth, I imagined there might be four separate characters sharing the lines of the two roles. During the dramaturgical process of cutting the text we discovered that Macbeth's lines were either about driving towards his goal or sensitively reflecting upon his choices. With Lady Macbeth, the splitting of the text became about the splitting of her personality towards madness. With this loose rationale, the doubling actors made tentative text selections, so they would know when I fed in the lines during Immersion, which might be theirs to respond to. We all acknowledged that within this prison 'world' the two actors playing

Lady Macbeth would be the same-sex lovers of the two Macbeths. These agreements, the text and the roles, as well as placing ten small, slatted benches in the empty space, were the major choices made before we began.

As I look at the scribbles from Immersion in my rehearsal script, I see descriptions of images and actions, staging ideas, arrows and sketches. The drive and energy of the emerging story 'world' are palpable, the meta-narrative clear and distinct. Below is a list from my notes, not in narrative chronology but grouped associatively, that gives some idea of the emergent imagery from Immersion. To distinguish between the doubled roles, the characters developing were referred to as Conscience and Ambition (Macbeth), and The Lady and Princess (Lady Macbeth).

Body culture

- Army drills against wall, push-ups (clapping in between), sit-ups (holding ankles), skipping, boxing, bodies hanging from balcony
- Conscience and Ambition wrestle as prisoners circle them
- Fighting – prisoners hide in cells, watch silently
- The rhythm of fight then flight – stillness and silence.

Set

- Pushing benches into a circle to make an enclosure (could be palace), Benches as weights, bench presses, coffins, cell walls
- Walking along benches as they are placed down (Lady)
- Everyone has their own bench – they carry it, sleep on it, hide behind it
- Benches vertical, men moving behind them (Birnam Wood).

Witches

- Witches snort coke, deal coke, witness and watch
- Witches tattoo prisoners
- Witches are messengers
- Prisoners/witches steal letter written by Macbeth, Princess tries to grab it, they taunt him, throw it around turning it into a game.

Duncan's murder

- Duncan and Macbeth kiss (betrayal)
- Dog pack sniffing dead Duncan on ground, snarling, howling, then back to men

- Conscience crawls like a dog – Lady leads him by his hair
- Lady on top of Conscience, seduces him
- Lady and Princess wrestle Conscience to the ground, drag him off, tie him up.

Banquo's murder

- Prisoners strip naked to shower against wall
- Conscience tries to hold Ambition back – he rapes Banquo over a bench – dogs sniffing and howling – Ambition takes shower
- Ambition whispers to accomplices/witches
- Conscience paces against the wall as Banquo is knifed in shower block
- Banquo runs frantically through space naked (ghost)
- Ambition stands against wall (Princess goes down on him).

Malcolm and Macduff

- Silence, stillness, night, Malcolm cries alone in cell
- Malcolm stands alone in a pin spot of light
- Macduff pushes Malcolm against wall – Malcolm spits in his face
- Malcolm carries Macduff who is howling (his wife murdered).

Macbeth and Lady Macbeth

- Lady urges on Conscience and Princess tries to restrain Ambition
- Macbeths and Ladies slow dance
- Lady is raped by Ambition
- Lady crying, it's over between them
- Lady kills Conscience then kisses him
- Conscience hangs himself from the chair, Princess screams, cuts him down
- Princess does a demented strip (Out, damned spot), prisoners taunt and cat whistle
- Princess kills Lady then bathes her gently, whimpering.

Locations evoked

- Exercise yard, the gym, tattoo parlour, dining hall, witches drug den, shower block.

Several actors came and went from inside the Pulse to make sound and music offers but other than that, all actors remained constantly in the space. They all had the same experience of the way this narrative was told through action, sweat and pace, violence, sex and death. They all found their relationship dynamics: who belonged to who, who needed protection from who and what happened, when and how. Although it was slippery, hinted at, merely suggested, I knew we had found the 'world' for the story to live in. 'Shakespeare's story is not "set in a prison," neither is it "prisoners playing *Macbeth*." It sits somewhere between the two and floats in and out of both realities' (Director's Note 2008). In an interview regarding the development process for *Manbeth* I describe how, by creating four characters from two roles while using Shakespeare's text and plot, we developed an alternative visual narrative that heightened the play's themes.

> ... although the Macbeths were best friends, they were in constant verbal and physical conflict giving the usual internal doubt of Macbeth's soliloquies a visible driving dynamic. The Ladies were thrown together as the only outsiders in an aggressive hostile environment, and after rejection by Macbeth they became vulnerable and unprotected. The sleepwalking scene became a sad, psychotic duet giving the madness of Lady Macbeth a visible and profound despair. I had hoped that once the audience accepted the convention of four characters instead of two, that the understanding of the narrative revealed through the poetic text would gain clarity rather than be diminished.
> (Gerstle cited in Erez 2010, 54)

Immersion straight to Rendering

Unlike the process for *Five Kinds of Silence* and *Stage Beauty* where we Mapped and then Rendered without doing Immersion; in this case, we had done Immersion but were left with no time for Mapping. We had the equivalent of one full-time week to Render the piece before Opening. This difference had consequences for the Rendering process (for both me and the actors) and this is reflected in the nature of the final staging. Immersion is about the raw, instinctive 'big picture' of an emerging imaginary 'world' and not about verbalizing the story moment-by-moment in 'extended time'. This means that all the actors were continually present – they were literally in the space during the sweep of the narrative. If they had been Mapping each line, only a few actors at a time might have been on the floor. Consequently, in the final staging, all the actors remain visible in the space. They fluidly shift characters (those who doubled) and shift roles – playing their character as well as serving the space through moving benches. At other times they are seen by the audience secretly watching each other.

As you can see from the lists and notes I made, Immersion evoked the meta-world of prison and gave me ideas for locations and activities in scenes (a drug deal, showering, eating in the dining hall, in the exercise yard, secretly having sex and being tattooed), as well as how to play the turning points (whispered secrets, murders and suicides). What it didn't provide was detailed action tied to each line.[6] Also, recurring motifs organically emerge during Mapping because thematic pre-occupations in the narrative are generally repeated. But when you Render from Immersion, the 'big picture' focus and pace at which you work means motifs will appear, but they may not be repeated. The building of recurring motifs then becomes part of the Rendering or construction process.

The actors were not yet secure in their lines, so we embarked on a 'brushstroke' Render – not a specific line-to-line movement pattern in space but a generalized spatial action plan for each scene. It proved difficult for the actors to Render line by line. The psycho-linguistic process dominated their 'composer'. They were reluctant, unsure and could not respond from impulse. My intuition told me to access the Pulse again. We began working through the script by Pulsing each beat before Rendering. We put on music, and I read the beat into the space as the actors re-connected with previous images, layering them and developing new ones. This served to re-energize the material and enliven the actors.

Reception

> Before the audience arrived, we would work physically for twenty minutes. I'm guessing the space was loaded with the smell of our bodies. At the end of the show, we were all out of breath and the floor was awash with sweat – it was one of those extraordinary moments in theatre – we'd all worked to the end of our physical endurance.[7]
>
> (Woods 2013)

Manbeth: Macbeth Amplified took the notion of physical acting to an extreme. It was Shakespeare on speed. As one reviewer remarked:

> The piece is powered by a physicality which amplifies the violence and intensity of the original. The constantly moving bodies climb the chunky struts which support the ceiling, roll, fight, choke each other, always grabbing and touching, fusing sexuality to violence with startling effectiveness … the ensemble generates a heady atmosphere, filled with sweat and pain, revealing the animal in man.
>
> (Bowen 2010)

Right from the beginning I trusted the energy and irreverence these ten young men brought to the Pulse floor. They revelled in the freedom to be bold, sexual and athletic while speaking Shakespeare's text, so it was essential that I wrangle the energy and frame the heightened excess in a disciplined way. It was the Rendering layer that allowed me to do this. I was rigorous in the creation of structure, shape and form and then meaning, language and the clarity and comprehension of the story. I wanted the audience to be inside this landscape, to smell and taste it, but not lose Shakespeare's intent.

> An interpretation preserves the original intention or spirit of the text. Rather than bringing the text forward to us, it takes us backwards. In this sense *Manbeth* is a triumph: it is hands down the strongest, most supple interpretation of The Scottish Play I've seen in a long while … This is a murky, muddy world in which every player must slip and slide in and out of multiple characters to keep his head above water. This requires theatricality – genuine theatricality.
>
> (Captain's Blog 2010)

Figure 17 Gabriel Partington and Thomas Conroy, *Manbeth: Macbeth Amplified*, August 2008.
Credit: Photo © Jeff Busby.

At no point did I question the alternative version we were presenting, it was poetically clear to me, but I was not sure how an audience would interpret the two Macbeths and two Lady Macbeths. Once it was reviewed, I understood the value of this process:

> ... sometimes one is absent while the other takes the fore, but there is a constant undercurrent of duality and connection between them. The naturalness of it is striking; there feels no need to question it, as the division creates two distinct characters, the one creeping ever closer to insanity, unrestrainedly violent and the other the more rational, calculating side. This melded into a perfect portrayal of the internal conflict for which *Macbeth* is so renowned.
>
> (Bowen 2010)

It is Pulse that enabled the linking of the two Macbeths. The fluidity of the Pulse floor allowed the actors to have hyper-spatial awareness of each other. Every action they took involved their intention towards the other. Through Pulse they expressed their intimacy physically, through action and space, touching, shadowing, protecting, bullying and distancing. As the reviewer remarks, this became the visual language for the audience. It was the same for the two actors playing the Lady Macbeths. They relished the opportunity to embrace the sexuality of her character, and in the heightened prison 'world' of the Pulse, courageously offered up a fusion of violent, sexual and sadistic behaviours. While their duet expressed physical intimacy, they also managed to represent isolation and vulnerability, counter-balancing the mentality of the pack and the menace surrounding

CASE STUDIES

Figure 18 Lachlan Woods and Alexander England, *Manbeth: Macbeth Amplified*, August 2008.
Credit: Photo © Jeff Busby.

them. 'Suddenly she was not the woman known so well from the endless productions of *Macbeth* over the years – now she was darker, her sexuality more dangerous and her strength palpable' (Bowen 2010).

'In any all-male scenario, the issue of homoeroticism is inevitably raised. In this production it is tackled head on; rather than a sprinkling of token moments designed to "tick the box" we get a thread of homoerotic desire woven right into the fabric of the piece' (Captain's Blog 2010). With this process there are never token moments because the fabric of the staged narrative has been woven layer by layer organically, and during Rendering the repetition of motifs ensures it is integrated. All action is evoked by the source text and emerges from the improvisation floor. If anything, Rendering is a process of elimination. You only take from Immersion and Mapping what is essential to tell the story. '*Manbeth: Macbeth Amplified* was stunning: the whole world of the play was as important as the individual scenes. It was that rare thing – a piece of total theatre which was organically complete' (Murphet 2013).

Future considerations

The dramatic texts (classical and contemporary) explored in these case studies were written in and for a heteronormative context. They are character-based, defining gender, race and sexuality. They are narrative focused, such that the storytelling depends on the gendered features because the characters exist within a social and political hierarchy. Over the past decade the process of presenting these stories has been fraught with tension. Diversity and inclusion are now embedded in contemporary social policy and our theatrical ecology has responded. New theatre writing is embracing this shift in both content and form. But it is particularly challenging, and yet liberating, for our presentation of dramatic writing from the past. From now on, adaptors need to be inclusive, consider gender fluidity and 'colour blind' casting, while making sense of the written narrative considering such altered circumstances. Of course, experimental theatre artists have always played with these ideas, but now practitioners working in conventional forms and mainstream environments need to take note. The Pulse rehearsal process facilitates kinaesthetic dramaturgical translation. As the case study above shows, fluidity is a defining feature of all its aspects. Immersion and Mapping allow for 'discovery in action' of character adaption, re-invention of relationship connections and solving of narrative leaps.

AFTERWORD

I remember how confused I was, as a teenager, when I watched mainstream theatre. I mostly saw static, visually unattractive storytelling where it seemed all that mattered was the words. Television on stage. As an emerging practitioner therefore, my focus became form (the body) and space (composition). I wanted to find a way to make the performance of a speaking actor in a naturalistic play, physically dynamic. Due to rehearsal experiences as a young actor, I also wanted to create a rehearsal culture that supported collaborative input. I wanted the staged outcome to be the culmination of discovery in rehearsal, rather than a presentation of the director's pre-conceived ideas. The Pulse approach is my response to those early theatrical experiences.

There are training/directing challenges for actors and directors using Pulse. It is hard work and not for the faint-hearted. It is physically rigorous, pushing actors beyond their perceived limitations – physically, emotionally and imaginatively. On the other hand, for actors who are physically disconnected, Pulse will connect them, and it is a gift to witness a group of distracted teenagers suddenly move like a flock of birds. As a director you will need the ability to improvise, multi-task on the floor, spontaneously solve problems, and 'hold the room' during delicate and emotional work. You must be able to embrace being in 'the unknown' despite looming deadlines, and be able to watch, listen and wait as well as pounce on opportunities when they arise. To a certain extent, a novice director can practise such skills during the process, but they would benefit enormously by engaging in some of the Pulse training before using the directing process. As mentioned before, Pulse is based upon spontaneous physical interaction where negotiation for consent in-the-moment is not possible; part of any training project must therefore involve sensitively setting up structures so psychological and physical safety are present.

Not long ago, when teaching in the UK and North America, I was interested to find that acting with a script was still primarily approached through speaking. Acting classes were taught in very small rooms with a couch for scene studies, and Pulse and Bogart's Viewpoints were seen as movement practices not acting methodologies. Now as then, Stanislavski's influence dominates conventional actor training and the direction of text-based dramatic theatre. Currently there is a generation of actors in training and the profession who have been disadvantaged by lockdowns and isolation and the normalization of the screen as a learning platform. Due to excessive screen time their brains are being rewired by the process of skimming, and they have little stamina for staying deeply focused and in the moment. Electronic stimuli have taken the place of image making from 'within', where the imagination was once stimulated by music, words and sensations (nature). I have found when working with some of these actors that their bodies lack muscularity, they shy away from heightened physical expression, and they have limited spatial awareness and diminished emotional and physical stamina.

Global theatre ecology is also experiencing societal transition. Dominant patriarchal paradigms are shifting, operating norms are being questioned, the representation of gender, sexuality, race and age is being re-defined, and diversity is demanding to be represented. Emerging from this context are smaller, intense, flexible and adaptable trainings and hopefully the Pulse approach contributes to this. Trainers using Pulse can re-acquaint this generation with their physical being, retrain the brain to build new pathways for the imagination, allow them to practise single and dual focus attention and give them, in this social media environment, the unusual experience of silence, duration and embodied stillness. Members of any Pulse ensemble regularly experience 'ecstatic collectivity' – the joy of communal, physical practice. In this current training environment Pulse would remind the isolated artist of 'what it is like to belong, to be part of something larger than ourselves, to be indifferent to our own egos – to be reunited with humanity' (De Botton 2023, 237).

Directorially, Pulse can be a story adaptation process. It assists in the reinterpretation of previously fixed identities of character, making it an investigative tool for the re-imagining of classic dramatic texts and in terms of casting, Pulse adapts to the nature of the individuals who are using it. As an approach, rather than a defined methodology, Pulse can adapt to meet our changing contexts, and I am hoping the readers of this book will 'grab' the tools, improvise with them, find their own working solutions and keep evolving Pulse as a 'living and breathing' practice.

NOTES

Chapter 1

1 'Psycho-physical training is one in which body and psyche, outer expression, and inner sensation, are integrated and inter-dependent. The brain inspires the emotions, which then prompt the body into action and expression. Or the body arouses the imagination, which then activates the emotions. Or the emotions stir the brain to propel the body to work. All the components – body, mind, and emotions – are part of the psycho-physical mechanism which makes up the actor' (Merlin 2001, 4).

Chapter 7

1 When I begin to work on a project my awareness expands to encompass my entire environment. It becomes heightened to anything that is tangentially connected to that project. This is a state of *unbounded yet focused awareness*. I become a piece of blotting paper. Sources might be, the morning newspaper, the car radio on my way to rehearsal, people-watching at a café, conversations overheard on public transport, a painting hanging in a restaurant or the fiction I'm currently reading and watching. I record these impressions as notes, images or sound bites and feed them into my creative process. I call this *incidental research*. This means sources that come *to me* rather than the research I do to intentionally *find* sources. Enjoy being a creative magnet without discriminating. If it comes to you, there is a reason for that. These offers may inform your character; they may unlock an idea, trigger a revelation or solve a problem incidentally. The subconscious is at work, so be prepared to notice it.

2 Actors need time and space to assimilate what has happened in the Mapping layer before they can have agency when Rendering. Once I tried to Map a beat and then straight away Render it. I wanted to see if I could work through the script dipping in and out of the two layers concurrently. What I found was that actors couldn't shift out of the 'submerged' state to engage their 'rational' minds quickly enough for the process to be efficient. They were resistant to moving from a state of autonomy and freedom of expression to the constrictions of a distilling process where their intellect must be fully engaged. It is interesting to note, however, that I have not found this difficulty in the reverse. During Rendering, when I have gone back into Immersion and/or Mapping (turned off the lights, put on music and let the actors play) to find transitions or loosen things up, everyone embraces the sudden freedom. They easily 'dive' quickly and joyfully back 'into the water'.

3 Neurobiologists of learning and memory say that the release of the chemical messenger noradrenaline during exercise promotes memory formation, and that the more senses you

engage in the process, the stronger the memory. Being mindful of your body's position also reinforces quality and clarity of memory. During Mapping, engaging your body and senses whilst expressing a line of thought helps you encode that memory. When you mentally replay it afterwards by doing the 'recall', you are telling your brain – this memory has high value and is worth keeping, which means you are more likely to consolidate it while you sleep. Perhaps this is why actors generally know their lines by the end of Mapping.

4   'We are not our experience. We're the consciousness that witnesses that process. We're not our feelings. Feelings, emotions and thoughts pass through us. When we laugh, we're not laughter, we're experiencing laughter; we're aware of it: we hear it and feel it. Once we become aware of ourselves laughing, we notice a space between our awareness and the laughter – between the one who is doing and the action that's being done. It's from this perspective, that we're able to play with the sound of laughter, and even the feel of it' (Zaporah 2015, 215).

Chapter 8

1   '... that Pulse revealed to me very clearly what Kushner was writing about. The free association allowed for all sorts of juxtapositions physically and vocally that we would not otherwise have found. That hour was a revelation to me because I understood the richness of the poetry of theatre' (Abrahams 2013).

2   During the Mapping phase, the voice/dialect coach for the production fed in the text in a general Yorkshire accent and the actors spoke only on accent during their rehearsal day.

3   I had seen Pericles done professionally only once, employing a stage revolve and large wings. I knew that it was rarely produced, possibly due to the epic sweep of the journey it entailed. Pericles crosses boarders, spends time in several countries and cultures and sails on stormy seas. But this was one of the aspects that drew me to the story. The staging would be complicated and challenging using an empty space, and I could not conceive of it, but I knew that if I placed it in the hands of Pulse, that solutions would be found.

4   The actors had been training together for three years and intimately, physically interacting, so consent had been implicit. In different circumstances or if I was directing this material now, I would certainly have needed to explicitly frame the consent parameters and ascertain verbal voluntary participation.

5   With Pulse actors, it is inevitable that if there is something in the space (objects, furniture, costumes) during Immersion and Mapping they will integrate it into their explorations. Sometimes materials become recurring motifs and cannot be removed from the organic development of sequences. So, if you don't want it in the show, don't have it in the space during Pulse.

6   Working in 'extended time' allows for a line to be fused with action and emotion facilitating detailed 'recall'. When Rendering from Immersion this fusion line by line hasn't occurred. Once actors know their character's staging context, they will be able to work sensorially to find an emotional bridge to their lines.

7   As preparation for all Pulse shows, the actors, in make-up and costume, ready to perform, come into the space twenty minutes before the audience enters, to do a non-speaking Pulse with sound and light. In command of the narrative, their character, the play's relationships, and familiarity with not only their lines but those of all the other characters, they are filled with content. The space is atmospheric, a sound source from the piece is chosen and the lighting operator is on the board improvising with the actors. The Preparation Pulses for *Manbeth; Macbeth Amplified* were impactful. Not wanting to exhaust themselves before the show began, the ensemble often created slow, sad, tender imagery that was beautiful and extraordinarily moving, so much so, that technicians and front of house staff would gather to watch. This juxtaposition in mood was the perfect prelude for what was to come.

REFERENCES

Bailey, John. 2009. 'Reviews: Invisible Stains'. *Capital Idea*, 28 October 2009. http://apentimento.blogspot.com/2009/10/reviews-invisible-stains-when-rain.html.
Baird, Julia. 2020. *Phosphorescence*. Sydney: HarperCollins.
Bowen, Joanna. 2010. 'Melbourne Reviews: Manbeth/Band of Creatures & OpticNerve'. *Australian Stage*, 20 July 2010.
Boyd, Chris. 2008. 'Five Kinds of Silence'. *Herald Sun*, 4 July 2008.
Byrne, Tim. 2016. 'The Mill on the Floss'. *Time Out*, July 2016. https://www.timeout.com/melbourne/theatre/mill-on-the-floss.
Captain's Blog. 2010. 'Manbeth'. *White Whale Theatre*, 25 July 2010. https://fortyfivedownstairs.com/review/review-of-manbeth-on-captains-blog/.
Chekhov, Michael. 2001. *On the Technique of Acting*. New York: Harper Perennial.
Damasio, Antonio. 2000. *The Feeling of What Happens: Body and Motion in the Making of Consciousness*. London: Mariner Books.
De Botton, Alain. 2023. *A Therapeutic Journey: Lessons from the School of Life*. London: Penguin Random House.
Edmundson, Helen. 1994. *The Mill on the Floss*, adapted from George Eliot. London: Nick Hern Books.
Erez, Eli. 2010. 'An Interview with Tanya Gerstle and Lachlan Woods'. *MASK: The Academic Journal of Drama Victoria*, 33.2, Summer/Spring: 52–5.
Fuhrman, Andrew. 2016. 'The Mill on the Floss (Theatre Works and OpticNerve)'. *Australian Book Review*, 5 August 2016. https://www.australianbookreview.com.au/component/k2/101-arts-update/3517-andrew-fuhrmann-reviews-the-mill-on-the-floss-theatre-works-and-opticnerve.
Gladwell, Malcolm. 2006. *Blink: The Power of Thinking without Thinking*. London: Penguin.
Green, Peter. 2009. Radio Review, 'Invisible Stains'. 3MBS 105.5fm, 22 October 2009.
Hatcher, Jeffrey. 2006. *Compleat Female Stage Beauty*. New York: Dramatists Play Service.
Luckhurst, Mary. 2012. 'Trans-Institutional Mixed Learning Models: Understanding and Performing Classical and Modern Play-Texts'. *Final Report*, The Higher Education Academy UK.
Merlin, Bella. 2001. *Beyond Stanislavsky: A Psycho-Physical Approach to Actor Training*. Great Britain: Nick Hern.
Moffat, Christine. 2012. 'VCA's Compleat Female Stage Beauty'. *Theatre Press*, 27 October 2012.
Nachmanovitch, Stephen. 1990. *Free Play: Improvisation in Life and Art*. New York: G. P. Putnam's Sons.
Oida, Yoshi, and Lorna Marshall. 1997. *The Invisible Actor*. London: Methuen.
Rutenberg, Brian. 2013. 'Brian Rutenberg: Studio Visit 34'. 20 November 2013. https://www.youtube.com/watch?v=hQ20DFHOTO8.
Rutenberg, Brian. 2016. *Clear Seeing Place*. New York: Permanent Green.
Stephenson, Shelagh. 1997. *The Memory of Water & Five Kinds of Silence*. London: Methuen Drama.
Wood, Charlotte. 2021. *The Luminous Solution: Creativity, Resilience, and the Inner Life*. Sydney: Allen & Unwin.
Woodhead, Cameron. 2008. 'Silence Speaks Volumes about Domestic Violence'. *The Age*, 28 June 2008.
Zaporah, Ruth. 2015. 'Action Theatre'. *The Actor Training Reader*, edited by Mark Evans. New York: Routledge.

Unpublished

Fleming, Alice. Prompt Copy Script: *Invisible Stains*. 12 October 2009, Faculty of the VCA and Music, The University of Melbourne.
Gerstle, Tanya. Programme: *Manbeth*, 'Director's Note'. 20 August 2008, Faculty of the VCA and Music, The University of Melbourne.
Gerstle, Tanya. Programme: *Invisible Stains*, 'Message from the Director'. 21 October 2009, Faculty of the VCA and Music, The University of Melbourne.
Gerstle, Tanya. Programme: *Stage Beauty*, 'Director's Note'. 25 October 2012, Faculty of the VCA and Music, The University of Melbourne.
Gerstle, Tanya. Programme: *Pericles Punished*, 'Director's Note'. 5 June 2013, Faculty of the VCA and Music, The University of Melbourne.
Kissane, Carla. Rehearsal Process Report: *Invisible Stains*, 'Week Nine'. 26 September 2009. Faculty of the VCA and Music, The University of Melbourne.

INDEX

Note: Page numbers followed by "n" refer to end-notes.

Abrahams, Gary 135–6, 145
abstract 43, 58, 65, 87, 132, 137
action vocabulary 29–33
    attitude to action 32–3
    physical gesture (*see* physical gesture)
    training challenges 31–2
Alfreds, Mike 3
approach
    outside-in 155
    Pulse approach (*see* Pulse)
Architecture of space 34, 38, 90, 107, 143
associative imagery and meaning 38–9
audience
    breaking the fourth wall with 40
    experiencing emotional 'truth' 74–5
    improvised performance and 103
    viewing experience, rehearsal 121–2
awareness
    focused awareness/attention 51–3, 185 n.1
    hyper-spatial 180
    kinaesthetic 15–16
    macro and micro 133, 147
    working in macro 17–19

blindfold tasks 55–6
Bogart, Anne 3
Breaking the fourth wall 18, 30, 39–40, 64

Canvas 10
    speaking on (*see* speaking)
    working with music 96–9
    work in macro 17
    work in micro 15–16
Cartwright, Grant 107, 136, 147, 150
Chekhov, Michael 3
collaboration 47, 85–6, 127
Commencement 34, 38, 63, 77, 92, 99, 100
Commitment to action 18, 39, 42, 61, 64, 78, 90

composer/performer 9, 18, 20–1, 35, 45–7, 110, 140, 147, 155–6
    access your composer 31, 64, 71
    activate your composer 9, 22, 28
compositional consciousness 21, 47, 101
Compositional Principles
    architecture of space 34, 38, 90, 107, 143
    commencement 34, 38, 63, 77, 92, 99, 100
    denouement 35–6, 48, 63, 77, 89, 92, 100
    depth of field 34–5, 47, 90, 102, 117, 143
    find the ending 36, 64, 66, 68–9, 92, 100–1, 108
    form and chaos 37, 63, 69
    juxtaposition 43–4, 48, 64, 84, 91–2, 100, 106, 111, 118, 135, 143, 147, 171
    recurring motifs 29, 35, 37, 45, 48, 77, 91, 160–2
    shatter the space 36–7, 89, 100, 102, 147
compulsive monologue 45, 86
consent 3, 14, 128, 183, 186 n.4
Content 10
    confronting content 167–9
    contrast 28, 43, 47, 71–2, 106, 118
    juxtaposition 43–4, 48, 64, 84, 91–2, 100, 106, 111, 135, 147, 171
    recurring motifs 29, 35, 37, 45, 48, 77, 91, 160–2
    repetition 29, 71, 77, 89, 91, 106, 111, 129, 147, 162, 181
    'smelling' the dramatic potential 18, 29, 39, 64, 67, 89, 91, 100, 107
    unit of action 29, 35, 37–8, 106
Contrast 28, 43, 47, 71–2, 106, 118
counting task 54–5
creative impulse 19

Damasio, Antonio 8
deep diving 130, 146

Denouement 35–6, 48, 63, 77, 89, 92, 100
Depth of field 34–5, 47, 90, 102, 117, 143
design elements
   costume 96
   light 100–2
   music 96–8
   objects 95–6
   and Pulse structure 131
design strategy, Pulse structure 131
Development to climax 26–7, 36, 77, 91, 107, 109
dramaturgy 10, 32, 39, 97–8, 111, 118, 127, 130, 137, 158, 172, 175, 182
dual consciousness 20, 22, 24, 62, 155
duet and chorus 17, 28–9, 42, 71–2, 102, 106, 110
Dynamic tension 28–9, 77, 89, 91, 100, 107

Edmundson, Helen 126, 160
Eliot, George 126, 160
embodiment 8, 21, 23, 143, 172
emergence of character 153–4
emo-choir 81
emo-juxtapositions 84–5
e-monologue 77–9
   crying/laughing 77–8
   sadness 78
   solo crying monologue 77–8
emotional gesture 42–3, 73–5, 92, 155
   anger and fear 79–80
   'come here' task 81–2
   crying/laughing 77–8
   emo-choir 81
   emo-juxtapositions 84–5
   e-monologue (see e-monologue)
   emo-transformations 82–3
   exploring 75–7
   punctuations 83–4
emotional signifiers 42, 73, 77–8, 156
emo-transformations 82–3
ensemble practice 1–2, 47, 106, 122, 126–7, 175
   awareness, field of 51–3
   blindfolds 55–6
   counting 54–5
   and function 154
   Hug Sculpture 56–7
   Hug Tag 58–62
   physical transitions 57–8
   walk/stop 53–4
ethical framework 7, 125
extended time 136, 139, 156, 159, 178, 186 n.6

feeding in the text 136, 145, 147, 150–1
Finding the ending 36, 64, 66, 68–9, 92, 100–1, 108
Five Kinds of Silence (play) 126, 133, 167–9, 171
flow 56, 76, 86, 110, 133–4, 141, 144, 153, 167
Fluid Sculptures 66–70
   continuous speaking 70
   finding the ending 68–9
   finding your way in 68
   moving in space 69
   observers 67
   players 67–8
   working in parallel 68
Form and chaos 37, 63, 69
four layered Pulse rehearsal 127–9
   immersion 132–6
   intuitive investigation 131–2
   mapping 136–40
   rendering 140–4
Free Pulse 105–6, 109, 115–16
function 128, 132–3, 154. *See also* four layered Pulse rehearsal

generative sources 11–12, 37, 44–5, 57, 65–7, 87–9, 96, 99, 102
Geometry of space 25, 34, 90, 107
group consciousness 3, 60, 167

Hastings-Edge, Luisa 137
Hatcher, Jeffrey 126, 171
horizontal layering 159
Hug Sculpture 56–7, 65–6
Hug Tag 58–62
   being in unknown 61
   commitment to action 61
   dual consciousness 62
   ensemble consciousness 59–60
   instinctive reaction 60
   Kamikaze action 62
   personal detachment and physical touch 60
   suspension of disbelief 60

imaginative responses 57
Immersion 132–6, 186 n.5
   advice for director 134–5
   non-scripted physical storytelling 163–7
   recurring motifs and metaphoric resonance 160–2
imprinting 22, 26, 33, 46, 110, 133, 147, 153, 156, 168

INDEX

improvisation and Pulse 9–11
improvised speaking 97
   compulsive monologues 86
   pausing 87
   run/stop/speak 87–8
   verbal monologues 88–9
   verbal Pulse 90
   vocal (sound) Pulse 89
impulse 15, 17, 147
   creative 19
   first impulse 15, 20–1, 67–8
   imaginative 87, 142, 162
   personal 19
   spontaneous 153
   working from 23–4, 54
Intuitive Investigation 131–2, 145, 149, 154, 159, 161, 163, 168, 172, 175
Invisible Stains case study 8, 111–13
   conception 114
   content and form 120–1
   episodes 120
   events 115–16
   rehearsal process 115–18
   viewing experience 121–2

jazz conduction 151
Jo, ha, kyu 27, 34, 36, 46, 72, 89, 93, 102–3, 111
Juxtaposition 43–4, 43–4, 48, 64, 84, 100, 106, 111, 135, 143, 147, 171
   dramaturgical 118
   emo-juxtapositions 84–5
   in speaking monologue 91–2

key working concepts
   breaking the fourth wall 18, 30, 39–40, 64
   commitment to action 18, 39, 42, 61, 64, 78, 90
   'smell' the dramatic potential 18, 29, 39, 64, 67, 89, 91, 100, 107
   what does it need? 18, 35, 39, 47, 64, 89, 100
   working in parallel 18, 39–40, 64, 68, 71
kinaesthetic
   awareness, development of 15–16
   dramaturgy 137, 182
   script analysis 133, 149
Kushner, Tony 157

language 64, 66, 119, 145–6
   performance 47, 99, 141
   shared language 18, 22, 24–9, 32, 114, 135
   of training 8–9

Languages Other Than English (LOTE) 41, 119
Lawton, Richard 120, 122
Leigh, Mike 3
Liddeaux, Hannah 21, 117, 121
line learning 149–50

macro 17–19, 31, 62, 133, 147
Manbeth: Macbeth Amplified (play) 126, 133, 174–81
Mapping 136–40, 186 n.2
   as abstract process 137
   advice for director 138–9
   confronting content 167–9, 186 n.5
   reception 169–70
   social norms and 171–4
metaphoric resonance 117, 126, 162, 168
micro 15–16, 31, 62, 87, 133
The Mill on the Floss (play) 3, 126, 131, 160–2
Murphet, Richard 24, 103, 151

Nachmanovitch, Stephen 9
Natale, Darren 31, 107
Newman, Zahra 106, 146, 150, 154, 161
non-scripted physical storytelling 163–7

organic process 3, 7, 19, 22, 33, 58, 108, 130, 181

paradox 23–4, 43, 118
Penman, Meredith 48, 137, 143
performance improvisation 1–2, 9, 11, 32. *See also* Pulse Sketch
Performance Principles
   contrast 28, 43, 47, 71–2, 106, 118
   development to climax 26–7, 36, 77, 91, 107, 109
   dynamic tension 28–9, 77, 89, 91, 100, 107
   geometry of space 25, 34, 90, 107
   jo, ha, kyu 27, 34, 36, 46, 72, 89, 93, 102–3, 111
   plateau 27–8, 36, 100
   repetition 29, 71, 77, 89, 91, 106, 111, 129, 147, 162, 181
   sustaining action 26, 70, 91, 106–7
Pericles Punished (play) 126, 131, 163–7
personal impulse 19
Phillips, Stephen 25, 44, 46, 74, 139, 148
physical acting 127, 144, 172, 179
   character and 155
   language 145–6
   Manbeth: Macbeth Amplified 126, 133, 174–81

physical gesture 82, 98, 106
    dragging and carrying 31
    fluid sculptures 66–70
    head turn 30
    hugging 30
    Hug Sculpture 65–6
    Liquid Jams 70–2
physical imagination 8–9, 30, 52, 56–7, 105, 128, 139, 144, 172
physical improvisation 3, 125
physical intimacy 14, 128, 180
physical transitions 57–8
physical vocabulary 22, 31, 38, 42
Plateau 27–8, 36, 100
psycho-physical training 8, 46, 185 n.1
Pulse 1
    improvisation and 9–11
    phases
        action vocabulary 29–33
        kinaesthetic awareness 15–16
        making connections 17–18
        Pulse Sketch 33–40
        shared language 24–9
        sound to physical world 40–4
        speaking on the Canvas 44–9
        working attitudes 18–24
    as rehearsal device 157–9
    rehearsal structure 129–31
    time management and 159
Pulse Canvas 7, 9, 58–60
    consent 14
    improvisation (see Pulse Sketch)
    Scales 10, 15–17
Pulse jam 107
Pulse Sketch 1, 9, 97, 99, 117
    associative imagery and meaning 38–9
    building blocks of 10–11
    compositional principles (see Compositional Principles)
    physical vocabulary 38
Pulsing frameworks
    content 109
    durations 109
    entrances and exits 108–9
    numbers of players 108
    solo 106–7

reaction 17, 20, 60, 137
recall 110–13, 117, 134, 136, 141–2, 151–2, 186 n.3, 186 n.6
Recurring motifs 29, 35, 37, 45, 48, 77, 91, 160–2

rehearsal concepts
    character, emergence of 153–4
    directing 146–8
    emotion 155–6
    feeding in text 150–1
    function 154
    line learning 149–50
    physical acting 144–6
    recall 151–2
    serving the speaking actor 148–9
rehearsal device 157–9
rehearsal practice 127–131
    attitude 128–9
    culture and 127–8
    structure 129–31
rehearsal process 131–44
    director, advice for 134–5
    immersion 132–6
    intuitive investigation 131–2
    Mapping 136–40
    rendering 140–4
Rendering 140–4
    advice for director 141–2
    fluidity of space, place and character 175–8
    immersion 178–9
    outcomes for actor and director 142–4
Repetition 29, 71, 77, 89, 91, 106, 111, 129, 147, 162, 181
respect 12, 23, 79, 128
response 16, 19, 60, 137
    behavioural 65
    emotional 68, 140, 156
    empathetic 75, 82
    imaginative 57, 134, 138
    instinctive 139
    performance 117, 132, 165
    physical 43, 65–6, 132
    psycho-imaginal 155
    verbal 66
Rhythm 10, 24
    commitment to action 18, 39, 42, 61, 64, 78, 90
    development to climax 26–7, 36, 77, 91, 107, 109
    dynamic tension 28–9, 77, 89, 91, 100, 107
    improvising spoken monologue 90–1
    plateau 27–8, 36, 100
    shattering the space 36–7, 89, 100, 102, 147
    sustaining action 26, 70, 91, 106–7
Rutenberg, Brian 109, 136–7

INDEX

safety 12–14, 47, 61, 101, 122, 127, 183
Scales 10, 15–17, 24–5, 29, 97, 105–6
score 31–2, 68–70, 89, 99, 131–3
sensory research 132, 167, 175
serving 148–9
shared language 18, 22, 24–9, 32, 114, 135
Shatter the space 36–7, 89, 100, 102, 147
side coaching 8, 21–2, 97, 102, 108, 130, 138
   architecture of space 34
   commencement 34
   contrast 28
   denouement 36
   depth of field 34–5
   development to climax 26–7
   directing through 146–8
   dynamic tension 28
   find the ending 36
   form and chaos 37
   geometry of space 25
   Hug Sculpture 56–7, 65–6
   jo, ha, kyu 27
   juxtaposition 43
   plateau 27
   recurring motifs 35
   repetition 29
   shatter the space 36
   sustaining action 26
   working in macro 17
   working in micro 15–16
singing 41–2
skill focus tasks
   emotional gesture (*see* emotional gesture)
   improvised speaking 86–90
   physical gesture 64–72
'smelling' the dramatic potential 18, 29, 39, 64, 67, 89, 91, 100, 107
solo 17, 28–30, 32, 35, 42, 70–1
   recurring motifs 36, 38
   solo crying monologue 77–8
   verbal solo 45
Space 10–11
   architecture of space 34, 38, 90, 107, 143
   depth of field 34–5, 47, 90, 102, 117, 143
   geometry of space 25, 34, 90, 107
speaking 44–9. *See also* improvised speaking forms on Canvas
   compulsive monologue 45
   fragment 45–6
   verbal solo 45
   how to 45–6
   what to 44–5
   when to 44
   why to 46–9
Stage Beauty (play) 126, 131, 167, 171–4
Stanislavski, Konstantin 3, 73, 183
Stephenson, Shelagh 126, 167
Strong, Sam 129, 141–2
Structure 10
   commencement 34, 38, 63, 77, 92, 99, 100
   denouement 35–6, 48, 63, 77, 89, 92, 100
   finding the ending 36, 64, 66, 68–9, 92, 100–1, 108
   form and chaos 37, 63, 69
   improvising spoken monologue 92–3
   jo, ha, kyu 27, 34, 36, 46, 72, 89, 93, 102–3, 111
   rehearsal structure 129–31
Sustaining action 26, 70, 91, 106–7

theatre-making 106, 126, 128, 159, 167
Themed Pulse 109–10, 116–17, 157
Therese, Kaz 39, 43
time management 126, 159
training outcomes
   immersion 135–6
   mapping 139–40
   rendering 142–4

Unit of action 29, 35, 37–8, 106

verbal gestures 40–1
   Languages Other Than English (LOTE) 41
   music as playing partner 42
   singing 41–2
   whispering 41
verbal improvisation 132, 136, 145–6, 151
verbal monologues 88–9
verbal Pulse 90
verbal solo 45
Victorian College of the Arts (VCA) 114, 163, 167, 169–70, 175
vocal gestures 40
vocal (sound) Pulse 89

walk/stop task 53–4
What does it need? 18, 35, 39, 47, 64, 89, 100
Woods, Lachlan 33, 116, 119, 122, 171
working attitudes, Pulse
   performer, advice for 19–21
   trainer, advice for 22–4
Working in Parallel 18, 39–40, 64, 68, 71